T0288026

Halal Investing for Beginners

Halal Investing for Beginners

How to Start, Grow and Scale Your Halal Investment Portfolio

Ibrahim Khan
Mohsin Patel

WILEY

This edition first published 2023

Copyright © 2023 by John Wiley & Sons, Ltd.

All rights reserved. No part of this publication may be reproduced, stored in a retrieval system, or transmitted, in any form or by any means, electronic, mechanical, photocopying, recording or otherwise, except as permitted by law. Advice on how to obtain permission to reuse material from this title is available at http://www.wiley.com/go/permissions.

The right of Ibrahim Khan and Mohsin Patel to be identified as the authors of this work has been asserted in accordance with law.

Registered Office(s)
John Wiley & Sons, Inc., 111 River Street, Hoboken, NJ 07030, USA

John Wiley & Sons Ltd, The Atrium, Southern Gate, Chichester, West Sussex, PO19 8SQ, UK

Editorial Office
The Atrium, Southern Gate, Chichester, West Sussex, PO19 8SQ, UK

For details of our global editorial offices, customer services, and more information about Wiley products visit us at www.wiley.com.

Wiley also publishes its books in a variety of electronic formats and by print-on-demand. Some content that appears in standard print versions of this book may not be available in other formats.

Designations used by companies to distinguish their products are often claimed as trademarks. All brand names and product names used in this book are trade names, service marks, trademarks or registered trademarks of their respective owners. The publisher is not associated with any product or vendor mentioned in this book.

Limit of Liability/Disclaimer of Warranty

While the publisher and authors have used their best efforts in preparing this work, they make no representations or warranties with respect to the accuracy or completeness of the contents of this work and specifically disclaim all warranties, including without limitation any implied warranties of merchantability or fitness for a particular purpose. No warranty may be created or extended by sales representatives, written sales materials or promotional statements for this work. The fact that an organization, website, or product is referred to in this work as a citation and/or potential source of further information does not mean that the publisher and authors endorse the information or services the organization, website, or product may provide or recommendations it may make. This work is sold with the understanding that the publisher is not engaged in rendering professional services. The advice and strategies contained herein may not be suitable for your situation. You should consult with a specialist where appropriate. Further, readers should be aware that websites listed in this work may have changed or disappeared between when this work was written and when it is read. Neither the publisher nor authors shall be liable for any loss of profit or any other commercial damages, including but not limited to special, incidental, consequential, or other damages.

Library of Congress Cataloging-in-Publication Data is Available:

ISBN 9781394178049 (Cloth)
ISBN 9781394178056 (ePDF)
ISBN 9781394178063 (ePub)

Cover Design: Wiley
Cover Image: © Daisy and Bumble/Shutterstock
Author photos: Courtesy of Ibrahim Khan and Mohsin Patel

SKY10089892_110424

To our patient, superhuman wives, without whom nothing would ever happen half as well in our lives, and to our wise parents, who pushed us at the right times and hugged us at the right times – may Allah reward you all immensely.

Contents

Foreword *ix*

Acknowledgements *xi*

About the Authors *xiii*

Introduction *xv*

PART I The Basics of Investing and Personal Finance **1**

Chapter 1 Personal Finance Essentials 3

Chapter 2 Breaking Even 5

Chapter 3 Islamic Wills 13

Chapter 4 Pensions 17

Chapter 5 Your Rainy Day Fund 21

Chapter 6 Going Halal for the First Time and the Purification of Wealth 27

PART II How to Develop Your Investment Strategy **35**

Chapter 7 Your Investment Mindset 37

Chapter 8 Building the Blocks 51

Chapter 9 How to Do Basic Due Diligence into an Investment Company 71

Chapter 10 Tax-Saving Strategies 77

Chapter 11 Weighing up Risk and Reward 81

PART III Investment and Sharia Considerations for Popular Investment Categories **87**

Chapter 12 Stocks 89

Chapter 13 Fixed Income 121

Chapter 14 Alternative Assets 153

PART IV How to Construct a Robust Portfolio **211**

Chapter 15 Portfolio Theory 213

Chapter 16 Case Study: Conservative 221

Chapter 17 Case Study: Moderate 225

Chapter 18 Case Study: Aggressive 229

Parting Thoughts *231*

Notes *233*

Continuing Your Education *243*

Helpful Resources *245*

Index *247*

Foreword

While Islamic finance has grown at an institutional level around the world, it has often been underserved at a grassroots level. The average person still has questions about what Islamic finance is, how it differs from traditional finance, and why they should invest in sharia-compliant products. There are several impediments to the growth of Islamic finance in the UK, including regulatory, political, and access to sharia-compliant capital, as well as a lack of human resources. One significant barrier that is frequently overlooked is a lack of Islamic financial literacy. This is an area in which Islamic Finance Guru (IFG) has excelled.

What began as a blog has grown into a global platform with millions of beneficiaries worldwide; IFG has become a household name in Muslim personal finance. Throughout this journey, I consider myself fortunate to have kept in touch with and collaborated on various projects and initiatives with my two dear brothers, Ibrahim Khan and Mohsin Patel. Their work is truly legacy-building, and I pray that they see the fruits of their efforts and hard work in the Eternal Life.

It was only a matter of time before they were approached by a major publisher to write about Islamic finance, so this book comes as no surprise. I read through the book and was very pleased with the hands-on approach it provides. It greatly simplifies investing and provides people with a road map for navigating the halal investing world. This book is more than just a theoretical write-up; it is the culmination of years of deep learning, insights, and personal experiences. This book is both a "hack" and an "accelerator"; it is thousands of hours of learning condensed into a few hundred pages.

It will truly save people years of learning time and fast forward their journey into the world of halal investing. Ibrahim and Mohsin have curated a powerful tool to educate this generation of Muslims about halal investing.

May God accept my dear brothers' efforts and take them from strength to strength in facilitating halal globally.

Mufti Faraz Adam
Amanah Advisors

Acknowledgements

We would like to thank the IFG team – particularly Sarah Brooking – for their support throughout the writing period, countless evenings of reviews and edits, and for working so tirelessly on our mission to level up Muslims financially.

A sincere note of thanks to Mufti Faraz Adam who has been a quiet, thoughtful and dynamic font of wisdom to us for many years, and for taking the time to comment thoroughly on this book as well.

And, finally, a thank you to the entire Wiley team for seeing the potential and then making this all happen in such a professional, seamless way.

About the Authors

Ibrahim Khan is the CEO and co-founder of Islamic Finance Guru and its sister company, Cur8 Capital, one of the most prominent Islamic investing platforms globally. He read Philosophy, Politics, and Economics at the University of Oxford, then went on to specialise in Islamic finance through a Master's and a traditional Alimiyyah degree. He worked for a number of years in corporate law, first for Ashurst and then for Debevoise & Plimpton. He holds a Diploma in Investment Advice & Financial Planning and a Certificate in Investment Management. He is based in London.

Mohsin Patel is the COO and co-founder of Islamic Finance Guru and Cur8 Capital. He read French and Russian at the University of Oxford. He subsequently specialised in Islamic finance through an Islamic Finance Diploma. He worked in corporate law at Squire Patton Boggs, before going full-time at Islamic Finance Guru in 2019. He holds a Diploma in Investment Advice & Financial Planning and a Certificate in Investment Management. He splits his time between the UK and the UAE.

Introduction

I first realised there was a problem when a financial advisor approached me about managing my money.[1]

I was working as a trainee in corporate law at the time and invited him into our plush London offices. This didn't disconcert him in the slightest – he was very familiar with these sorts of settings.

He walked me through his beautiful models. I should be accumulating in my youth and decumulating in my retirement. Pensions were good, as was insurance. Financing should be used strategically as a tool throughout my life to smooth out purchases and get onto the property ladder quicker, and tax-efficient investments should be used to build my nest egg.

This was all brilliant and made perfect sense to me. I was ready to go full-on Wolf of Wall Street – but there was one big catch.

Literally nothing he had offered to me was *sharia-compliant*.

I rang my best friend and long-time business partner Mohsin that evening.

"We need to figure this one out, Mohsin. We're going to have savings soon and we need to manage them properly. And it's completely barmy that in a twenty-first-century world a quarter of the world's population still doesn't have financial products that they can actually use."

Mohsin agreed and, in an evening of discussion, debate, and idea creation, Islamic Finance Guru (or IFG) was born: a blog to share our research into halal investing and personal finance.[2]

Thus started an eight-year journey (to date) of research, discovery, and building financial products that helped scratch our own itch. In that time, we gained Islamic qualifications, sat our financial advisor exams, qualified as corporate lawyers, got married, and had kids.

Today, only through the grace of God, IFG is one of the most prominent Islamic investing websites globally, with its own suite of financial tools and investment products.

Over this journey, we've had the privilege of interacting with thousands of Muslims also on the same path as us. We've interacted with students just starting out on their journey, single mums looking to stabilise their finances after a divorce, a scam victim who is fearfully looking to invest again for the first time, billionaires who made their money in crypto, and – because we deal mostly with Muslims – lots and lots of doctors. Despite the variety of these backgrounds, these individuals actually had a lot in common when it came to the challenges they were facing in their investment journeys.

These challenges were:

1. Wondering what is halal or haram in the investment world – from the most basic products to the most complex.
2. Being keen to learn about personal finance and investment strategies that were sharia-compliant.
3. Looking for advice, coaching, and guidance on their investments.
4. Wanting to understand what halal investment options there actually were for them to take up.

Much of our content on IFG and in this book has been inspired by the questions we've received over the years from our audience members. We have written hundreds of thousands of words, shot over 150 videos, and given talks up and down the UK and abroad on these topics.

But what we had never done till now was condense it all down into one neat package. This book is our attempt at doing just that. It is a distillation of all those conversations, articles, videos, and lectures – suffused with a healthy dose of practicality to get you moving from "learning" to "doing". We hope you enjoy it and learn something new.

The Why

But before we dive into the action, it is important to remind ourselves what is at stake here.

The religious texts are very clear – hoarding and passively sitting on cash are frowned upon. The Qur'an says, "But as for him who is stingy and self-satisfied, and denies the good, We will pave his way to difficulty."[3]

More broadly, zakat is a 2.5% compulsory charitable donation on every Muslim's stagnant wealth every year. Interestingly though, zakat does not generally apply to investments. In other words, zakat is effectively a wealth tax, encouraging the circulation and investment of money, rather than it sitting in cash. We can see therefore that the *sharī'a* – the Islamic legal code – has always been pro-investment.

But today this message has taken on a particular urgency. According to an annual report on global wealth by Credit Suisse,[4] the global average net worth at the end of 2021 was $87,489, a staggering 12.7% increase from 2020 and the fastest annual rate of growth ever recorded.

Some quick back-of-the-napkin analysis of their numbers, accounting for Muslim populations, indicates that global Muslim net worth is approximately $16,702. In other words, the Muslim community is approximately five times poorer than the rest of the world.

This can be seen in Figure 0.1.

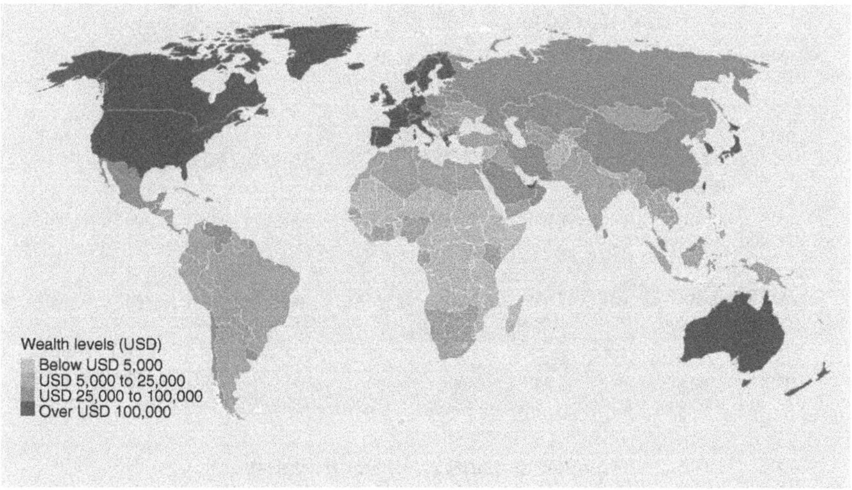

Figure 0.1 Global wealth.

Source: Davies et al., 2022 / Credit Suisse Group/ Public Domain.

With the exception of some of the smaller Gulf States, much of the Muslim-majority country belt stretching across North Africa and across the Middle East and subcontinent has wealth in the lowest two bands. This puts the task ahead of the Muslim community in a rather different light: we must look after our wealth not just for ourselves, but the greater good. This is particularly so for the most affluent Muslims.

As can be seen in Figure 0.2, the top 13% of the population owns 85.9% of global wealth. That means that if you're reading this book and are lucky enough to be in that bracket, there is an additional onus on you to ensure your wealth is (1) invested and growing; and (2) allocated to investments that do more than just give profit.

We actually ran the numbers on what it would take for the Muslim community as a whole to get back to a level financial playing field, and what we found was that if every Muslim earned around 12% per annum on

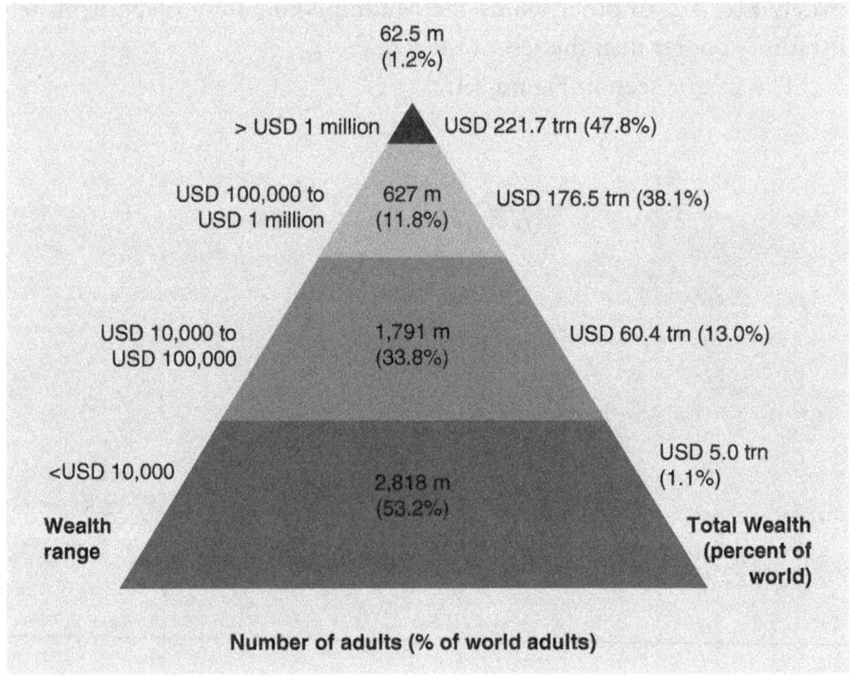

Figure 0.2 Global wealth range.

Source: Davies et al., 2022 / Credit Suisse Group/ Public Domain.

their savings – roughly 4–5% above the global average returns – it would take just 35 years to close that gap.

The goal is actually achievable and could even be attained in our lifetime. We've made it our mission at IFG to do precisely this – and this book is a key part of that journey. The more Muslims who are educated about investing well, the more they are likely to invest profitably.

Right, enough preaching, let's get down to business.

How to Use This Book

This book is divided into four Parts:

Part I - The basics of investing and personal finance
Part II - How to develop your investment strategy
Part III - Investment and sharia considerations for popular investment categories
Part IV - How to construct a robust portfolio

The first time you read this book, we would suggest reading from start to finish. Then, when you revisit the book,[5] you should just dip in and out of the Parts that are most pertinent to your personal situation. We would expect Part III in particular to become a reference section for your ongoing investment activities.

We also want to make sure that this book isn't just a theoretical primer full of nice platitudes that is read once and then sits on a shelf getting dusty. At the end of this book, we want you to have the toolkit to be able to take control of your finances and have the confidence to use those tools too.

Specifically you should be able to do the following:

1. Construct a personal finance foundation for your own life.
2. Measure your own risk appetite in order to decide what your overall portfolio will look like.
3. Explain what popular investment categories are to a beginner.
4. Discredit myths about investing the next time you hear them.
5. Have a firm grounding in the mainstream Islamic positions on popular investments.

We have also provided an investment checklist document that you should fill out for yourself as you progress through the book. You can get a downloadable PDF version.[6]

Structure of Each Part

First, we're going to cover some very practical personal finance foundations that will help you to think about how you allocate your money in life. This is all the essential, not-so-exciting stuff that forms the backbone to healthy finances. We'll be covering:

1. Breaking even.
2. Islamic wills.
3. Pensions.
4. Rainy day funds.
5. Going halal for the first time.

In Part II, we start drilling into investments but we're more interested in helping you understand the *why* and *how* of investing here, rather than the *what*. We cover:

1. Your investment mindset and dealing with different circumstances that you'll be facing.
2. The basic building blocks of investments: buying a house, achieving investment goals, and retirement.
3. How to do basic due diligence into an investment company.
4. Key tax-saving strategies.
5. How to weigh up risk and reward.

In Part III, we'll actually get down to the nitty-gritty. We cover various different investment options under the three big umbrella terms:

1. The stock market.
2. Fixed income.
3. Alternative assets.

For each investment we cover, we answer the following questions:

1. What is it?
2. What are the returns on offer?
3. Is your money safe?
4. Can you get your money back easily?
5. What are the sharia considerations (including zakat)?
6. How can you get access to it?

In Part IV, we pull everything together and move you to action. We cover portfolio construction – how you actually craft an investment pot for yourself – and present three realistic case studies of individuals at different life stages with very different incomes, goals, and ambitions.

Global Readers

Just a quick note for those readers among you who do not live in the United Kingdom. This book will regularly express money and examples in pounds sterling and certain aspects of our coverage will be somewhat UK-oriented. However, in most cases, what we cover in this book has global application as the lessons apply to investments generally, regardless of the particulars of each country.

Even for the very specifically UK-oriented discussions (of which there aren't too many), take this as a nudge to go on the internet and find out if your country has something similar. For example, if we are talking about tax incentives to invest in startups – and you are based in Bulgaria – check if Bulgaria has something similar.[7] Most governments the world over will be looking to incentivise the same behaviours, so chances are actually quite high that there is considerable overlap in the areas that they incentivise.

Halal Investing
for Beginners

PART I

The Basics of Investing and Personal Finance

1 Personal Finance Essentials

Most complex skills have only a few true experts. There are only a handful of world-class tennis players, surgeons, or lawyers in the world, and yet the tennis academies, medical schools, and law schools are full of prospective future experts. What happens to these hopefuls that winnows the field so dramatically?

Complex skills are based upon the learning and repetition of many smaller factoids, activities, and actions. Over time, these thought patterns, skill sets, and movements become so ingrained that a skilled surgeon can mentally walk their way through a complex surgery entirely in their head.

But the problem with these simple factoids, repetitions, and skill sets is that they are often not the glamorous end result usually associated with practising that craft. Hitting 100 balls alone on a tennis court is just not as exciting as playing on Centre Court at Wimbledon. And yet understanding and honing the basics incredibly well are what the later successes are based upon.

The same is the case when it comes to investments and personal finances. The glamorous side of investing is taking meetings with the next Mark Zuckerberg, looking into his eyes and deciding to invest all your money in his company because you can see where this rocket ship is headed. It's having films like *The Big Short* made about your decisions. It's picking the next stock, cryptocoin, or asset class before it becomes huge and making enough to retire off the back of it.

But before you get the right to do that without improperly risking your wealth, you must grasp the basics of personal finance. Unless you do that, you're going to be as out of your depth as any of us would be if we were to inexplicably find ourselves on Centre Court against a world-class tennis player.

This chapter starts with the absolute fundamentals and the rest of the book builds on that.

Personal finance, when done well, is not just "a thing" you do once and then forget about, it is your ongoing relationship to money. Indeed, you already do have a relationship with money before you started reading this book. It might be a happy-go-lucky relationship but where you're not honest with each other. It might be a tempestuous relationship that goes through extreme highs and lows. It might be a relationship where you are settling for satisfactory rather than true love. It could even be an abusive relationship.[1]

The aim of this book is to give you a perspective on the implications of your current relationship and to sketch out alternatives.

The key ingredients to the base layer of personal finances are:

1. Breaking even.[2]
2. Getting an Islamic will.
3. Getting your pension (or regular savings) up and running.
4. Setting up a rainy day fund.
5. Going halal and purifying historic investments.

2 Breaking Even

The UK financial sector recently went through a major convulsion due to a mini-Budget announced by the then Chancellor of the Exchequer, Kwasi Kwarteng.

The government announced that it would be spending aggressively to stimulate growth while making swingeing cuts to taxes. However, the markets reacted extremely badly to this and the pound hit its lowest points ever against the dollar. Meanwhile, there is a crisis brewing in the pensions sector as a result of these market dislocations.

Why did the markets react this way? Surely in a time of recession, extra spending would be welcome? The answer is the markets are concerned that in the long term the government's economic plan is unsustainable. The government is spending more than it makes, and, frankly, more than it can even safely borrow.

It's the same for our personal finances too. A very helpful way of understanding our own finances is to think of ourselves as a company.

The maths is simple. You have two scenarios:

1. Incomings – outgoings = +ve number

or

2. Incomings – outgoings = –ve number

In scenario 1, you are making a "profit" and, in scenario 2, you are making a loss. Scenario 2 is only sustainable for as long as your reserves last, or as long as you can borrow money in a sustainable way.

Scenario 2 is the one to avoid, as, if you stay there for any length of time, you will go bankrupt. That, of course, is a *bad* personal finance situation.

So how does one move from scenario 2 to scenario 1, and how does one increase the +ve number in scenario 1?

Well, again, there are two mathematical answers to that:

1. Increase your incomings.
2. Decrease your outgoings.

Or, even better, do both.

Increasing incomings can include:

- Negotiating a salary raise.
- Taking on an extra job.
- Starting a side hustle.
- Getting your spouse to start part-time work.
- Investing in income-generating assets.
- Selling your old clothes and items, not just binning them or throwing them away.
- Ensuring you are claiming all government grants and benefits you are eligible for.
- Ensuring you are not in the wrong tax band.
- Ensuring you are effectively making tax returns that account for losses, charitable giving, etc.
- Ensuring that you are investing wisely and getting a tax rebate where they are possible (more on this later).

Decreased outgoings means cutting costs. The first step is to understand what your costs are. Imagine having to allocate each of your bank transactions to a category and then getting a month-by-month summary of what those different categories look like. You might have a category called takeaways and realise that you're actually spending £150 per month on takeaways. Or you might have a category called fuel and realise you are spending more on fuel in the summer because of holiday travel. These are all insights on which you can take action.

Doing this activity doesn't have to always result in cutting things out either, but it will force you to ask yourself the question, "Do I need this?" and that really is half the battle.

If you do it well, you'll know month in, month out what your necessary expenses are – things like mortgage, bills, fuel, and medical costs. You'll also pinpoint what your more flexible payments are – things which are not strictly necessary but you buy them anyway. This could be things like buying gifts for Eid, going on holiday, or redoing your kitchen.

So how does one go about tracking their transactions? Well, we've tried the whole spectrum of options and what we found actually gives great insights is to pretend we are a company and run our own expenses as a company. So we subscribe to a paid software which is actually designed for businesses – an app called FreeAgent.[1]

That's just our preference though, and if you are starting out, we would try the many personal finance tracking apps that are out there: Emma and Money Dashboard are a couple of examples. Frankly, today even the main banking apps do a pretty good job of this. We personally have experience of Starling, Monzo, and HSBC and they all do a reasonable job.

Once you have this basic financial data about yourself, you can think about where you can make some savings.

Here's a practical list of ideas on how to cut expenses:

1. Refinance your mortgage – making sure you're not paying too much here as the cost really adds up over time because we're dealing with large amounts.
2. Switch utility companies or get a packaged deal with one company.
3. Go on a cheaper holiday or do a staycation.
4. Sort out car insurance a month in advance – this is when prices are cheapest.
5. Insulate your home and police the usage of gas and electricity.
6. Wear jumpers at home.
7. Buy second-hand rather than new.
8. Switch to a discount store rather than shop in a larger supermarket.
9. Get a more fuel-efficient car.
10. Sign up to store memberships, such as the Tesco Clubcard. These can unlock better pricing and in some cases you get money back.
11. Talk to a debt management company and get your debts renegotiated.

12. Move to a cheaper flat or house if renting, or consider downsizing if you've bought.
13. Cut unnecessary and unused subscriptions.
14. Eat at home and plan out your meals for the week.
15. When you go shopping, shop with a list and don't make any other purchases apart from the things on the list.
16. If you buy something new, sell something old.
17. For larger purchases, don't make impulsive buys, sleep on it.
18. Rather than buying things, check on websites like Gumtree, Facebook Marketplace, Freecycle, and others where people are giving away free stuff.
19. Take a packed lunch to work and make your own coffee rather than buy it.
20. Really study how food can be stored and made to last and what food is okay to eat after its best-before date.

We fully appreciate that if you implement all of the above suggestions religiously, you will automatically become "that interesting chap" at work and among the neighbours, but even if you implement just 25% of the above list, you'll end up saving a ton and retain your street cred.

Okay, now you've cut your expenses, you're hopefully making some savings every month. This is the free cash you have per month. So if you have £3000 coming in each month and you figure out that you spend £1,700 per month, that's £1,300 of free cash you have.

This is the capital you need to start doing something with in a way that is smart and sustainable in the long term. We'll talk a lot more about this investment aspect in the rest of the book.

Then you should turn your mind to any debts. If you have anything that is short-term and relatively easy to get off your back, you should do that now. Whether it's a loan from a family member or friend, or whether it's some small haram debt you've incurred, just get the direct debits going and get it paid off if it's doable in the short term. It's best for your own mental well-being and Islamically it's the right thing to do as well. Prioritise this before any investments.

For long-term debts – things like mortgages, student loans, or perhaps large family loans – as long as you are not violating someone else's right or going against what was agreed, it is wise to set up a sustainable standing order to pay it off in the long term. But don't think that you cannot invest until the debt is repaid, you can and should continue to build your long-term portfolio in parallel.

Getting onto the Housing Ladder

Talking of long-term debts, there is one particularly important long-term debt to call out: home financing.

We know an elderly man with four children who are now grown up. Each member of his family lives in their own London home, but none of this entire family pay any rent or mortgage payments.

How did they achieve that?

The simple secret is that, forty years ago, this man bought four homes on a mortgage for his children. They cost in total about £100,000 at the time. Today, with inflation and house price increases, that portfolio is worth in the millions.

Figuring out how to get on the housing ladder is possibly the single biggest strategic personal finance move you can make because of these long-term outcomes.

This is not the book to cover the halal and haram of Islamic mortgages or other home financing solutions.[2] We have covered this extensively in analysis on our website and YouTube channel, but we will assume you are comfortable with at least one form of Islamic home financing available.

The reason why getting on the housing ladder is such a key step of your personal finances is because home-related costs are usually the most significant every month, and because, for most people, the most expensive asset they own is their home.

We have a "should I buy or rent?" calculator on our website[3] which can be an effective tool for modelling out whether you should buy or rent. In the vast majority of cases it makes sense to buy rather than continue renting.

The reasoning behind that is pretty simple: with rent you pay £1,500 a month and none of that ever comes back. You add that up and add inflation and that is a hefty sum over 20 years. And you're still paying rent with no end in sight.

But if you buy a house, on the other hand, you typically face a lower monthly payment, and a portion of your monthly payment is going towards the purchase of your home, which you will see the upside of when you sell it.

Fast forward 20 years, and you're sitting on an asset that has appreciated considerably in that period, and your monthly home financing costs have now come down considerably or may even have stopped completely.

Let's put some numbers on this to really clarify the point. Babar wants to buy a house worth £400,000. He is going to put a deposit down of £80,000 and he has taken out a mortgage of 25 years paying 5.5% per annum.

If he were to rent that same property instead, he would pay £1,800 per month and he would look to invest his £80,000 in an investment. Let's assume he finds an investment that yields him 8% per annum. On this analysis, using our buy/rent calculator, Babar should buy his house as he would otherwise end up losing around £125,000.

Of course, there are exceptions to the general rule. If you have access to a great investment that is consistently returning double-digit returns that is quite safe too, this may be a better option instead. But history tells us that usually those safe, consistently-returning, double-digit investments are either not actually consistent, drop in return, or aren't safe.

Of course buying a home is not just a financial decision, consider Figure 2.1.

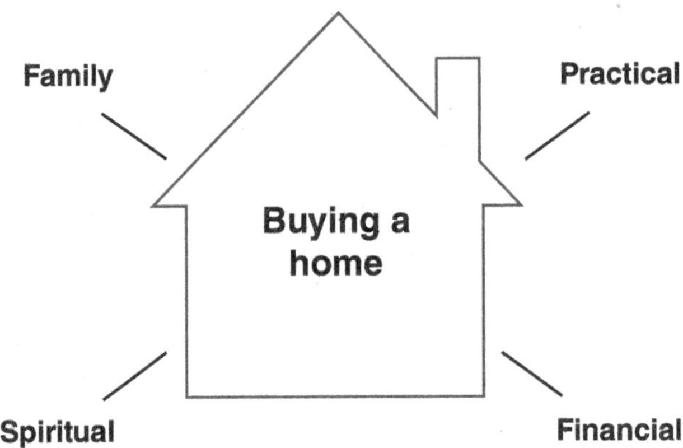

Figure 2.1 Key considerations.

Source: www.Islamicfinance.guru.

From a financial perspective, you are basically assessing the following conundrum: (1) should I take the deposit money I've saved and lock it up into a property and pay monthly mortgage payments?, or (2) should I take the deposit money and invest it, and pay rental payments on my house instead?

To answer this you'll have to think practically. Do you need to rent because you might move regularly, for example? Or perhaps even if you know renting might make more financial sense, you want the safety and security of buying a house without having to worry about making x% return a year on what would have been your deposit money. Or maybe you don't want the hassle of renting and a potentially bad landlord.

So when making this decision, first think it through financially, and then think it through practically. Sometimes practicality *can* outweigh the financial.

3 Islamic Wills

Now that we have hopefully brought our financial ship back onto an even keel, and are at least breaking even every month, we can turn our attention to other urgent priorities.

Not to put a downer on things this early on in the book, but you will die at some point. And when you do, money is a key part of that conversation.

Muslims in the West should pay particular attention as you will need to get a specific type of will done in order for it to be sharia-compliant. This is something you should look into as a priority if you haven't already got one.

In a well-known hadith, the Prophet Muhammed (PBUH) said: "It is not permissible for any Muslim who has something to will to stay for two nights without having his Last Will and Testament written and kept ready with him."[1] This is particularly important if you don't live in a country governed by Islamic inheritance laws, as this usually means that if you die intestate (i.e. without a will), your affairs will be settled according to the law of the land – not the sharia.

Try not to leave it to the very last minute either. During the early part of the COVID-19 pandemic, there was an almighty spike in our IFG wills service, and we were getting emotional emails and calls from customers on ventilation machines in hospital, some of whom unfortunately passed away and our will was in use far earlier than we would have wanted. This is not an unusual occurrence outside of the COVID-19 pandemic either. We once got a call from a man in a taxi on his way to hospital for heart surgery.

Sorting out your Islamic will is an important way of organising your personal finances too. As part of the process of writing your will, you need to figure out your full portfolio and unlock access to many long-forgotten pensions and investment accounts. You'll finally have to figure out how to do something about that land your mother left you in Delhi.

But there are serious money-saving benefits too. Having a will means you can plan your inheritance tax much better and often side-step it. In the UK an individual gets £325,000 as their tax-free allowance on inheritance tax, and, including your primary residence, up to £500,000. If you are married, you can, with some tax planning, unlock up to £1 million free from inheritance tax.[2]

But if you are above the thresholds, then the taxman will charge your estate 40% above the tax-free threshold. That is a very significant amount of money and it's worth spending some time to figure it all out now.

We regularly deal with families who have estates in the millions who haven't yet properly thought through inheritance tax planning. Thankfully they are now thinking about it and getting the relevant documentation in place to navigate the issue, but there are hundreds more families out there who are unnecessarily paying huge amounts of inheritance tax.

As a side note, avoiding inheritance tax legally is not morally dubious either. The HMRC literally encourages people to get a will to ensure they do not end up paying more tax than they need to.[3]

Having a will also allows you to leave a record of all your assets. On average, people without a will lose around £10k of their assets simply because they don't write down what they own and their heirs have no idea about those assets or how to get access to them. There is around £50 billion of unclaimed or lost assets currently in the UK alone[4] and other countries report similar large sums.

Writing a will is pretty cheap and quick these days. For people with simple estates under £100,000 who are without children, we have compiled a list of free Islamic wills online[5] that you can use.

For those with larger and more complex estates, there are now plenty of online Islamic will options (of which our Cur8 app is one) that can allow you to get your will done quickly and cheaply. We have written a detailed guide to Islamic wills and your options in an article you can access.[6]

For those with estates above £5 million, you are typically advised to talk to a tax advisor in parallel to your Islamic will drafting, as the two things feed quite closely into each other.

A little-known way to get your will done online and drafted by a professional, cheaply, or even for free, is to use an Islamic charity's will offering service. We are partners with a number of major Islamic charities today and most of them offer an Islamic will service at a substantial discount or for free.

If you do go for this option, we encourage you to leave a small donation and remember the charity as part of your legacy giving.

4 Pensions

We're now breaking even and ready to die. Let's now work on giving you the money you need for your retirement.

For People Living in Countries That Charge Tax

This is where we start thinking more about actually putting money to work. And one of the easiest places to start with this is your workplace pension, if you are an employee. That's because in the UK, employers are legally obliged to contribute to your pension, provided you also contribute your legal minimum. There are similar rules in most other developed countries.

The current rates are that you put in 5% of your gross salary and your employer will put in 3%. Many employers will actually exceed this. This is basically free money.

For example, if your gross salary is £4000, you'd be putting in £200 from your untaxed money, and your employer would be putting in a minimum of £120. That's you effectively getting a 60% return.

For self-employed individuals too, contributing into a pension can be an excellent way of extracting tax-free amounts from your company (up to £40,000 every year). However, remember, pension money is locked away until you retire.

There are no other investments that offer you these kinds of returns so consistently. So if you're wondering if you should opt in to your pension – YES you should!

But that's only one problem solved for a Muslim because we also need the investment to be halal. Unfortunately, the choice of things to invest in is not amazing in a workplace pension, as you have to invest in an Islamic fund, given that most other funds will not be adherent to Islamic sharia stock screening criteria.[1]

The upshot of this is that you are likely to be investing in an equities-only fund, meaning that you do not get the diversification[2] available to non-sharia investors. However, this is still better than not taking the free money.

As part of the process of setting up your pension, make sure you remember to switch away from the default investing option to the halal fund option. If you don't do this, you will be investing in haram funds which can cause massive purification headaches later down the line.

With some pension providers, you can search the investments online yourself. An easy way to find the right options is by searching "Islamic" or "sharia". Otherwise you might need to speak to HR or the pension provider to sort it out. Also remember, ethical does not equal sharia-compliant!

A potential hack if you're not happy with the choices in your workplace pension is to start your own SIPP (self-invested personal pension) and ask your workplace pension provider what you need to do to transfer the money in your workplace pension to your SIPP.

A SIPP is simply a stockbroking account you can use to buy various Islamic funds and stocks using your own discretion. With the SIPP you are in control of your pension investments. This is both the beauty and danger of the SIPP. It is typically only advisable to go down this road once you are a little more experienced and ready to analyse and pick individual stocks, or if you're just planning to hold large Islamic funds. The last thing you want is to prematurely start taking big risks with your retirement money and end up frittering that away.

Just make sure you don't close your workplace pension and lose the free money you're receiving through that. Be sure to confirm that before you ask about the switching process.

What you want is for everything to stay the same from your own and your employer's point of view, but then funnel that workplace pension money (both your own contribution and your employer's top-up contribution) away into your own SIPP every 6 months or so.

If you're struggling to access a sharia-compliant fund within your workplace pension, remember that, in the UK, this is a legal obligation. You should ask your employer to provide a sharia-compliant option as part of their pension package.

If they are not receptive, there's a good way to convince them. We have spent £10,000 obtaining a written legal opinion on this from one of the country's leading barristers. We've made this available for free[3] for you, as we feel so strongly about this. Take this to your HR and in 99% of cases they will start to see things differently. Barristers have a wonderful way with words.

For People Living in Countries That Don't Charge Tax

We regularly speak to, and help, expats who are thinking about their retirement and don't currently have a pension.

The initial appeal of a pension in countries that charge tax is the fact you won't have to pay any tax on it, or as much tax on it, and the free contributions employers have to make.

However, when that incentive isn't there, it is very easy to end up piling up money with no real retirement plan anywhere to be seen. You're enjoying the sun, piling on the pounds, and liberally using terms like "yalla" while you order £35 sandwiches. But do that for long enough and, scarily, you can actually end up worse off than you would be if you stayed in dark, dank, mould-infested Britain.

For people in this situation, the solution is that you are effectively going to have to create your own pension pot so that you are confident that by the time you retire, you have the relevant income sources coming in to sustain yourself.

We will talk in a lot of detail throughout the rest of this book about investment strategies and what asset classes you can choose for your portfolio, but if you are in this group of people who need to build up a pension, just keep in mind that there are different phases of a typical pension cycle (See Figure 4.1).

In the first 30 years of your career, you are in the accumulation and earning phase. At this stage you can be a lot more aggressive and long-term about your investments and think about capital gain. Your investments are increasing in value but they're not necessarily giving you an annual cash distribution.

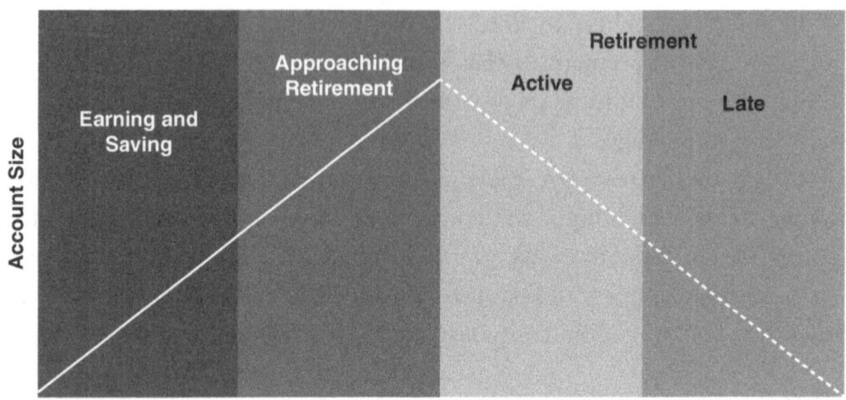

Figure 4.1 The savings lifecycle.

Source: www.Islamicfinanceguru.

Then as you approach retirement, you start shifting your investments into lower risk asset classes that are cash-generating but with less capital gain. That means that once you do retire, your pension is set up to do exactly what it needs to do: sustain you through the income it is generating.

5 Your Rainy Day Fund

We've now broken even, got our *kafns*[1] ready, and oiled our zimmer frames. After all that positivity, we now want to turn our attention to lighter subjects: what happens if calamity unexpectedly befalls you?

Before we talk about the specifics of a rainy day fund, we want to tell you, from our own experience, why they're important.

When the COVID-19 pandemic hit and people were staring job losses in the face, many people faced – for the first time in their adult working life – a genuinely desperate situation. The last time something remotely on the same scale had occurred was the global financial crisis of 2008. Your authors were fresh-faced undergraduates at the time, and although the matter was of keen interest to us as a dinner-party conversation, the global financial crisis just did not affect us the same way it affected a 40-something working in banking at the time with two kids and a mortgage.

Perhaps you were affected by the global financial crisis or perhaps, like us, you managed to dodge it. But picture yourself in the position of our 40-something employee with two kids and a mortgage who has just been laid off and is on his drive home wondering what on earth his next steps are. *That's* what the rainy day fund is for.

We bring this up because the very concept of a rainy day fund is the kind of thing that is very easily overlooked.

In the good times, everything seems good. This is often reflected in the markets too. You keep hearing on the news about how the stock market has gone up *again* today (more on that in Chapter 12 on Stocks in Part III).

Everything around you is green. Your friend Javed, whom you previously encountered struggling to understand the markings on your shatterproof ruler in Year 6, tells you he has recently started investing in the stock market as he steps out of his Porsche.

Your neighbour who works in the local council department dealing with park maintenance explains how he has funded his retirement entirely through a cryptocurrency called Dogecoin. You Google this name and realise that the emblem on this coin is a dog. Your investment portfolio is being outperformed by a corgi.

Some others have picked out yet another niche that you didn't even think was an investment, usually a collectible like Pokémon cards or luxury watches.

Sound familiar?

That's because it is familiar. This is what happens in good times. We saw this during the pandemic. With the amount of money being pumped into the economy by various world governments, combined with the new-found time that people had sitting at home without a commute or any events to go to, people entered the investing markets for the first time and the sheer buying demand caused prices to rise.

Charles Schwab, the US stock broker, did a survey on this exact point in 2021 and found that 15% of investors had only started investing in 2020.[2]

We know from the thousands of queries that we get every month how tempting it is to go all in when everything around you is positive. In the moment, it feels right. It feels like you can't fail. It feels like *this time is different* and you need to take advantage of it.[3]

Let us assure you that markets work in fairly predictable cycles. It usually goes a little something like Figure 5.1.

The problem, of course, is that you can make a case for the market being in any number of stages at any given time. Those who are extremely positive (commonly known as the "bulls"[4]) will, even at a time of seeming euphoria in the markets, convince you that things are just getting started. At the same time, those who are eternal market pessimists (commonly

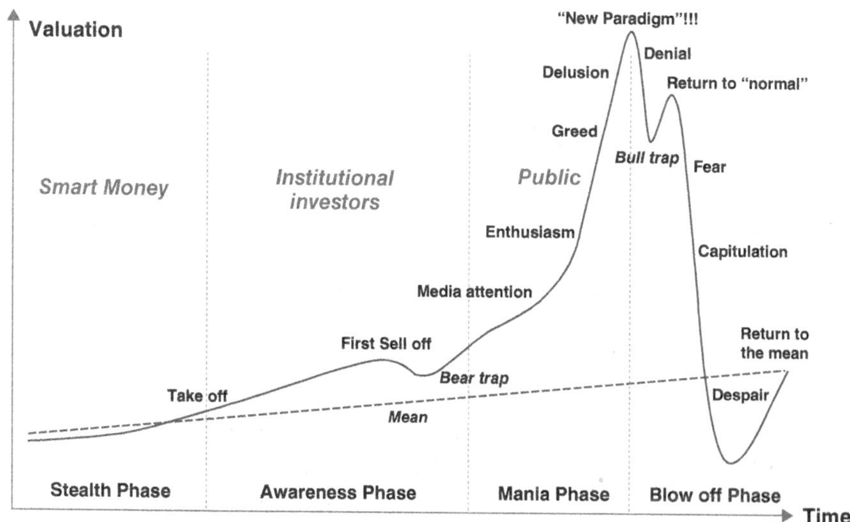

Figure 5.1 Investment stages.

Source: Jean-Paul Rodrigue/ Hofstra University/ Public Domain.

known as the "bears") will convince you that things cannot possibly go any higher and a huge sell-off is around the corner.[5] In our experience, the truth is somewhere in the middle. And actually, the point of giving you all of this backdrop on how markets work is to tie it back to the rainy day fund.

You see, the thing about investing is that it doesn't mean anything in and of itself. It only has significance if one or ideally both of these things happen:

1. The act of investing makes your life goals more achievable (e.g. you bought your dream house because you started investing); and
2. Your investments have an impact, irrespective of any financial return (e.g. you invested in an early-stage company which made a breakthrough on treating a particular disease and went on to save thousands of lives).

If we accept that investing on its own is pointless, then we also accept that we need to do other things which make our lives and the lives of our families easier and better.

The rainy day fund is exactly that. It is a collection of money which you draw upon in times of need to make sure that you and your family can retain a certain standard of living, even in a situation where your income has dried up. And even if you aren't running into crises every year or so, this emergency pot is helpful to pay for those unexpected annoying costs like boiler repairs and car repairs.[6]

How Much Should You Save in a Rainy Day Fund?

This is a question that we get asked very regularly. The conventional answer is 3–6 months of expenses. Simply calculate your monthly expenses, assume zero income coming in, and multiply that by anywhere between 3 and 6 to get the size of what your rainy day fund should be.

Where exactly you land between 3 and 6 months is a matter of personal appetite. If you're very confident that you would be back up and running within 3 months, build your rainy day fund accordingly. On the flip side, if you think it might take you somewhat longer, adjust your rainy day fund.

You can also adjust for other important factors too. A common one is that if you have a lot of support around you and you know that you have extremely reliable people you can call on in times of need who will have the amount of money on hand that you need, it's inefficient for you to be building up a big rainy day fund.

Similarly, access to lines of credit such as credit cards might affect how much you really need to save in a rainy day fund.

The bottom line is that it is important for you to recognise that the concept of a rainy day fund is important. How much you choose to save in one is a personal choice though, and we have outlined some key factors here as to what might affect that.

From a personal perspective, we like to keep some liquid cash (i.e. cash we can quickly access) as a buffer but we are in the fortunate position of having strong family support, and/or lots of other tools at our disposal that we can call on in an emergency scenario, such as lines of credit.

Should You Invest Your Rainy Day Fund?

Another common question once people have decided to save a rainy day fund is what they should actually do with the money. Should you keep it in the bank? Or should you invest it and try to make a return on it? The golden rule here is that if you would struggle to get hold of money almost immediately in an emergency scenario, you should leave it in cash.

On the other hand, if you are confident that you would be able to get your hands on some emergency money through family, friends or other means, then there is a good argument for investing your rainy day fund.

That being said, if you do decide to invest your rainy day fund you need to have two big concepts in mind, concepts which will become increasingly important as we dive deeper into the book: *liquidity* and *volatility*.

Liquidity simply refers to how easy it would be to encash that investment. For instance, an investment in a physical property would not be very liquid. House sales take months to go through, after all. But an investment in the stock market is liquid because you can simply open your share trading app and hit the sell button. Of course, you need to factor in the time it takes for the broker to send the money to your bank account and the fact that you would only be able to sell during market hours (that rules out weekends, for example). This should help you to understand the concept of liquidity.

However, you will shortly understand why an investment in the stock market is not a good idea. Although it is liquid (you can encash the investment easily), the stock market can be volatile. This simply means that prices go up and prices also can go down. Generally speaking, the stock market is best as a long-term investment because it generally goes up over time. But the thing with a rainy day fund is you need to be able to sell it *at any time*. And if you happen to need to sell it when your stock is having a bad day, week, or month, you will not have the opportunity to ride out that volatility by just staying invested for the long term. You would be forced to sell at a low price because you need to get your hands on the money immediately.

So what we're really looking for in an appropriate investment for your rainy day fund is something which is liquid and not volatile. Examples of this are:

- Instant access savings accounts
- Fixed income funds
- *Sukuk* funds.

If you do decide to try and make a return on your rainy day fund, just make sure that you are putting it into something where you can *easily get hold of your cash* and where the value of your money is going to remain fairly stable.

Are Rainy Day Funds Completely Necessary?

Having just explained in detail why rainy day funds are important, we will now seek to argue that they are not *absolutely* necessary for everyone.

Let us start by saying that for the vast majority of people, a rainy day fund will be necessary. However, a rainy day fund can also be extremely *inefficient* if you know that you would be able to get access to emergency funds quickly if the need ever arose, from another source.

Examples of this are if you have close family on hand who you know would be willing and able to help you out on a short-term basis, if you have a line of credit that could cover emergency needs, or perhaps if you have access to cash through your own business which you could temporarily loan.

Please note though that this is to be treated with caution and is a personal judgement call. It is better to err on the side of caution if you are at all unsure, as the risks are too high otherwise.

6 Going Halal for the First Time and the Purification of Wealth

After a spectacularly pessimistic start to this book, you'll be pleased to note that from hereon in, things start to get exciting. We'll be talking about where to invest, how much to invest, and the various ways you can make money.

But first, let's set you up so that you're not just going to be rich, but rich the halal way.

Jeremy became a Muslim in 2010. As is normal, he declared his *shahada* (testimony of faith) in front of the Friday congregation. Afterwards dozens of people came up to him, hugged him and congratulated him.

"One thing multiple people independently advised me during these hugs," he told me afterwards, "was that I need to eat halal meat now. They were really concerned about that."

Needless to say, Jeremy quickly started shopping at the halal meat store rather than his usual butchers. Halal food was now sorted, but halal finance not so much. It wasn't until many years later that Jeremy stumbled by chance across a book on Islamic finance. He quickly realised that he needed to make some significant changes in his life and that's how we met.

Jeremy's story is not unusual, even for those born Muslim. Islamic finance and the rights and wrongs of things according to the sharia are not always given emphasis as we are growing up. We all know that pork is impermissible, as is alcohol. But a large number of Muslims are completely unaware that concepts like *riba* (interest) and *gharar* (uncertainty) would render financial products like premium bonds, conventional mortgages, and conventional insurance impermissible.

The *Qur'an* is really explicit about this:

> O believers! Fear Allah, and give up outstanding interest if you are "true" believers. If you do not, then beware of a war with Allah and His Messenger! But if you repent, you may retain your principle—neither inflicting nor suffering harm.[1]

Dealing in interest is the only thing in the entire *Qur'an* that attracts such a severe injunction as to have Allah and his Messenger declaring war on that individual.

But unfortunately, because finances are perhaps not as visceral and physical a thing as alcohol or pork, for many of us, this gets overlooked until we stumble across it or look into it.

Going halal for the first time can seem daunting as you feel like you'll need to do open heart surgery on your entire finances. For some people, that is honestly not too far from the truth, but, for most, going halal for the first time is actually not that difficult if you have a good game-plan. In this chapter we set out that game-plan for you.

One thing to note though, if you are a new Muslim: your entire past financial activities – including profits – are acceptable for you to continue to live off and benefit from. However, you should look to purify and rejig your portfolio from the date you became aware of the rulings around Islamic finance and investing.

Income

The first thing to do is take stock of your financial affairs, particularly your income. Is your career a halal career? If it is not, then your entire earnings would not be permissible under the sharia and you would again fall into significant censure from the sharia. In a famous hadith of the Prophet, he describes the case of a man: "His food is haram (unlawful), his drink is haram, his clothing is haram, and he has been nourished with haram." The Prophet rhetorically asked: "So how can [his supplication] be answered?"[2]

If you're unsure if your income is halal or haram, then we point you to a detailed analysis we did[3] and if you are still unsure, we recommend you discuss this with a scholar who understands your industry and can give you their opinion on the matter.

Financing

The big no-no in the sharia is dealing with interest, so naturally one of the first places you should review is your debt finance situation.

If you have any conventional financing arrangements, try to pay those off as quickly as you can, without causing yourself excessive difficulty. The basis behind this is that the sharia encourages one to get out of a religiously compromised situation as soon as possible.

If you regularly use overdrafts, that needs to change. Overdrafts are simply a conventional loan with interest built in.

Credit cards are slightly different. So long as you pay the loan back in full prior to being charged interest, scholars typically allow that. The pro tip that we always give to people is the minute you get your credit card online details through the post, set it up and set the payment to be taken in full at the end of every month. Just make sure that whenever you spend money on the credit card, you could use your debit card if you wanted to, you're just choosing to use your credit card.

Student loans and other very long-term loans should be accelerated to the extent possible, but without putting yourself in excessive difficulty.

Investments

Where you have existing investments that are non-compliant, things get a little trickier.

For individual haram investments, e.g. shares in an alcohol manufacturer, you should divest from such assets as soon as you can. Let's say you bought £5000 of Diageo shares which are now worth £5200, you should sell those immediately and give away the extra £200. Conversely if they were worth £4800, you can keep the entire amount.

The reasoning behind this is that you should only keep the capital and give away the profit, as your capital was fundamentally from halal sources while the profit has arisen from the haram company's activities.

Of course, a company may not be so obviously haram as an alcohol manufacturer but it may be haram nevertheless. There are multiple steps you need to take to analyse a company to check whether or not it is halal to invest in. We'll cover this in a lot more detail in Part III.

A more complex problem occurs if your haram investments are commingled with halal investments. In this situation you need to work out the haram component in order to purify it. The typical circumstance where this would present itself is when you have been holding a conventional fund (i.e. not an Islamic one). Some of the underlying shares held in the fund will be halal while others will be haram.

Let us say you invested £5000 in a fund 5 years ago. This fund is not a sharia-compliant fund. Let's take "Aviva Investors Multi-Manager 40–85% Shares Fund 2 GBP Acc" as an example. You can get the factsheet for it here,[4] we will also provide some screen captures from this account. As you can see in Figure 6.1, we've got a clear view on about 21% of the portfolio. The rest we have to just approximate for. The key aim here is to work out: how much of the profits that I have made derive from haram sources?

The most effective, practical, approximate way to get to that point, is to work out what assets in the portfolio are actually haram and then assuming that that is the percentage of your profit that will be from haram sources.

The idea is to end up with a percentage of haram sources in the portfolio overall, so you can say clearly something like "My portfolio has 44% haram assets, so 44% of my profits are haram."[5]

On the top 10 holdings we can see, the stocks can be dealt with straightforwardly. You can work out if they're haram or halal using a sharia screen app or work it out manually using the guidance in Part III of this book. In this instance, the majority of these investments actually look sharia-compliant, bar HSBC, Diageo, and British American Tobacco. Therefore, in this case it would appear that around 27% of this portfolio is haram.

	Company	Sector	Fund (%)
1	Shell PLC	Energy	3.79
2	AstraZeneca PLC	Healthcare	3.35
3	Unilever PLC	Consumer Defensive	2.32
4	HSBC Holdings PLC	Financial Services	2.15
5	Diageo PLC	Consumer Defensive	1.93
6	BP PLC	Energy	1.85
7	British American Tobacco PLC	Consumer Defensive	1.67
8	Glencore PLC	Basic Materials	1.44
9	Rio Tinto PLC	Basic Materials	1.21
10	GSK PLC	Healthcare	1.20

The Top Holdings shown in the factsheet excludes cash and equivalents.

Figure 6.1 Top holdings.
Source: Aviva/ Public Domain.

However, it's never that straightforward, alas. If we look further into the fund holdings, we realise that only 74.14% of the overall fund is in equities. Therefore, we can more accurately say that 27% of 74.14% is haram, i.e. around 20.3%.

The remaining amounts include a couple of other problematic areas. The "Defensive" section in Figure 6.2 represents bond holdings. Bonds are interest-bearing instruments and therefore impermissible. The "Absolute Return" section is also likely to be impermissible, as it would typically involve derivatives, which are not seen as permissible financial instruments.

If we add all that up, we get:

20.3% haram equities + 14.49% bonds + 8.08% derivatives = 42.87%

Unfortunately in this case, around 42.87% of the profits would be derived from haram assets. Therefore, if over 5 years, you have profited by £1000, you will have to give away about £420.

We appreciate that for many of you, you may be making this calculation after years of being invested in the wrong funds out of ignorance. If these calculations result in significant and material losses to you, your pension, and retirement prospects, and you will be placed into hardship as a result of this, we would recommend you consult an Islamic scholar and seek a bespoke fatwa that allows you a little more leeway.

Fund Positioning

	Fund (%)
Growth	74.14
North America	31.31
United Kingdom	12.28
Emerging Global	7.37
Europe	6.64
Pacific Basin	5.61
Emerging Markets Debt	5.56
Japan	3.82
Global High Yield	1.55
Defensive	14.49
Global Sovereigns	10.41
Corporate Global	4.08
Uncorrelated	8.08
Absolute Return	8.08
Cash and Fx	3.29
Cash	3.25
FX	0.04

Figure 6.2 A typical Aviva pension fund.

Source: Aviva/ Public Domain.

Where you own bond funds, where the entire earnings are unfortunately haram, you should look to give away the interest component while keeping the original investment. If your bond fund investments are substantial, you may want to consult an Islamic scholar and get a bespoke fatwa that allows you to increase your capital portion in line with inflation so that you don't end up losing most of the value of the investment otherwise.

Zakat

Zakat is the 2.5% annual charity contribution on standing wealth that every Muslim needs to pay. Unfortunately some people do not realise that they should be paying zakat, and have many years of historic *zakat* to approximate and pay off.

The good news is that you don't necessarily have to compound the due zakat payments, nor do you have to adjust for inflation, however the bad news is, you definitely still have to pay it.

Some individuals opt to make a note of the due amount in their will and defer the payment until they pass away. However, the advisable route is to pay it off in your lifetime and as soon as possible.

Summary

- Understanding and applying the basics are fundamental to your financial journey.
- If you do not have an Islamic will, get one now.
- If your employer will contribute to your pension, make sure you are enrolled in your pension, otherwise you are turning down free money. Just make sure you are not inadvertently investing in anything haram via your pension.
- A rainy day fund is a priority for most people.
- Be prepared to genuinely scrutinise all aspects of your life from the perspective of "Is this halal?"

PART II How to Develop Your Investment Strategy

The first time you play cricket, you're introduced to something called "the box". This is a plastic covering that is designed to protect your crown jewels if you are a boy. Every so often, a particularly daring boy will want to prove his mettle and decides to go into bat without wearing a box. I've[1] seen with my own eyes this ending pretty badly.

In Part I, you learned the rules of the game and you're now raring to go. Part III is ultimately where you will get that chance. Part II is "the box".

We're going to cover four important concepts that will end up determining the success or failure of your investments in the long term far more than the actual individual investments you choose.

We'll be covering:

1. Investment mindset.
2. The basic building blocks of an investment life.
3. How to do basic due diligence into an investment company.
4. Tax saving strategies you must be aware of.
5. Weighing up risk and reward.

7 Your Investment Mindset

In early 2021, an online army entered the stock market, flipped it on its head, rejoiced gleefully, and heralded a new era of "social investing".

We're talking about the online community known as "r/wallstreetbets", a sub-community of stock market enthusiasts within Reddit. This entire ecosystem came to public prominence when the GameStop saga started in January and February 2021.

What had happened in the months prior was that a few people had identified the fact that GameStop – a US retailer selling video games – had been identified by professional fund managers as a favourite to go bust.

When businesses perform poorly, certain fund managers get very excited. That's because it opens up the possibility of "shorting" that company on the stock market. Shorting is a mechanism that allows you to borrow shares from an existing shareholder, sell those shares on the market (and get the proceeds), as long as you promise to give those shares back to the shareholder from whom you borrowed them. Where the share price decreases in that time, you have a net gain.

The shareholder is no worse off – since all you do is borrow 10 GameStop shares from them and return 10 GameStop shares to them. But the winner is the person shorting because they benefit financially from the share price going down. If I borrow 10 shares when they are worth $10 each I would bag $100. If those shares halve in price, it only costs me $50 to repurchase them and give the shares I owe back to the owner.

Shorters get a bad reputation as the practice of shorting is seen as highly unethical. It accelerates the downfall of a business and leaves them little chance of surviving if there is negative headwind around the stock. It makes life difficult for that company to raise financing, for example.

Poorly performing businesses are therefore very attractive for shorters. They are prime candidates for share price declines because the market is efficient and it will punish bad businesses.

Right?

Well, traditionally, yes. But in the modern world where thousands of "unsophisticated" people can band together to save a stock from the horrible throes of shorters, it can completely flip the market on its head.

The problem with shorting is that if it goes right, the most you can ever gain is 100%. A stock can only ever fall to zero, and if that happens, you would not have to give the shares back to the shareholder so you get to keep all the proceeds you earned from the initial sale.

On the flip side, if the trade goes against you and the stock actually *goes up*, you end up having to buy the stock at a higher price in order to fulfil your obligation of paying back the shareholder his or her shares. And as you know, there is no limit to how high a share price can go.

So when the Redditors got involved and started buying GameStop shares furiously, that sent the price up drastically. This band of people, all unknown to each other apart from through online pseudonyms, literally caused a hedge fund who had shorted GameStop to go bankrupt.[1]

All of this serves as a very useful backdrop to understanding investment philosophy. It is absolutely vital to remember one critical rule about investing: investments serve you, not the other way round. Don't let emotions get the better of you – the disciplined investor is a rich investor.

One thing we often see with investing – particularly those who are very hands-on – is the tendency to become obsessed with the investments themselves. We have seen people who literally the week before had no idea about what the stock market was, become obsessed with the stock market to the point where they are refreshing their app almost every ten minutes to check the latest prices on their portfolio.

There are two core things wrong with an obsessive approach to investing – and we say this as self-professed investing geeks. The first is that from an investing perspective, it is generally not a fruitful exercise to be so short-termist in your approach. The most sensible investment approach, particularly in the stock market, is to have a long-term view and invest as though you do not intend to sell for several years.

The mere ability to be able to view prices for certain things like stocks on a live basis is not a reason to obsess over the price and to keep buying and selling for tiny gains. It is bad for your mental health, and it is generally long-term investing which brings the most capital gain.

The second is that from an Islamic perspective, there are better things with which to occupy our minds. Investing is an important piece of the puzzle that is life: it is important that we are responsible and that we have a sound financial house. However, that should not be at the expense of our mental health, nor should it be at the expense of other obligations we have with respect to time we spend with our families, work, spiritually, fitness and other important aspects of our day-to-day life.

Investing done badly can have consequences far deeper than simply losing money. It can cost relationships and other untold damage.

So set yourself firm rules around what success actually means, and, irrespective of which camp you belong to for how you go about your investing, set parameters around the tracking of your investments to ensure that you don't become obsessive in a bad way. Mentally get yourself in a place where making or losing money doesn't hurt you any more. Once you take the hurt out of it, investing becomes a cerebral activity, not an emotional one.

The best way to take the emotion out of investment decisions is to plan for the exit and the unexpected. Let's unpack that.

Plan for the Exit and the Unexpected

It is vital that you go into investing with a very sound understanding of how to behave in the post-investment phase. Like most important things in life, you must go in with a plan of what you want out of it, and how you plan to achieve that.

This period can be compared to pre-match preparation. If you've ever played or watched sports at any level, you will know that teams spend a large amount of time preparing for a game. This will include the team's fitness and tactics, and it will also include an analysis of the opponent's strengths and weaknesses to ensure that the team is best prepared to win the game. At the elite level, teams of sports scientists will be looking to extract every single marginal gain possible, including being involved in the team's travel plans and making sure that comfort levels are high so that the athletes are in peak condition for the game.

This period is akin to what many investors do before they invest. They spend a decent amount of time researching. They watch videos, read books like this one, read articles, talk to friends; they hover over the invest button and then get occupied with something else and find another area to research and get comfortable on.

Solid preparation and research are vital to making an informed and confident foray into investing.[2]

It is vital that in this planning phase you focus first and foremost on what *you* want and need out of your investing. Whether you're young and seeking growth at all costs, whether you're sitting on significant amounts of cash and looking for a defence-first approach, or whether you're approaching retirement and figuring out how best to stay invested whilst protecting your nest egg – we all have goals that we need to make explicit in our minds.

You must ask yourself this question: *what does success look like?*

The answer to that question will determine not just what kinds of investments you make, but crucially it will help your behaviour to remain rational after you have invested your money too. Particularly if things do not go to plan.

Imagine the following scenario: you finally get comfortable enough to invest and due to your particular investment strategy, 40% of your portfolio is invested in the stock market. Global events take a turn for the worse and the stock market tumbles, with the markets down 50% overnight.

What do you suppose your reaction would be here? You might be surprised to learn that many people panic and sell off their investments in such a scenario. You might read that and think that this seems highly irrational, but the chances are that many of you would also find yourselves among these people panicking.

In this day and age when prices are available readily and you can sell shares in the stock market at the click of a button, remaining invested during a crashing market can be difficult. This is only exacerbated when all you are hearing on the news and reading online is about a global crisis.[3]

But actually if you went into the game with a very clear plan and a sound understanding of your investments, that would allow you to be much more level-headed about your strategy. People panic-sell when their knowledge levels at the start of the game are not high in the first place. But those who are sound in their knowledge actually see crashing markets as an opportunity to buy investments which are irrationally priced by the market.

Having a good sense of what success looks like and what would trigger you exiting a position is important before you start investing because it will allow you to react properly even if things do not go to plan.

To go back to our sports analogy, if the opposition lines up slightly differently to how you expected or they change tactics mid-game, the best prepared teams will know exactly how to counter that move. Poorly prepared teams would not.

A properly prepared investor chooses investments according to his or her goals and also has forecast and played out a series of scenarios. We strongly encourage you to forecast this either before investing or immediately after in order to keep the rational part of the brain at the forefront of the decision-making process.

You should have a list of pre-set rules and moves ready to be played in case of certain scenarios happening. Let's say you have a portfolio which is comprised of the following:

25% stocks
20% fixed income
30% real estate
10% venture capital
10% private equity
5% gold

There are lots of permutations as to how things might play out over the years. Some of these asset classes are very illiquid and take years to play out (e.g. venture capital and private equity) and others are much more liquid (e.g. stocks and gold).

You might have rules that say, for example, that if gold prices rise such that the value of your gold becomes anything more than 5% of your portfolio, you will sell the portion above and lock in that profit. Similarly, you may also have a rule that says if the stock market crashes and "If any stock

I own goes below 35% of my buy-in price, I will buy more." Another one might be: "If I receive dividend income from my fixed income and real estate exposure, I will re-invest that into gold." Having pre-set rules this way takes the emotion out of investing and puts your investments on an emotionless autopilot.

But what if you think you can't control your emotions and want to entrust it to someone else instead?

How Hands-On Should You Be?

One of the best things about running IFG is that we get to interact with such a wide variety of investors that we really have seen the whole spectrum.

When we first started IFG as a blog, we had naively believed that everyone was like us. That they would be willing to spend hours and hours getting deep on investments, understanding all the nitty-gritty, and that they would actually enjoy it. Our mind boggled at the thought of someone who would hear the words "Self-Invested Personal Pension" and manage to maintain a steady heart rate.

Today we have come to realise that there are different profiles of people. It is likely that you resonate with one of these characters described now.

Take Ahmed, a friend of ours who works what many would deem to be a fairly standard 9–5 role. I[4] spent a lot of time trying to convince Ahmed that investing was for everyone, not just the elite. I introduced him to books that I recommend to everyone, such as *One Up On Wall Street* by Peter Lynch[5] and encouraged him to read commentary and follow smart people on Twitter to really get a sense of things.

Ahmed was in the 5% of people who actually took this seriously. He went away, and became obsessed with it. He went on to build his own social media list of smart people he liked to listen to, developed theses around different companies, and even became proficient in understanding how to read charts through technical analysis.

When I next met up with Ahmed, he was telling me what he had been up to and how he had started investing in the stock market. He had gone full growth mode by investing in smaller cap stocks listed on the US markets as he felt that was where there was most growth potential.

To his good fortune, Ahmed couldn't have picked a better time to get into the market. The stock market was in heavy bull mode, and his stocks went up significantly. He made some great money on the stock market and although he got a bit of a shock when the bear market set in, the seed was sown: Ahmed now felt extremely confident handling his own investments and navigating not just the stock market, but also other types of investing.

Compare that to Bilal. Bilal is actually a finance professional. He has an Economics degree and has only ever worked in the City at top investment firms. He is regularly involved through his work in some of the City's highest-profile transactions. The type of guy who you would think would be the perfect candidate to be very hands-on with his own investing.

The surprising thing about Bilal is that he considers himself incompetent to run his own investments. As much as I've tried to convince Bilal that he can take a leaf out of Ahmed's book and get deep in the weeds of his investments (and that actually he already has a lot of the skills), he refuses to do so. I have a couple of theories as to why this might be the case:

1. As a finance professional, he is all too aware of the complexities that go into the transactions that happen at work where he deals with extremely high value and often complex transactions. The mental load of adjusting to his own portfolio is quite difficult to make.
2. Quite simply, as someone who deals with finance and investing on a day-to-day basis, it is hard to muster the enthusiasm to translate that to his own portfolio. This is a common phenomenon across different industries where people simply do not want to take work home.

But the thing with Bilal is, once you get him going on investments, he'll actually become hands-on quite quickly, because he has that background and will have an opinion on things. He won't ever become as hands-on as Ahmed though.

The third character that typifies the range of characters is Usmaan. Usmaan is a medic. He is not particularly interested in getting into the nitty-gritty of investing but, interestingly, he is also not that interested in investing at all. Usmaan is still fairly early on in his career, and unlike Bilal who at least recognises the importance of investing, Usmaan has a relaxed attitude to investing. He knows he has a rather good public pension which means his retirement should actually be quite comfortable. He doesn't really feel the urgency to invest and, even if he wanted to invest, he knows he would be somewhat paralysed by struggling to decide what to invest in and likely also by sharia compliance. When Usmaan does invest, he'll likely want to give all his money to someone he trusts to manage his money for him and ideally never be bothered about investment decisions again.

The fourth character is Zainab. Zainab actually wants to invest but is blocked from doing so due to the nature of her job. She is a professional in the finance industry who is privy to sensitive information that would potentially categorise her as trading on inside information if she were to act on that information. Zainab therefore needs to find a legal avenue to actually be able to invest. Usually this means Zainab goes completely hands-off like Usmaan.

Even if you do not fit one of these personas exactly, it is likely that you will resonate with one of them. The one you resonate with the most will determine how hands-on your investing should be. As we have mentioned earlier in the book, there is no right or wrong way of investing. There is just a way of investing that is suitable to you.

There are broadly the following options:

1. Do all the investing yourself, including choosing which asset classes you want to invest in and what percentage each one makes up of your portfolio, and choosing the underlying investments yourself.
2. Decide to leave the choosing of underlying investments to other professionals, but choose who those providers are. For example, I will buy this particular stocks fund or real estate fund.
3. Decide to leave everything to a professional who will decide the construction of your portfolio in terms of which asset classes go in, and who will then choose the investment providers to then give your money to. Those investment providers will then ultimately deploy your capital.

Even if you simply want someone else to manage your money, we would certainly encourage you to gain a basic understanding of investments. This allows you to be conversant in the world of finance and investing which in turn makes you better equipped to properly understand what makes a good wealth manager or not.

Of course, whatever decision you make, you will have to navigate the sharia lens. So whether that is picking investments yourself, you will need to have the necessary understanding to be able to navigate the halal from the haram. Part III of this book will greatly assist you on this.

If you are opting for approach (2) or (3) above, you will need to satisfy yourself that the investment providers or the wealth manager you choose has a sharia strategy. In many cases, a sharia strategy is simply an overlay whereby the providers/wealth manager will be investing in well-known sharia products that already exist on the market. It is therefore worth your time digging deep into what exactly a provider or wealth manager is going to do for you that is actually value-add and not something you could just do yourself in 30 minutes.

If they are simply accessing sharia-compliant products that are themselves readily available on the market, then you must question what this person is actually doing to earn their fees. Ask them questions like: "If I could invest in non-sharia-compliant products, is this the asset mix you would allocate for me?" The answer to that question is usually very telling.

In summary, pick your investment lane, understand the fees associated with that, and never ever compromise on the quality of investment that you are exposed to.

The Three Types of "Hands-On"

Here's a little secret that is surprisingly hard to grasp: there is no right or wrong way to invest.

It seems crazy, given that the whole financial industry is predicated on the idea that there are some people who know how to invest and there is everybody else. And while it is definitely true that professionals who spend their careers investing are savvier and can be worth the money, it is also true that you need to have your own philosophy to investing, otherwise it can become a rather misguided and fruitless endeavour with no internal consistency to your decision-making.

The beauty of investing is that it is intensely personal. It is a cocktail of many things which can only come from you. Your risk appetite, your wealth levels, your time horizons, your upcoming life events, your hunches, and, yes, how much time you are willing to put in.

Because even the choice to hand everything over to a wealth manager is a proactive choice. So too is the choice not to do anything with your money. As is the choice to take any other position on the spectrum of investing which includes becoming a seriously advanced DIY investor.

So let's discuss investment philosophy from the perspective of three different camps:

Camp 1: hands-off (Usman and Zainab).
Camp 2: hands-on (Bilal).
Camp 3: hands-on plus (Ahmed).

Hands-Off

The unfortunate truth for investment geeks like us is that the overwhelming majority of people simply have no interest or desire to manage their own investments.

The somewhat surprising reality that we have discovered over the years is that the profile of such people is not what one would typically expect. This profile of the individual actually includes *seasoned finance professionals*, as well as other senior professionals in other industries. This shocking realisation has led us to the conclusion that investing is only partly about knowledge; it's also about how much of a priority you are willing to make it.

There are many personal tasks we all have to do, and usually they are a bit dull. Consequently, many of us are open to paying a premium to get the convenience of knowing that our problems are being taken care of by someone else. Whether it's getting a takeaway instead of cooking from scratch or getting the car oil changed by a mechanic rather than doing it ourselves. Investing is no different, and the argument the people in this camp make is that they have neither the time nor the expertise to become good at investing – so it makes sense to give their investments to a specialist.

The only choice that remains then is who to hand over your investing to. Unlike a bad takeaway where the consequences are, at worst, 24 hours long, entrusting the wrong person or firm with your hard-earned money can lead to financial ruin.

The first option you could take here is to pick a reputable, regulated financial advisor with experience in Islamic investing, who will be paid around 0.5% of your total savings pot every year and will invest that money for you. Financial advisors will usually prefer listed stocks and Islamic bond products and they'll guide you through broader personal finance issues such as life insurance, wills, etc.

The second option you could take here is to choose one investment platform and put in a few hours of work one time and set up a couple of direct debits to long-term investments. This could be a regular investment in a stocks, property, or fixed income fund – and then you're done with it. After that, your investments are on autopilot for a good few years at least.

Hands-On

The hands-on camp is an interesting bunch and can often be among the most sophisticated investors.

This camp has usually ended up here having been in both the hands-off camp and the hands-on plus camp. They found the hands-off camp a little too disarming: it is hard to completely trust someone with your money after all. They then went the other way and tried to go hands-on plus, i.e. choosing individual investments like stocks but then realised that it was too much time, effort, and headache and they probably were not getting amazing results either.

What ends up happening is that this camp still remains hands-on: they don't typically give their money to a wealth manager or financial advisor. Instead, they seek out opportunities to invest their money with people who know what they are doing for a particular asset class. They will know that they want exposure to, say, real estate, stocks, crypto, and private equity. And they will then seek out specialist firms in those areas and trust those people with their money.

Hands-On Plus

This is the camp that goes all the way to the core, getting deep on investing and choosing the actual investments themselves.

What usually happens is that an individual will end up becoming good at one particular asset class – be that stocks, real estate, crypto, or something else – and they will end up concentrating their investments in this one asset class because it's what they know best.

If investing is a layered cake, these guys dig right to the bottom (Table 7.1).

Table 7.1 Range of investment involvement

Cake layer	Involvement	Public markets	Private markets	Due diligence standard
Top layer	Hands-off	Let financial advisor decide	Let financial advisor decide	Need to pick a credible financial advisor
Middle layer	Hands-on	Pick a fund that invests in public market assets	Pick a fund that invests in private market assets	Need to get fund manager to pick right ones and ensure monies invested in credible investment companies
Bottom layer	Hands-on plus	Pick individual stocks	Pick individual companies, real estate assets, *sukuk*, etc.	Need to get individual assets right

There is no right or wrong answer as to which of the three levels of "hands on" you ultimately go for, and it might change for you over time. If in doubt, start with the hands-off approach first, and start to learn about investing in the company of others who are more experienced than you. Then, if you start to feel the itch to venture forth and do your own thing, embrace it.

Making Decisions as a Family

When it comes to anything regarding money and investing, it is likely that you are not the only person affected by your decisions. We have already discussed that inherent in investing is a goals-based approach, and for nearly all of you, those goals will involve your family.

Different households run their finances in different ways. For some, investing is a family decision and the husband and wife make decisions jointly. For other couples, either the husband or the wife will control the purse strings and make the decisions on investments without any real nod to their spouse.

While there is of course nothing wrong per se with any approach, we recommend that when it comes to investing, your significant other is at least aware of what you are up to and what is going on.[6]

This has multiple benefits for an investor. The first main benefit is that it is only fair and respectful that your spouse knows where the money is going. It also means that in an emergency event where you are potentially no longer even around, that they know where money has been invested and how to deal with it.

In addition, from a purely investing perspective, a cold read on investments can often be priceless. There have been many times where your humble authors have had a sensible dose of cold water splashed on our investment ideas by our respective spouses (who are not investment professionals by any stretch) and, in hindsight, they were absolutely right.[7] Having a sense of accountability can temper your investment decisions in the right way.

So our advice here is clear: if you are the kind of person who makes investing decisions alone, bring your other half into the equation. Let them know how and where you've invested your money, why you made that decision, and what you expect to get out of it. The mere act of verbalising this will help you to clarify your own thesis too.

Summary

- Investing is as much a mental game as it is a financial one.
- Always remember the *why* behind your investing journey and don't lose sight of it.
- Have an unemotional plan for your behaviour once you have invested – set rules and stick to them.
- Decide how hands on an investor you are and switch your strategy accordingly.
- Hold yourself accountable to your spouse for investment decisions if you typically make them on your own.

8 Building the Blocks

Earlier on we mentioned the fact that the beauty of investing is that it is an intensely personal thing and, as a result, is completely unique.

You can compare investing to building a house from scratch. While the fun bit can be seeing the house come together and then enjoying it by living in it and hosting your friends, there is an awful lot that needs to go into the planning and construction first before you can lay the first brick.

A house needs strong foundations, utilities companies need to come out and ensure they have laid the ground to ensure running water and electricity, regulation will ensure that parts of the land are sampled to test for contamination, and so on. Nobody buys a plot of land and immediately starts building. If the initial groundwork is not top quality, it will affect the enjoyment of your house later on. If you somehow skip the groundwork and start building, you will find that things go wrong and affect how much you are actually able to enjoy the house.

Investing is similar: it is part of your overall life plan and is not an isolated matter. In this chapter we will cover three crucial building blocks that all of us will need to face at some point or another:

1. Rent or buy?
2. Preparing for life's big events.
3. Retirement.

Rent or Buy?

One of the biggest decisions anybody faces early on in their financial life is what to do about housing. This is also partly driven by the local norms and local housing markets. In the UK, for example, property is considered to be a very stable and safe asset class that appreciates reliably over time. See Figure 8.1, which shows the trend of the average property price in the UK from 1985 to 2025. You can see the only real blip is around the 2008 mark which was brought on by the Global Financial Crisis and, even then, UK real estate was reliable enough to have bounced back by 2015.

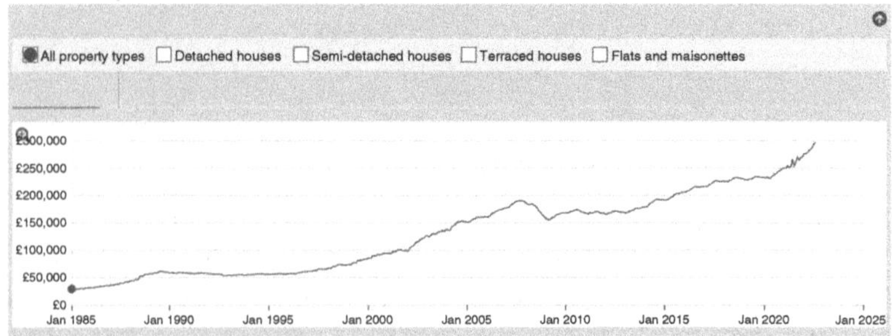

Figure 8.1 Average price by type of property in the United Kingdom, 1985–2025.

Source: HM Land Registry / https://landregistry.data.gov.uk / last accessed December 12 , 2022.

Figure 8.2 shows this more vividly, depicting the percentage change of property prices in the UK, from 1985 to 2025. Remarkably, there are just two serious periods of negative growth.

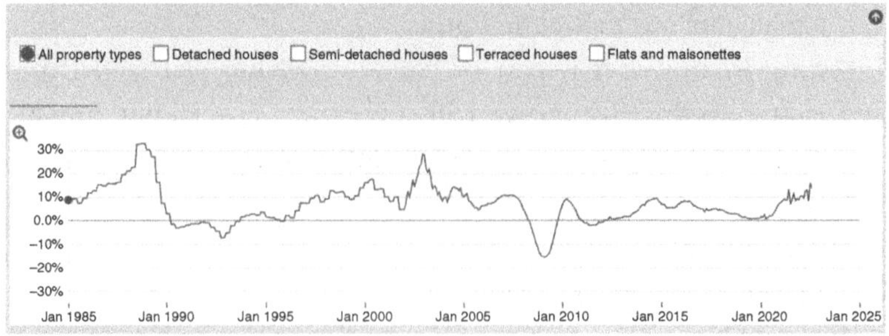

Figure 8.2 Percentage change (yearly) by property type in the United Kingdom, 1985–2025.

Source: HM Land Registry / https://landregistry.data.gov.uk / last accessed December 12 , 2022.

Compare this to the situation in the United Arab Emirates (UAE) as depicted in Figure 8.3.

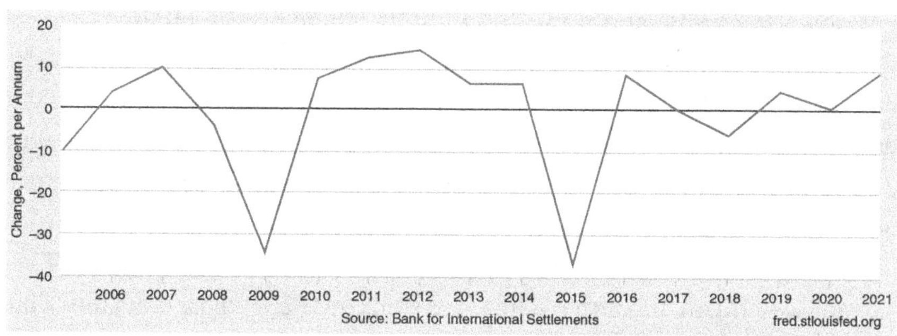

Figure 8.3 Real residential property prices for the United Arab Emirates, 2005–2021.

Source: Federal Reserve Bank of St. Louis / https://fred.stlouisfed.org/series/QAER771BIS / last accessed January 03 , 2023.

Based on Figure 8.3, if you buy property in the UAE, there's a very real chance that you might be down on your purchase price in the not-too-distant future.

We can see, therefore, that every market is unique when it comes to real estate and in certain countries you will need to adjust this advice according to how long you plan to be there, and the local housing price permutations.

But the choices facing you remain the same in any country. People broadly face two options when it comes to the accommodation they live in: either buy or rent. All other things being equal, we are inclined to buy in most situations.

The first is that there is a mental liberation in selecting a long-term property of choice with your family, setting down roots, gradually buying the equity in that house and generally treating it as your own. That mentality simply cannot be replicated in rented accommodation.

The second is that although it is common in investing circles to treat your own accommodation as a liability rather than an asset, the reality is that owning your home *can and does* give you a financial advantage. Consider the following situation:

Asad buys a property for £350,000, putting down a £50,000 deposit (just under 15%) and paying the rest over 25 years. Over the next 5 years his property appreciates by 30% and now that he has a young family, he has outgrown the house and wants to buy somewhere bigger. He is able to sell the house for £455,000. Even if we are conservative and assume he has bought no further equity in the house (which would be wrong), Asad would hand the bank the £300,000 he owes them, and walk away with £155,000. Admittedly, £50,000 of that was the original deposit he put in, but a gain of £105,000 sets him up nicely to upsize into his next home.

Of course, the flip side of all this is that properties require expense. They are not a standard investment like the stock market where you buy your shares and wait for the gain. Properties require constant upkeep and occasionally come with unexpected costs too.

In addition, it is important to bear in mind that the entry price for the potential gain that Asad got was not just his original £50k deposit, but also all of the foregone gains he could have had with that £50k had it been invested elsewhere. Property is illiquid and once Asad has upsized, his money will once again be locked up in his house.

Of course, the alternative to all of this is renting. Renting comes with a few advantages and disadvantages. The disadvantages are fairly obvious: you can never truly call the place your own, and your monthly payments serve only to pay your landlord rather than buy you any equity. The advantages of renting, however, are often underrated. The ability to pass maintenance costs on to a landlord can be a major win: no more unexpected boiler repair costs or other potentially costly maintenance.

The flexibility of location is another important advantage of renting. It allows you to move for your career or lifestyle, and follow opportunity around the country or even the world.

But as a pure financial decision, what you choose as your accommodation is going to be important. The property you live in is the only asset class that is a hybrid of a personal necessity combined with an investment.

Unless you live somewhere where property prices have a bad history, buying your property will rarely be a bad decision. The act of saving for a deposit forces saving in ways that can rarely be replicated due to the fact that your future home depends on it. And then making regular mortgage payments towards your property is such an ingrained expense that buying equity becomes an autopilot move.

In short, owning your own property can be a savvy financial move, as well as being mentally liberating. If you are in the UK or similar areas where property is stable and tends to appreciate, owning your own home makes an awful lot of sense. As such, it is often the first investment building block to really concentrate on.

Life's Big Events

While every investing journey is unique, as we discussed earlier, the stories of people's lives often rhyme. In our work at IFG, we hear that very regularly with the thousands of customer calls we've had the pleasure of taking. It usually goes a little something like this.

Young Zayd goes through school and eventually finds himself in the world of work – either via university or not. Soon, he settles down with his life partner Zainab and concerns himself with finding a deposit for an Islamic mortgage (having gone through a rabbit hole of researching whether conventional mortgages are *actually* haram and whether Islamic mortgages are any better).[1]

Zayd and Zainab settle into their new three-bedroom house. Now Zayd starts plotting out his future and realises how expensive life is. Zainab has indicated high hopes of having four children, but not before a once-in-a-lifetime trip to Zanzibar. Of course, prior to the Zanzibar trip, several Ikea trips are in order to start furnishing the new home. And all of this is set against the backdrop of wanting to go for Hajj as soon as possible.

How should Zayd and Zainab prioritise?

Even before thinking about what their investment portfolio looks like, they should make sure they have the basics right when it comes to their expenses and general financial hygiene.[2] Assuming all of that is in order, they can then start thinking about how to structure their portfolio to make sure they can hit their goals and cover life's big events.

Like Zayd and Zainab, you should have a clearly drawn-up list of goals that you want to meet over the short and medium term and allow your investing and saving strategy to work around this.

Remember that investing is not always just about putting capital into something and looking for a return. Sometimes the best investment you can make can be yourself.

You would be extremely fortunate to find an investment that increased by 50% in a short space of time. To get to that, you would have to take some pretty serious risk and put your money on the line. But you could upskill a little in your professional career and be savvy about your career to seek a job elsewhere and/or a more senior role and actually increase your salary by 50% or more relatively quickly. This "investment" move will have a much more long-term and meaningful impact than most other investments you could make.

Being honest with yourself is very important when setting out an investment strategy. With your list of goals, you need to honestly ask yourself if you can meet those goals with things as they are. If your income levels mean that you're unlikely to meet your goals, then one of three things (or possibly all) need to happen: (1) you need to make more money by finding another job; (2) you need to really strike big with your investments; or (3) you need to adjust your goals.

To help you practically on this, fill in the personal planner in Figure 8.4.

Armed with Figure 8.4, next fill in Figure 8.5.

Doing this exercise properly should spell out to you clearly what steps you need to take. If you are somebody who is well on track, your

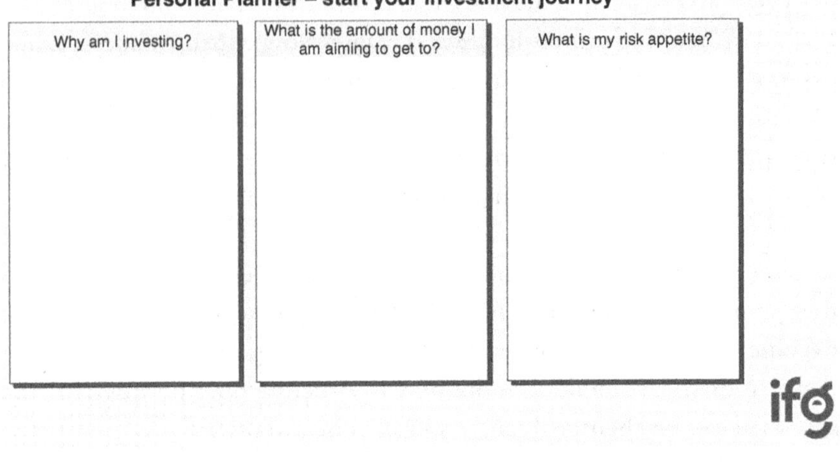

Figure 8.4 Personal planner – start your investment journey 1.

Source: the Halal Investment Checklist (p. 9). www.Islamicfinanceguru.com.

investment strategy does not need to incorporate much risk. That is simply because you are likely to meet your goals with your income levels anyway, so all you want from investing is a helping hand and extra return to shorten the time period.

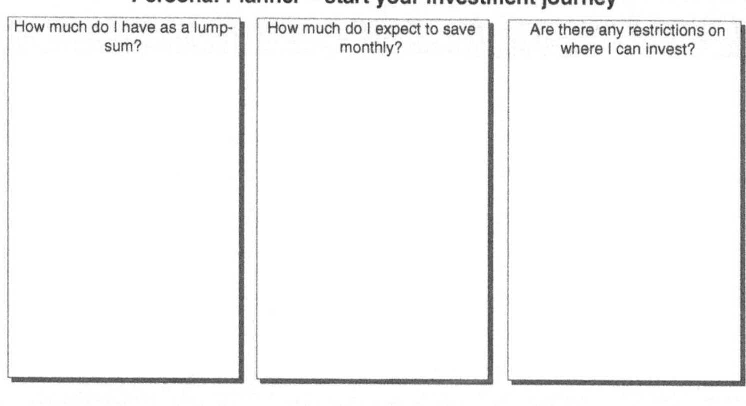

Figure 8.5 Personal planner – start your investment journey 2.
Source: the Halal Investment Checklist (p. 9). www.Islamicfinanceguru.com.

The further you are away from this ideal, the more risk you likely need to take with your investments – or the more you will need to consider changing your goals.

Figure 8.6 is a matrix that will help you understand what different types of portfolios are made up of.

A few important words of caution here though, as this is the part where many people falter. If you feel like you are far away from your goals, that

Investment Type	Low risk portfolio	Medium risk portfolio	High risk portfolio
Low Risk Investments	70%	20%	5%
Medium Risk Investments	25%	65%	65%
High Risk Investments	5%	15%	30%

ifg

Figure 8.6 Some examples of different portfolios.
Source: the Halal Investment Checklist (p. 13). www.slamicfinanceguru.

does not mean you have to go gung-ho to the point of absolute folly. You will be surprised at the power of consistent saving and solid investing. Sure, you will not meet your goals overnight but you might very well get there if you are realistic and sensible about your time frames. The danger of going overly aggressive and thinking you have no hope is that you are more susceptible to making really bad investments, because you are now playing in the world of high risk investments where the downside is far greater.

If you are playing in the world of high risk investments and feeling quite desperate, it also makes you more open to scams. Even though you might consider yourself to be the last person in the world to fall for a scam, do not underestimate the effect that pressure can have on you.

So even if you feel that you are far away from your goals, things probably are not as bad as they seem. Double check and triple check every single time you're putting money into something. Read reviews online, reach out to trusted people, and always remember the adage: "If it sounds too good to be true, it usually is."

It is also important to remember that your goals will not necessarily be met by investing alone. Investing is to your goals what an oven is to someone wanting to bake a cake. If you're missing a few ingredients, your cake is going to come up short. You can only make so much return safely and that will always be a product of the amount you are putting in.

Consider instead what you can do to bolster that. Be resourceful and entrepreneurial. We've already discussed salaries and seeking a raise either through your existing job or by going to work for a different company. There are other tactics you can use too: your spouse might be happy to work and contribute, or perhaps you can pick up a side hustle. You could do something simple like tutoring or side projects in the field you're in, or you could even start your own business. Have a look at "Breaking Even" (Chapter 2) for more ideas.

We know people in our network who have done some incredible things. One of our own employees changed his entire career trajectory by moving from the charity sector into software engineering by learning to code on the side; there's a guy we know who paid his way through university (and some!) by starting a business at university. It's not as hard as you might think; it simply requires consistency, patience, and a little bit of learned skill.

Retirement (and Pre-Retirement)

Let's take stock. We have got our investment mindset correct, decided on buying our own home or not, and figured out that it is vital to have a clear plan and set of financial priorities listed.

The next important grown-up thing we must do is discuss pensions. Financial retirement planning is a hefty topic and, for sharia-conscious investors, a particularly under-discussed area. We gave you a taster of this topic in Part I in Chapter 4, but it is time to really roll our sleeves up.

Before we unpack retirement investing, let's first spell out the characteristics of this phase of life to understand the particular nuances from a financial perspective. You'll need to understand the concepts of **risk** and **liquidity** which we discussed previously as they are fundamental to understanding this section properly and acting on it.

Let's start with the planning that comes before retirement. At this point, you are likely to still be in gainful employment and earning an income. Having likely spent your entire life with a regular monthly income, the prospect of going from that to nothing is a scary one.

Depending on what you are actually doing at this point in your life, there is not just a financial adjustment to make, but also a mental one. Prepare yourself. Just like the advice we gave when it came to investing, being in the right mental frame of mind is actually a crucial and often overlooked part of your financial retirement strategy.

There is a danger of just coasting into retirement since life at this point starts to slow down and can easily go on to autopilot. That would be a mistake though: it's crucial that you recognise the different stage of life you're entering into and that this needs a different game plan.

Much has been written about the social side of retiring. We do not propose to cover that here as that is beyond the scope of this book. But it is a very important part of your financial retirement planning to fully understand what you want to do with your time, how you'll stay active and have a good quality of life, and crucially, what sort of funds you need to live that quality of life.

Every decade of your working life you probably want to check in on your pension and make sure things are on track. But particularly in the last 20 years before your planned retirement you really need to make sure your pension is on track and ready to achieve your goals. At this point, you are probably fully invested in the stock market for your workplace pension. As we previously discussed, being invested in something for the long term is a great idea for growth. But when you have something coming up that you are going to need the cash for (in this case, retirement), you need to optimise for a lack of volatility and regular cash distributions.

If you recall, we discussed this in the context of investing your rainy day fund in Chapter 5. And in many ways, your pension pot is a glorified rainy day fund. The last thing you want to do with this pot of money is be fully invested in the stock market just before you retire and then you have a black swan event and the market comes crashing down, bringing the value of your pension portfolio down 30% right at the time when you need to encash it.

Now this might sound like an extreme scenario but it's possible and so the general wisdom is that with a pension you want to gradually taper down investments that are growth-focused and which can be volatile, in favour of more stable investments that offer a much more predictable return. Let's call this "retirement investments". See Figure 8.7.

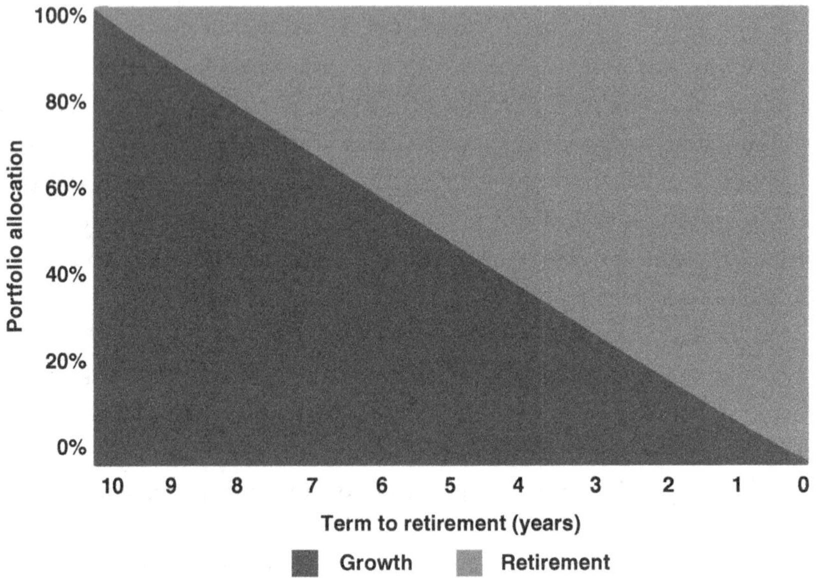

Figure 8.7 Retirement strategy.

Source: www.Islamicfinance.guru.com.

Implementing this strategy, often referred to as "lifestyling", will ensure that at the time you come to retire you will have a predictable pool of cash to draw upon. How you draw out that cash is also a strategic issue.

In the UK, the rules as at tax year 2022/23 are that you can withdraw 25% of your pension pot without paying any tax.[3] Following this, you are subject to income tax at the usual rates. While the tax implications will be different for every country, the concept of taking an income from your pension is not.

Since retirement is not a single moment in life, rather it is a period of around 30 years, you must treat this pot of money accordingly. It is helpful to split your pot of money up into three buckets: (1) cash that you need to withdraw immediately to fund your lifestyle and plug the income gap that will occur once you retire; (2) safe and steady fixed income investments that you can sell off each year to act as the first bucket described above; and (3) long-term investments that are growth-focused because your retirement will last several decades and you need to make sure you are still outstripping inflation and growing your pot.

When starting out in retirement, it is important to make sure that you have accurately forecast your cash needs for both the immediate and short-term future. That way, you can ensure you have enough cash on hand, that the money you will need in the short term can be locked away in safe, short-term fixed-income products, and the remainder can then go into longer-term investments over your retirement.

This ensures that you have enough cash to fund your lifestyle, while the rest of your cash is either earning a modest but stable return (the next 20%) or is locked away in higher growth (the 60%) for you to draw down on later.

When it comes to accessing the money from your pension, there are broadly four options:

1. Take 25% of your pot free of tax.
2. Buy an annuity.
3. Take flexible income (known as drawdown).
4. Leave all the money in the pension pot.

Let's analyse each of these options.

Taking 25% Tax-Free

In the UK, the rules as at tax year 2022/23 are that you can withdraw money from your pension pot immediately as soon as you get to the pension age. This is currently 55 although it is set to change in 2028 to 57.[4] The first 25% of that is free of tax and the remaining 75% is taxable.

Many people choose to simply take 25% of their pension pot immediately as it is tax-free and it may help to serve a particular purpose in your life. What you do with that 25% is up to you: you might need it for lifestyle purposes, or you could further invest this and take advantage of your ISA allowance and get tax-free growth there to further bolster your pot.

Remember, although growth within your pension is tax-free, you generally end up paying tax when withdrawing money from the pension. But with an ISA, not only is the growth in the ISA tax-free, the withdrawal is completely free of tax. This is because, generally speaking, money going into an ISA has already been taxed; it is usually someone's earnings. The 25% tax-free lump sum from a pension going into an ISA is one of the rare occurrences where you have an untaxed sum of money able to go into a vehicle where it can also grow untaxed and be withdrawn untaxed.

If you struggle to remember the taxation rules surrounding pensions and ISAs, remember that (except for the example above) *pensions are not taxed on the way in, but are on the way out; whereas ISAs are taxed on the way in, but not on the way out.*

This simply means that money going into an ISA has already usually been subject to tax (normally income tax), while money going into a pension is not subject to tax (but will be on exit).

Annuities

The tricky thing about retiring and planning for it is that, of course, we do not know exactly how long we will live. The clever folks at insurance companies, however, are willing to price this with their army of actuaries and they offer a product called an annuity.

While there are sharia-compliance issues with annuities which may well render it unsuitable for Muslims, it is worth discussing the premise and seeing if we can replicate it another way if you like the sound of it.

The idea with an annuity is that you effectively buy a guaranteed income for life. When you approach retirement, you can go into the market to purchase an annuity and you will be comparing annuity rates.

The way it works is that you trade a sum of money – typically some or all of your pension – and in return you get the annuity rate back as a guaranteed annual income for the rest of your life.

For instance, if you had an annuity that promised you a 3% rate and you put in £250,000, you would get a guaranteed £7,500 per annum for life.

So what's going on from a market mechanics perspective here?

Underneath the gloss, what is occurring here is basically an insurance transaction (hence the sharia-compliance issues). The annuity provider prices their annuity looking at plenty of factors in the market including macro factors like interest rates and competition in the market, but individual factors such as your own health and life expectancy. From their perspective, very crudely, they want you to die before they've paid you out the principal sum you put into the annuity (£250,000 in our example above).

So using the example above, if you lived more than 33 years, the insurance company would effectively have lost out, as by that time they would have paid out £250,000 to you.[5] If you die before then, particularly if you die long before 33 years, the insurance company would keep the £250,000 you put in, having paid out to you less than that. This is why those with medical histories that make them higher risk tend to get offered higher rates on their annuity (known as enhanced rates): the insurance company is pricing in the fact that they are more likely to die quicker so they can afford the rates to be slightly higher.

Of course, in the background, the insurance company is not sitting still on your £250,000. They have their own investment strategy to invest premiums that come in, so in reality that £250,000 will swell for them over the years. And the opportunity of growing that £250,000 yourself is something you gave up when you handed it over to buy the annuity.

So are annuities actually worth it then? Annuities are often criticised for the low rates they offer. But they do play a very important role in offering a guaranteed income. As we have mentioned earlier, financial decisions are not always just based on the numbers: there is a price and value attached to mental liberation – especially in a part of your life when you should be turning your attention to more interesting things, such as spoiling your grandchildren, mosque politics, and taking advantage of being rude in public without any repercussions.[6]

That being said, our sincere view is that while annuities are a useful tool, they are generally not a very attractive product. It boils down to the question of what are you actually protecting yourself against by entering into such an insurance transaction? It seems that what you are really protecting yourself against is bad market returns and you are paying a bit of a premium for peace of mind.

But if there were ways to ensure that you are not exposed to bad market returns, you could be much better off from a value perspective by not buying into an annuity. Generally speaking, insurance companies invest the money themselves in low-risk, fixed return products. If there were a way of Muslim investors replicating that, would that eliminate the need for you to buy an annuity?

In our view, the answer to that is yes. So let's take a look at the things you could do to effectively replicate an annuity but with a better rate, i.e. put money into something which spits money out for the rest of your life at a guaranteed rate.

Sharia-Compliant Annuity Replacement Options There are two primary candidates that we will consider here. There are more than this out there, but the two we discuss here are the two which are both easiest to grasp and to access and we want this book to be very practical and easy.

The first obvious choice to replicate an annuity is real estate. No doubt that the first thing that comes to your mind here is *hang on, that is nothing like the peace of mind or guarantee that an annuity offers.* And that is very largely true. However, the reality is that while we are seeking sharia-compliant alternatives, it is difficult to exactly match an impermissible product.

Real estate, of course, varies massively depending on how you actually have exposure to it. If you choose to use your £250,000 to buy a property in the north of England and rent it out to tenants, that is quite a hands-on approach which, although it may give you a nice net 7% yield per annum, also comes with a load of potential hassle and opens up the door for 2 a.m. phone calls telling you that the boiler is broken and that you need to fix it pronto.

There are other ways of having exposure to real estate that do not involve this. One such popular way is to hold it via publicly-listed REITs (Real Estate Investment Trusts). These are specialist property investment funds which are traded on the public markets, giving you the liquidity and the ease of something on the stock market, with the underlying exposure to something that is illiquid. There are sharia-compliant REITs available globally[7] and this provides a great option to invest an amount of money for ongoing dividends as well as capital growth.

The other option here is to invest in private real estate funds. Depending on the amount of capital that you have, there are investment managers out there running private real estate strategies, many of whom are sharia-compliant. If you have access to these funds and you can buy their minimum ticket (this will often be in the early millions), this could be a viable option.

In our work at Cur8 Capital, the very first private fund we offered was a real estate fund with a seven-figure minimum ticket (if you went directly to the real estate fund manager) which we opened up to our investor base to invest in from £5,000.

So real estate can be done in clever ways and give you a healthy annual income as well as capital growth, since property, when invested in well, should appreciate gradually over time.

The other option is to invest in fixed income products. More on the specifics of this in the Part III of the book but if you are able to get exposure to products like *sukuk*, you are effectively buying yourself an income similar to an annuity.

The Drawdown Method

The good news is that drawing down on a pension is much easier to get your head around and doesn't require as much mental gymnastics. It is what most people instinctively imagine to be the case with pensions.

Drawing down on your pension simply means taking money out of your pension pot as and when you need it – a flexible income. The remainder of the money stays in the pot and is invested in some way. This allows you to solve your immediate financial needs whilst taking into account the fact that your retirement phase is actually (statistically) a long period of time of around 30 years. You therefore want the remainder of the pot to be growing nicely, at least in line with inflation, but ideally doing more than that so you are replenishing what you already have in there. Given the long time frame, you can stay invested in longer-term investments, particularly if you are still towards the start of your retirement journey.

Any money you take from your pension pot is classed as income and you are subject to the income tax rates that you will have been used to during your working life. That is, a certain portion will be free of any tax (currently £12,570), the following portion (£12,571–£50,270) will be taxed at the basic rate (currently 20%), and anything from £50,271 to £150,000 is taxed at 40% (known as the higher rate). Any income beyond this is taxed at the additional rate, which is 45%.[8]

While we are on the topic of income tax, it is worth bearing in mind that as soon as your annual income goes over £100,000, your tax-free allowance of £12,570 dwindles down by £1 for every £2 you earn over £100,000. So once you hit £125,140, you have no tax-free allowance and that first £12,570 becomes taxable.

In a nutshell then, you can choose to take your pension as a series of lump sums paying tax on 75% of the lump sum each time, or you can choose to draw down on it annually and treat it as income subject to income tax rates.

What you choose to do is a matter for you to consider based on your personal circumstances, tax efficiency and whether you want to keep money in your pot for growth.

The considerations for each option can be viewed in Figure 8.8.

Defined Benefit Pension

Much of our discussion so far has been based on the prevalent pension schemes of today which are the defined contribution pensions, otherwise known as workplace pensions. However, there is another significant type of pension known as a defined benefit pension which many of you may well have.

Defined benefit pension schemes are a type of pension scheme where the employer guarantees a certain annual income to the employee in their retirement. These are seen as extremely attractive because, like annuities that we discussed earlier, they are a guaranteed income for life. In addition, they often rise in line with inflation. The amount of the annual payment can be linked to different things but is often linked to length of service and the salary you were on at the time of leaving.

Many large employers in the UK and globally, such as the NHS and the Royal Mail, have historically afforded their employees defined benefit pension schemes. Defined benefit schemes are now becoming vanishingly rare; employers now favour the much simpler defined contribution schemes. The reason is defined benefit schemes are much more complex to manage and can create large liabilities in the long term.

Flexible income (drawdown)	Lump sums	Guaranteed income for life (annuity)	Leave it where it is
"Pros"			
You can vary the income you take according to lifestyle changes.	A lump sum withdrawal could move you into a different, higher tax bracket.	Your income will be based on a few key factors, primarily the amount you bought the annuity with, your age and your health.	Delaying withdrawals may mean you need to withdraw higher amounts in the future, making your tax planning harder.
"Cons"			
The remaining money in your pension pot will be invested and could therefore rise or fall depending on how the investments perform.	The remaining money in your pension pot will be invested and could therefore rise or fall depending on how the investments perform.	Annuities offer you the ability to lock in certain protections for a price, such as a guaranteed minimum income or inflation-linked raises.	The remaining money in your pension pot will be invested and could therefore rise or fall depending on how the investments perform.

Figure 8.8 Flexible income drawdown.

Source: www.Islamicfinanceguru.com.

If you are the fortunate beneficiary of a defined benefit pension scheme, then you will have the comfort of a guaranteed income for your retirement. This income is treated as income for tax purposes and is therefore subject to the income tax bands as laid out in the drawdown section above.

In addition, some schemes provide a tax-free cash lump sum. Since each scheme can be very different, you should look at the rules for your particular scheme and take any advice necessary.

Pensions for Business Owners or the Self-Employed (Which Employees Can Also Take Advantage Of)

There are a surprisingly large number of pension wrappers that exist on the market. This is particularly relevant for those who do not fit into the neat world of employment where pensions tend to be very well catered for and documented.

For those who run their own business or are self-employed, the need for saving into a pension does not go away. So what mechanisms exist for such people? In the UK, the most common pension vehicle in this mould is known as a SIPP: a self-invested personal pension. The SIPP is incidentally also something that anyone can open (including employees who have a workplace pension) and from a sharia perspective, it is particularly relevant as a bit of a hack.

You see, when you have a SIPP, you effectively are just opening a new type of account with your usual share broker online. You can choose whichever share broker you like, chances are they will have a SIPP option and you will be able to open one. The beauty of this from a sharia mindset is that because you now have an account that is able to invest in everything that your share broker provider can give you access to, all of a sudden your pension has much more flexibility. Otherwise you are restricted by your pension provider as to which funds you can put money into.

Once your money is in a SIPP, you not only can choose from all the listed funds out there but you can also invest in individual stocks and other listed securities such as REITs.

As a business owner, paying into your SIPP is one of the primary ways that you can save on tax if you have surplus profits. Contributions to your pension are tax-deductible when it comes to corporation tax and can be a smart way of ensuring that you're tucking money away for your retirement (something many business owners neglect to do).

There's also a canny trick that we used in our days as corporate lawyers. We had heard all about the advantage of having a SIPP as a Muslim – you can imagine that the increased flexibility to invest in what you want sounded like a dream to the two of us. The only problem was that no matter how much fine print we read in the legislation, employers were simply not obligated to make employer contributions into a SIPP in the same way that they had to make contributions into your workplace pension.

We thought this was terribly unfair and, to be honest, it is not entirely clear why such rigidity exists. Perhaps this is to avoid burdening employers with requests from potentially thousands of employees to start putting money into individual SIPPs, which is understandable.

However, as young Muslims with one sharia-compliant fund to choose from in our workplace pension (which wasn't that appealing to us), the workplace pension just did not cater to our needs. We wanted to be more aggressive in our early days and while our non-Muslim counterparts had a plethora of funds to choose from, including ones catering to more aggressive stocks strategies like small caps, emerging markets, etc., we had nothing. So we moped around for a bit before we stumbled upon an almighty hack. This is a hack which is still not really practised or preached enough but can be very powerful.

The hack is as follows: you phone your workplace pension provider (we had Scottish Widows and Aviva) and tell them that you want to transfer the money from your pension into your SIPP but – crucially – that you want to leave your workplace pension open and active. Different providers have different rules around this but Scottish Widows, for example, advised that £2 would have to be kept in the workplace pension pot for it to remain alive and able to continue to take the next month's pension contributions as usual from both employer and employee.

So that's what we did. We would let the money build up in our pensions, enjoy the free contributions from our employers, and then funnel the money out into our SIPPs where we would have complete investing freedom.

Now this might not sound to you as exciting as it does to us, but in an investing world where Muslims have to fight for every little advantage, this was a huge deal for us! We spent our time publicising this hack through our reach on www.Islamicfinanceguru.com and telling anyone at dinner parties that could handle talking about pensions.

As a side note, people vastly underestimate the power of employer contributions. While many larger employers will do better than the statutory minimum, even at the statutory minimum levels, an employer is putting in £60 for every £100 you put in. Some employers go as far as to match contributions.

Let us be very explicit on this: that's a 60% return on your money before you have even invested it. Or doubling your money before you have invested it if your employer is kind enough to match your contribution.

This is an extremely big win and ensures you are up even before the money has been invested.

There's also another type of pension scheme known as an SSAS – a small self-administered pension scheme. These are often referred to as family pensions and are typically set up within family-owned businesses as it is possible for family members outside of the business to join the scheme too. They are typically set up by, and for, the director/senior management of a trading business and there are several advantages to this type of scheme.

The principal benefits are:

1. Flexibility on where the money can be invested.
2. Ability to lease your own premises (held in the SSAS) back to the company, thus availing of tax benefits.
3. Ability to lend from the SSAS to the company.
4. In addition, the usual benefits that come with a pension also apply to an SSAS.

If you think an SSAS would be a good fit for you, you will need to talk to your accountant in the first instance, and then to a specialist SSAS scheme provider.

9 How to Do Basic Due Diligence into an Investment Company

In 2016, I[1] was invited to a friend's house under somewhat unusual circumstances. I almost never get cold-approached for elaborate investment scams. This is probably primarily due to the company I keep: my inner circle would typically not fall for simple scams as they are in the corporate sector.

In this particular instance, I took the meeting with a large degree of scepticism and partly curiosity – as I do not actually get to see the pitch process of investment salesmen very much. I am very much the kind of person who does his own investments, and so I tend not to fall into the category that these folks target. They typically target people who want to make money quickly (who doesn't?) but who cannot match that up with decent investment or finance knowledge or experience.

The evening came round and my wife was surprised that I was going to a meeting where it was known beforehand that we were going to be pitched by a man I'd never heard of selling an investment product. I told her that I was doing it out of curiosity, and perhaps a little part of me also wanted to be amused and actually see how these guys operate.

The evening started cordially. The gentleman who had come round to pitch us was actually a known family acquaintance and so there was a degree of respect and willingness to listen to what he had to say. I wanted to approach the evening not as someone who does investments for a living, but as far as possible as someone who actively is not in the investments world. This, by the way, was true of the person who had invited me over and also the fellow guests. I was the only one there who was actually in the finance and investing industry.

It started off very promisingly. The man had clearly not just prepared his pitch well, but it was clear that this pitch had been delivered many times successfully. Some of you reading this book may even have heard this pitch, or perhaps fallen victim to it.

After being presented with biscuits and tea, the pitch began. We were told how he had been all set to move abroad with a well-paid teaching job before he came across an incredible investment opportunity founded by Dr Ignatova, a supposedly stellar individual who had created the next big cryptocurrency: OneCoin.

We were told how OneCoin was essentially the next big cryptocurrency. That although we'd missed the Bitcoin rally, the time to get into OneCoin was now.

I remained sceptical, but was curious to see how this pitch landed with others. I asked how many other people had invested in this. He proudly told me about the hundreds of thousands of pounds that people had parted with via him alone.

When I asked about the sharia compliance, he gave me an answer which was convincing enough. Incidentally, sharia compliance was not so much the main issue with OneCoin. The bigger issue was that it was a massive scam.

I must stress that this pitch was not by your classic snake oil salesman. This was a family contact and respected individual, and I do not believe he was being insincere either. My view is that he genuinely got wrapped up in it, and, given the rewards on offer like all pyramid schemes, was keen to make sure he did his job without thinking too much about the possibility that the thing he had invested his money in, and on which he had seen some paper returns, was a complete sham.

After he left, I turned to the other members of the group who had listened to the same pitch, thinking that they would also be just as sceptical as I was. To my surprise, they were quite taken by it and were actually half-considering investing in it. I quickly dispelled any notion of that, and explained why I thought it was a Ponzi scheme which not only makes it a terrible investment, but also calls into question the sharia compliance of it, given the spirit of a Ponzi scheme and the fact that it is designed to essentially favour only a few people at the top.

This story is one of the first times we saw up close and personally exactly why it is worth making it our life's work to put out content to try to educate the Muslim community on investments and making those investment opportunities available to them. We have several such stories of Muslims being taken advantage of, and it really does break our heart every time.

Our community is one whose characteristics also make it susceptible to scams. We are close, we talk frequently in our communities, we gather at places like the mosque and each other's houses, and news travels fast via the various WhatsApp groups and other conversations that go on.

So when one person targets the Muslim community and has some early success, it isn't long before a large part of the Muslim community has heard of the opportunity. And when they hear that this other person that they know has also invested in it or recommended it, it comes with that golden stamp of approval that we all seek: a trusted friend or contact who has done the same thing.

All of this serves as an important example of how to conduct basic due diligence into an investment opportunity or an investment company through whom you will be investing. Here are the key pieces of advice that you need to take away from this:

1. When investing for yourself in a single opportunity, try not to steer too far away from the mainstream opportunities. These are typically things like stocks, property, Islamic bonds, and (with a higher level of caution) startups and crypto, and other things for which there are well-established markets. You can often tell these apart because you will typically need to sign up to a broker to access the opportunity. For instance, you cannot turn up at Microsoft's office and ask to buy some shares. You would need to sign up to a reputable broker. It is an

indication of a reputable and mainstream investment if there is an established marketplace through which to buy the underlying investment. For example, you buy stocks or funds through a stock broker, crypto through a crypto exchange, property either directly or through an online real estate provider, gold you can buy directly or through an online provider, and so on.

2. When making an investment through an investment company, irrespective of the jurisdiction you are in, you should make sure that the company is regulated by an established financial regulator. And don't simply take their word for it: these financial regulators will typically have registers which you can search online. Take the time to check it yourself by going to that regulator's website. Always go to the primary source when conducting research on an investment company rather than relying on something that the investment company themselves provides you with. If they are legitimate, it will be obvious through these checks. If they are trying to pass themselves off as something they are not, they will discourage you from doing the research yourself and may provide you with details themselves that claim to prove their authenticity. Never blindly accept these without verifying them.
3. Take the time to read online reviews and ask around if other people have made such an investment before. In the case of OneCoin, for instance, even if other people in your network were telling you to go for it because they had too, a simple online search would have revealed some red flags. Look for investment forums, Twitter threads, and Reddit discussions where sensible people may have discussed this opportunity.
4. Remember the adage "If it looks too good to be true, it usually is." If someone is offering double-digit returns in an assured way through some novel investment with no risk, that should be a red flag for you to do more due diligence. Not every great opportunity is a scam: some opportunities are genuinely good but you need to make sure that you interrogate it properly with good people around you. Seek out that friend who regularly does investments, speak to friends and family who work in finance or professional services, and so on.

5. Always follow the money. Ask yourself and ask the investment company what actually happens to your money. Who are you sending it to? Is that entity regulated? Is it appropriately licensed to handle client money? Companies cannot simply handle investment money provided to them by a client in order to execute an investment without some kind of necessary legal overlay such as being regulated to handle client money or making sure that they use a third party who is. Find out if your money is protected while it is not invested, for example, what happens if the firm goes bust overnight? The flow of money should be clear to you and it should never fall into the hands of an unregulated entity and should ultimately end up with the underlying provider of the investment.
6. The people matter. If you are making an investment in property and the team behind the investment company do not have any experience of property investing, amber lights should immediately go on in your head. If a quick Google search of the names of the directors throws up concerning allegations of historic investment losses, that's another amber light that should flicker on. If you are not getting the right vibes from the team, or they are pressuring you to invest, trust that instinct. If you can, you should ideally look to speak to a member of the team through whom you'll be investing over a video call or in person. These days it is incredibly easy to impersonate people and to create entirely fictitious personalities online.[2]

If you stick to these tips, your money should be in good hands.

10 Tax-Saving Strategies

We have covered a fair amount of tax-saving strategies already in this book, but we wanted to pull everything together in one neat place to act as a reference point.

Investments

First, make sure you are doing the basics right. Ensure you have a pension and are contributing to it regularly. These are typically significantly tax-advantaged by most tax-charging governments. They also attract voluntary or legally required matched contributions from your employer and/or the government.

In the USA, the 401k scheme allows you to pay into your pension from your salary, therefore reducing your salary (and the tax you have to pay on that). In the UK, as a higher rate taxpayer you can get £100 worth of pension contributing with just £60.

When you invest your cash generally, look to do it through an ISA in the UK, an IRA in the USA, or the equivalent in your own country. These vehicles allow you to contribute up to a limit every year into this account. This amount then grows income and capital gains tax free for as long as you would live.

Then we get into the more exotic options.

There are remarkable investments all over the world driven entirely by tax-efficiencies. In the USA you have the 1031 exchange strategy to

Delaware Statutory Trust (DST). This strategy allows you to defer any capital gains tax (which can add up to 30% when including both federal and state tax) when you sell a property. The way it works is you take your exited cash and invest it into a DST, which is a very specific kind of eligible investment fund. If you hold your investment in a DST all the way until you die, your capital gains gets wiped out and beneficiaries immediately get a 30% uplift on what they would otherwise have got.

In the UK, you have the AIM index – a small cap stock index that is home to the likes of ASOS and Boohoo among others. Much of this index has stocks that are actually inheritance tax-free if you hold them for over 2 years.

Similarly, if you invest in forestry in the UK, the sale of wood from woodlands is free of income tax, corporate tax, capital gains tax, and inheritance tax.

Equally, if you invested in early-stage startups, you can benefit from the SEIS/EIS schemes, which are enterprise investment schemes to allow you to get back up to a 50% tax rebate on the amount you invested, as well as being free of income tax, capital gains tax and inheritance tax. Interestingly, with SEIS/EIS investing, you can also completely defer any capital gains taxes that you otherwise have due to pay.

For example, let's say you recently sold a property for a nice profit and have to pay £20,000 on a £100,000 profit. You can invest that £100,000 into an EIS fund and that £20,000 tax no longer remains due. You only pay that tax eventually once you exit from the EIS fund, which could be in a decade's time. One way of thinking about this tax strategy is that the government is effectively extending you an interest-free loan that you can use to invest.

Another little-known trick in the real estate world is to invest through an offshore entity situated in a place like Jersey or Guernsey. These entities do not charge taxes on the returns and are consequently tax-neutral. But what is even more appealing is that if you receive dividends from these companies into your own UK company, you do not have to pay any corporate tax on it. We came across this particular gem when we were structuring our first real estate deals for Cur8 through Jersey and Guernsey.

To be clear, we are not advocating tax evasion,[1] or even, tax avoidance. Our tax philosophy is to navigate your path through the complicated tax rules in a way that reduces paying unnecessary tax. To use the example of the offshore real estate companies we just mentioned, ultimately when you withdraw your money from your UK company, you will still have to pay dividend tax which will be substantial. But the point is – if you took the route of investing in your personal name – you likely would have had to pay more tax entirely unnecessarily.

Personal Finance

Taxes can eat away large chunks of income and profits so don't just limit your tax efficiency to investing. There are significant opportunities in personal finance generally as well.

For business owners with their own limited company, a child education trust (CET) can be a very effective way of funding your children's upbringing. From paying for private school to extracurricular tuition fees, to holidays, a child education trust effectively funds them all.

The way it works is that a grandparent needs to decide to donate a portion of their shares in the son's company, to the CET. Those shares could be of a particular class and distribute their returns regularly to the CET. The CET can take advantage of the £12,500 income tax-free component that every child has. The CET monies can then be used to pay for all things related to the child.

Separately, the son's company will employ his father and pay him roughly equivalent to all the investments he makes annually into the children. Everything nets off nicely.

The benefit to all this is, if you have two children and are already spending on various expensive educational things, by setting up this trust you effectively reduce your tax liability on that.

In my case, I have two children and am a higher rate taxpayer. That means that, for every £25,000 I contribute annually to the CET, I save around 40% in tax.

If you are a business owner, there are several other areas to look into. Research & Development tax credits can recoup substantial amounts of tax payments, patent boxes can reduce your corporation tax by half, and thinking about offshore structuring for certain things can also take a scythe to your taxes.

This is not a book on tax strategies so we'll leave it there, but the point of this chapter was to make you aware of the possibilities that you could take advantage of immediately and to ensure that you think about the tax aspects as a standard point of due diligence whenever you are making a significant financial decision.

11 Weighing up Risk and Reward

When we were both early in our savings journey, with only a few thousand pounds to our name, we decided to make a big risky investment. We invested almost all of our net worth into a cryptocurrency we believed in (and still believe in) called Hedera Hashgraph (HBAR). Our view was that this is a currency very likely to make a significant upward move with sound fundamental value too (so not just a hyped memecoin).

Both of us were looking to put down a deposit for a house at this point - and houses in London require a deposit of £80,000 at least. With a paltry £5,000 to our names each, we were way off our goal.

So we made the educated, well-analysed decision to take a big risk on the basis that if it went well, we would be materially closer to our deposit target, while if it went south, we were young enough to recoup that money quite quickly.

Fate was with us and HBAR rocketed and gave us a 6× multiple on our initial investment. Suddenly our £5k was looking a lot more substantial at £30k. At this point we both exited half of our HBAR investment and banked £15,000 each, leaving a remaining £15,000 invested.

We made this exit on the basis that our risk-reward calculus had now shifted, when measured against our goal. We were now materially closer to our deposit goal – likely 2 years closer. We were still believers in the potential of HBAR so we didn't want to fully exit, but we definitely wanted to reduce the overall investment risk and save our portfolios from being so concentrated in a volatile cryptocurrency.

We are extremely lucky in that we love investing and started very early with small amounts of money. We got most of our mistakes out of our system in those teenage years which set us up with the necessary experience to make the right decisions when managing a live investment situation like the above.

Compare our situation to the story of Ja'far, a friend who invested a small but significant amount in a memecoin. Over the period of a month his £5,000 investment rocketed to £300,000. Unfortunately at this point he did not de-risk his position and instead doubled down into the coin further and actually quit his job to become a full-time crypto trader.

Sadly, in the next three months, the coin fell sharply, and Ja'far ended up losing most of his profits and having to go back into the job market once more – but this time in a recession.

What we got right and Ja'far got wrong was the management of risk and reward. There is a strong relationship between those two concepts. Usually you will find that the more the risk, the more the potential reward on offer; and the less the risk, the less the reward on offer usually is.

As Figure 11.1 outlines, different asset classes sit in different places along what investment theorists call the "risk curve". Cash is very low risk but also very low return. Property is somewhere in the middle, while alternative assets are higher risk but also higher reward.
If you find an investment under the risk curve – that is an investment to be avoided. For the same level of risk you should be able to find a better returning investment by just investing in whatever is above it on the risk curve.

There are usually three main ways investments are carved up:

1. low risk
2. medium risk
3. high risk.

Low Risk

Lower-risk investments are usually quite stable, with no crazy spikes or troughs in their value. You would typically expect to yield somewhere between 0.5–5% in annualised returns. Lower-risk investments will rarely lose you money.

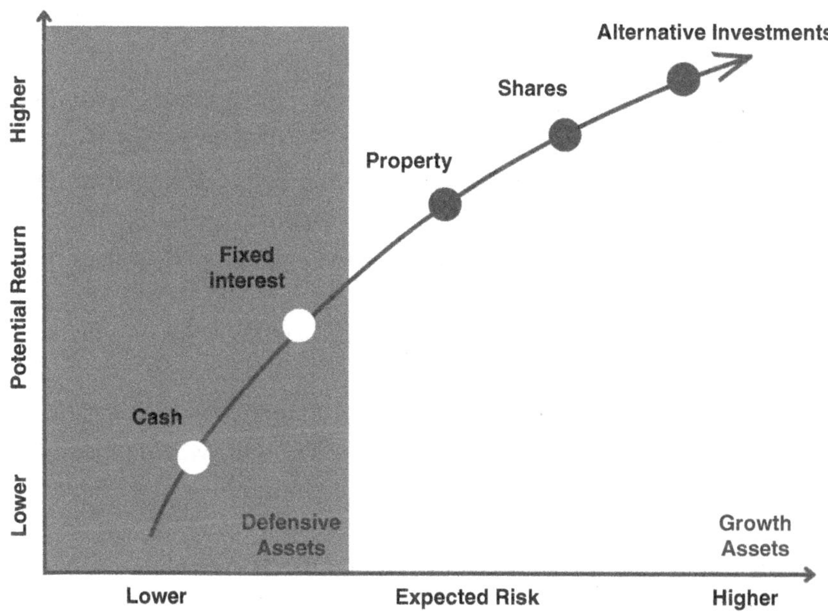

Figure 11.1 Asset risk.

Source: www.Islamicfinanceguru.com.

Examples of lower-risk investments include holding cash, investing in a savings account, buying a government sukuk bond and, arguably, holding a commodity like gold.

Certain properties can also fall into this bucket. Investing in a Class A, mature, well-tenanted, and larger property with multiple occupants would be an example of such a property investment.

Medium Risk

Medium-risk investments can be a little bit more volatile, and return in the region of 4–10%.

You may end up making a small loss if things go badly, though you are unlikely to lose all of your original investment.

Examples of a medium-risk investment include most stock market funds and adding leverage[1] to a property investment (because now there is an additional risk of not being able to meet your monthly payments).

High Risk

High-risk investments are usually very volatile and often illiquid (i.e. hard to sell and exit from), but they will typically return 10% and above in annualised return.

High-risk investments can sometimes result in you losing your entire initial investment, and – if you're unwise enough to venture into haram derivatives and other exotic instruments – lose even more than your initial investment.

Higher-risk investments include cryptocurrencies, startup investing, small cap investing, and many more.

An important caveat here though: By pooling higher-risk investments into a fund, you can dramatically reduce the risk of what would individually be a basket of high-risk investments, into something a little more moderate.

Mixing and Matching between Risk and Reward

In Part IV, we will examine the ins and outs of constructing a well-balanced portfolio set up to achieve the goals you have identified for yourself. We will walk through examples of different portfolio types.

But to give you a reference point ahead of Part III, where we dive into a dizzying array of different investments categories, look back at Figure 8.6 in Chapter 8, showing three portfolios with low, medium, and high risk associated with them.

The lower-risk portfolio is heavy with low-risk assets, while at the other end of the spectrum, the higher-risk portfolio allocates a substantial 30% of the portfolio to higher-risk investments.

We have now covered enough ground for you to be able to identify your answers to the two most fundamental questions for your portfolio:

1. What goal are you investing for?
2. What type of portfolio risk is most suited to achieving your investment goals?

There is one final question remaining, to which we will devote much of the remainder of this book:

3. What investments should I put into each of my three buckets of low-risk, medium-risk, and high-risk investments?

Summary

- Renting or buying your home is a major decision and merits a lot of thought.
- Investing is not always just a case of taking money and making more money. Consider your wider life – a 50% salary increase could be game-changing.
- Retirement planning needs to start early, and the plan needs to start being executed around 10 years before the planned retirement date.
- There are plenty of options on how to withdraw your pension. Do some research and consider the best route for you.
- Be reluctant to fall for opportunities which seem too good to be true. Always remember to do your basic due diligence into investment companies.
- Tax hacks can bolster your portfolio.
- Your portfolio mix is a function of your assessment of risk versus reward.

PART III

Investment and Sharia Considerations for Popular Investment Categories

In this Part of the book we will systematically work through some of the most popular and prominent investments you should know about. For each investment we will cover the following questions:

1. What is it?
2. Returns on offer.
3. Is my money safe?
4. Can I get my money back easily?
5. Sharia considerations.

We start with the most important asset class of them all: stocks.

12 Stocks

What Is It?

The stock market is probably the first thing you think about when you think of the word 'investments'. Typically associated with imagery of Wall Street traders screaming buy and sell orders across a trading floor, the stock market can be a daunting prospect for novice investors.

Stocks (another name for which, by the way, is "shares") are the perfect example of public investing. Many of the investment opportunities that we mention such as fixed income, property, forestry, etc. are actually examples of private investing. That means they are not publicly listed, easily bought and sold on an exchange, and have to adhere to different regulations around governance and disclosure.

When a company "goes public", they list on the stock exchange that they choose to list on and the investing public is then able to purchase shares in that company (typically via their stock broker).

The stock market is therefore a collection of companies who have chosen to list on the stock market. As you will be aware, not all companies are public. Listing on the stock market comes with a significant burden for the company as they must make sure that they abide by the relevant regulatory jurisdictions.

Companies choose to list on the stock market for several reasons, but key amongst them are: (1) increased profile; (2) ability to ask the market for more money if it ever needs to raise finance; and (3) it provides an exit opportunity for early investors.

Stock markets differ from country to country and even within one country you might find several different stock markets that are aimed at different types of companies. For instance, the UK has the FTSE (the Financial Times Stock Exchange) which is owned by the LSE (the London Stock Exchange) and it also has the AIM (the Alternative Investment Market). The US has the NYSE (New York Stock Exchange) and NASDAQ (National Association of Securities Dealers Automated Quotations).

Stock markets are primarily made up of trading companies. These are simply trading businesses that you probably come across in your day-to-day life. BT, Vodafone, Shell, and the like, if you are in the UK. And a similar story for the biggest brands you come across on a daily basis wherever you are.

Of course, not all large companies choose to be listed companies. There are examples of many large companies which choose to remain private such as JCB, Dyson, and – just to make you feel hungry – Nando's. Naturally, there are more private companies than public companies, given that so many companies exist the world over and given how tightly regulated the stock markets are and how expensive it is to float your company on the stock market.

However, for you, the investor, investing in these companies via public means such as the stock market can be a fantastic way to invest your money and own a slice of your favourite brands.

Returns on Offer

Data suggests that the stock market averages a 10% annualised return if you reinvest your dividends.[1] This makes it an extremely attractive asset class and means that you would double your money approximately every 7 years.

Handy tip: you can use the rule of 72 to figure out how long it would take to double your money. The rule of 72 is quite easy: you simply take the number 72 and divide by the projected annualised return. In this instance, that would be 72 divided by 10, giving you 7.2 years. Being a mathematical calculation you can also use it to figure out the annualised return if you know how long it would take to double your money. For instance, with UK property, there is a rule of thumb that you double your money every 10 years (NB: as it happens, the data actually suggests this is not true[2]) but assuming it were, you could do 72 divided by 10 to give you a projected annualised return of 7.2%, if that were true.

Of course a 10% per annum return in the stock market depends on which stocks you are investing in – you may do slightly better or slightly worse in reality, although 10% per annum is a good target to aim for.

You could dial it up or down though, depending on your risk appetite. For instance, if you wanted to be more aggressive and really go after growth, you could limit yourself to those areas of the stock market where growth is more explosive, for example, smaller companies.

These companies, particularly if you are hands-on and a stock picker, can really catapult a portfolio, if chosen well. Naturally, there is increased risk with this approach so you can also really negatively affect your portfolio too. We hope that is something you have come to learn anyway over the course of this book.

Equally, if you want to play it particularly safe in the stock market, you could limit yourself to certain companies which are incredibly defensive and accept lower returns and a safe dividend in exchange for the safety and security.

Capital Growth vs. Dividends

When investing in the stock market, there are two types of return on offer: one is the capital growth (i.e. when the shares increase in price) and the other is dividends.

Dividends are a very popular income stream and offer passive income for people who are confident in a company's ability to continue paying dividends. Dividends are simply payments made by companies to their shareholders from the profit of the business.

From a sharia perspective, receiving dividends is totally fine as they are just a share of the profits made by a company in which you have an ownership stake in. The only thing to watch out for is whether the underlying business itself is permissible (see the following section on how to check if a stock is sharia-compliant).

Companies usually pay out a dividend as they don't have anything better to do with their profits. This is why most dividend payers tend to be big established companies whose high growth phase is behind them. Instead of reinvesting all of that generated money, they give a proportion of it to investors. It's also a nice financial incentive for investors to invest in their company.

Most smaller companies don't pay out dividends. Some of them are yet to make a profit while others instead reinvest their profits in the business to pursue growth. That money could then be used for growth initiatives, such as funding research and development or expansion projects.

Growth investors tend to stay away from dividend stocks as they are looking for companies that are still in their growth phase. Because these companies will be reinvesting most of their money to pursue growth initiatives, they have the potential for larger capital gains.

Dividend investors want dividend stocks as they want the dividend payments and have a lower risk tolerance. As dividend stocks tend to be more established companies with a proven track record of success, they tend to be less risky than growth stocks. As such, the potential for capital gains is usually lower. This is fine as the aim for many dividend investors is to build a reliable dividend income stream. For example, a portfolio of £500k with a dividend yield of 4% could provide you with a tidy annual income of £20k.

Most companies pay out quarterly or even twice a year. Some even pay out monthly. Any dividend payments made throughout the year are referred to as interim dividends. At the end of the year, the last payment will be called a final dividend. Ultimately the payment schedule will vary based on the company. The total dividend yield will still be the same. The payment will just be spread out over the payment schedule with the final dividend typically being the largest payment.

On rare occasions, some companies will even issue a one-off special dividend. This could be because they have extra money they would like to distribute or in response to a major win by the company.

When dividends are issued, there is a formal process they go through. Here are the key dates you need to be aware of:

- **Declaration/announcement date:** This is the date when dividends are announced along with the ex-dividend date and the payment date.
- **Ex-dividend date:** To receive a dividend, you need to be holding shares of the company at the ex-dividend date. So any shares purchased on the ex-dividend date or after will not be eligible for a dividend (until the next time). You might have noticed that big stocks' share price falls the date after it goes ex-dividend. This is because once a stock goes ex-dividend, that money has been marked out to go to the shareholders and has effectively been taken out of

the company. So the market corrects the company's valuation accordingly, reducing the amount of the company's valuation by the amount that is leaving its coffers.

- **Record date:** This is usually the day after the ex-dividend date and is essentially when the company checks to see which of its shareholders are eligible for the dividend.
- **Payment date:** On this day, the company distributes the dividends to each eligible shareholder. It may come a bit later if your shares are held in a nominee account with a stockbroker (e.g. AJ Bell). In that case, the company pays the stockbroker who will then pass it on to you. Historically many dividends were paid by cheque but this is not so common now.

There are a lot of factors you need to consider when looking at dividend stocks. Here are some key considerations.

1. Dividend Yield The dividend yield tells you what the size of the dividend is relative to its current share price. For example, a company with a share price of £100 and a dividend yield of 5% will give you a dividend of £5 per share you hold.

Dividend yields are reported in two ways. Either they will be reported as the trailing dividend yield or the forward dividend yield. The trailing dividend yield tells you what the dividend yield was for the previous year. The forward dividend yield is the predicted yield for the coming year. You need to be sure which yield figure you are looking at – particularly as dividends aren't guaranteed and can be cancelled, cut, or even increased. More on this later.

There is no rule of thumb answer to what makes a good yield. It depends on many factors. Beware of really high dividend yields (8% or more). A high yield may look initially attractive but it tends to be a good indicator that a company is in trouble. One reason for such a high dividend yield could be because the company has recently had a big drop in price, so its historic dividend amount now looks like a much higher percentage of its total value. However, often, such companies will end up reducing their next dividend payments anyway.

Conversely, a low dividend yield may initially look poor but could mean the company is prioritising growth, which could be great over the long term.

A sensible range would be between 2% and 6%; 2% is close to the S&P 500 average in recent years and should therefore be the minimum you look for.

2. Dividend History Ideally you want a company with a long track record of regularly paying dividends. You may want to avoid companies that have a patchy history of paying dividends. That being said, you might want to be flexible with dividend misses during crazy periods such as last year's COVID crisis. In that case, paying a dividend while a business is in trouble may not be the best option for the company. However, often companies will do so to avoid disappointing their investors and maintain their payout streak.

Companies regularly reducing their dividend is a bad sign and could hint at future troubles. You want companies that ideally raise their dividend over time.

3. Dividend Payout Ratio This tells you how much the dividend is relative to the profit. You work it out by dividing the total dividend by profits. So, if a company has profits of £1m and pays out a dividend of £100k, its dividend payout ratio would be 0.1.

This ratio can help you interpret how sustainable a company's dividend is. If it's a large ratio, then this could mean the company may struggle to continue paying the dividend if it falls on hard times. A low ratio could mean the company has ample room to potentially raise the dividend and not break the bank.

That being said, you shouldn't look at the payout ratio in isolation. It should be combined with other information to allow you to make a more informed decision.

4. Dividend Cover This is the inverse of the dividend payout ratio and is another measure for how sustainable a company's dividends are. This time you divide the total profits by the total dividends.

Revisiting our earlier example of a company, we see £1 million in profits with a £100k dividend results in a dividend cover of 10. This is really healthy.

Any dividend cover less than 1 is a major red flag as it means that the dividend is unsustainable, given it exceeds the profit. To be safe, it may be best to stick with dividend stocks that have a cover ratio of at least 1.5.

Dividend Investing During a Crash

A common tactic that many people go for is to simply wait for bear markets before going for dividend stocks. That's because you have to remember that the share price of a company can sometimes become disjointed from the actual performance of that business – and therein lies opportunity.

For instance, if company X routinely pays a dividend of 20p per share and that is unaffected during a stock market crash but the price of the stock has gone from £8 per share (2.5% yield) to £3.50 a share (5.7% yield), that represents a great time to buy a dividend-bearing stock, assuming that you are confident that the business will still be able to pay out the 20p per share dividend.

What's more, you have locked in that yield forever. So even as the share price hopefully goes back up, your yield is still the same as you have secured your shares, and you will also be nicely placed to benefit from the capital appreciation of the shares too.

Investing for Capital Gain

The other type of stock market investing is where you invest purely for capital gain without worrying about dividends. The aim here is clear: sell for higher than you buy.

The natural questions that follow are: how does one go about picking these and what are the time frames involved? There are many different answers to this and we will attempt to shed some light on this topic that might help you to get started before you explore further yourself with some of the resources we point to.

In short, there are two broad factors to look at when investing in a stock: (1) the fundamental analysis; and (2) the technical analysis. We will explore each in turn.

Fundamental Analysis Choosing a stock for its fundamentals simply means that you choose it based on the company's business, performance, news flow, financial reports, etc. When it comes to generating ideas for stock picking, there are a range of techniques. From a personal perspective, we like to first identify where the markets are where we would actually like to hold stocks. For many folks this is the US stock market as it is the biggest and most liquid arena to be investing. We personally have always liked the UK markets for the simple reason that we know this market quite well. We have in recent years switched most of our exposure to the US though.

As far as idea generation goes, we always encourage investing in things where you have an understanding. We have the benefit of running a tech business, and we are therefore exposed to many of the tech stocks that you see on the market but as actual customers. We know what their sales tactics are like, we know their products well, and we also know which products we just cannot get rid of even if we wanted to (which therefore often make great stocks to be buying if their product is just that good and essential)!

One way that you can therefore generate ideas for stocks investing is to look at your life around you. This is one of the ideas espoused in the famous Peter Lynch book, *One Up on Wall Street*.[3] Simply paying attention to great brands and products around you can often be a trigger for investing in these great and growing businesses. Sometimes these companies might not even have the attention of analysts or large funds which can mean the big moves in price are yet to come.

I[4] had a few such pleasant instances in the stock market and they are very pleasing when they come off. One of them was a British company called Ideagen. I identified the stock while searching for small cap companies with a market cap below £500m. I liked the initial look of them due to the headline fundamentals: growing revenues, growing profits, healthy metrics that I like to look at such as Return on Capital Employed (often shortened to ROCE) where I target 15% or more.

This then prompted me to look further at the business: I looked at their website and offering through the eyes of a customer. Many people miss this out when investing: you are buying a piece of a business, not simply a ticker on the stock market. So it makes sense to act as a customer.

Their products looked very neat. They were providing bespoke software solutions for highly-regulated industries, such as aviation. Their client list was stellar. It struck me that a company doing such interesting products with such a good client list was going places and with such a low market cap (only around £100m at the time), it certainly had legs.

My general practice for doing further due diligence is to look at previous years' annual reports. I like to see management delivering on what they have said they would deliver on in previous years. I also take some time to read other real-world indicators like job posts. This is an underrated tool in the stock picker's armory: it allows you not only to see that they're likely to be growing if they are recruiting well, but the wording of job posts also gives you a clue as to the working culture at the company as well as what their burning priorities are right now. With all this information, you can quickly triangulate and form a basic view on whether or not you like the company enough to invest.

I invested in Ideagen for just over 50p per share and it was a fantastic performer. It unfortunately got taken private in July 2022 at 350p per share. It is always bittersweet when good performers get acquired, but it was a great lesson for me in spotting gems of companies relatively early on. The best companies are incredibly easy to hold as they just keep performing very well.

Other ways to generate ideas are quality publications such as *Investors Chronicle*, *Seekingalpha*, and other finance-dedicated newspapers or magazines.

Another way to generate ideas is to think about the kinds of qualities you want to see in a company, and then run those through an online screener tool. For instance, I mentioned earlier that I like the metric of ROCE and I like to see growing sales – these are things you can plug into a screener as a way of filtering the stock market.

There are plenty of good screeners out there including Sharepad, Trading View, Finviz, Koyfin, and MarketSmith. You might want to start out with free tools such as Yahoo stock screener before moving on to more advanced ones.

Depending on what types of stocks you are looking for will also determine what kinds of qualities you want to see in a company. For instance, if you only want to invest in large, blue-chip companies, you will not see aggressive year-on-year growth because the companies are just not set up to do that.

For those of you looking at smaller companies, the Jim Slater book, *The Zulu Principle* is a must-read.[5]

Some Popular Fundamental Styles

While this book is not meant to be an in-depth manual on stock analysis and methodologies, it is helpful when analysing the stock market to understand the approaches that some legends of investing have when looking for stocks.

Of course, these are not prescriptive by any means. You should use them as a point of interest rather than a prescribed formula for success. The fact that different investors have different approaches should be enough to tell you that there is no one-size-fits-all approach to investing. You should use these approaches for your stock education and you may find that you have some of your own convictions which can contribute too.

Benjamin Graham Benjamin Graham is the original "value investor". He made his name on buying stocks which, in his view, were trading for less than their intrinsic value. This approach of value investing remains extremely popular today, particularly when markets get very heated and investors become worried about overpaying for stocks.

To learn more about his style, Graham's book, *The Intelligent Investor,*[6] is a seminal book worthy of a place on any serious investor's bookshelf. Graham advocates buying stocks that are the subject of market irrationality and therefore unloved. He looked to buy stocks that come with a margin of safety to help overcome any human error involved when selecting the stocks.

While his writings are from the 1940s, Graham's style is timeless. Here are some parameters you can set up in a screener to filter for companies that would be favoured by this approach:

- Market cap greater than $100m
- PE ratio of 15 or less
- Price to NAV of 1.5 or less
- EPS growth of 33% or more over the last 5 years
- 5 years of dividend payments
- Dividend cover of 1.2 or more
- Positive cash flow.

Warren Buffett Buffett is comfortably the most famous investor of our lifetime, with a hugely successful track record and his juggernaut company Berkshire Hathaway, which is effectively an investment company.

Buffett's style took a lot of inspiration from Graham, but I[7] have a personal leaning towards Buffett's style since he also brought to the fore important qualitative business factors when investing, such as the quality of the management and competitive advantages.

Buffett's style is a mixture of value and growth, with Buffett not being afraid to buy stocks at reasonable prices as opposed to just undervalued prices, and focus instead on holding them forever.

To learn about Buffett's style, the best thing you can do is sit down one day with the letters to his shareholders[8] and get a sense for his approach. The metrics set up for the Benjamin Graham screener will help bring Buffett-like stocks to the surface too, though much of the analysis comes in analysing these companies for the qualitative things we mentioned above, such as quality of management and sustainable competitive advantages.

Peter Lynch We have already mentioned the book *One Up on Wall Street*,[9] so it comes as no surprise that we include Peter Lynch on the list of legendary investors.

Like Buffett, Lynch is a living legend but is perhaps somewhat less well-known outside investing circles compared to Buffett. I[10] have a real affinity towards Lynch which stems primarily from his writing: he is simply effortless. One thing about real masters of their trade is they make everything look and sound easy. And when you read Lynch's books, you very much get the sense of someone who has a knack for explaining complex things in a really straightforward way, which is an extremely rare skill.

Lynch's writings are often written for people like you and me, which is a big part of his appeal. Despite having been in the financial industry himself, his books lean towards titles with the idea of beating the professionals at their game. He famously looks for stocks with "ten-bagger" potential, i.e. the potential goes up by 10 times.

Here are some parameters you can set up in a screener to filter for companies that would be favoured by Lynch's approach:

- Market cap greater than $500m
- PEG (price/earnings-to-growth) maximum of 1
- 15% or more EPS growth last 3 years
- Include industries that you are familiar with.

Jim Slater Jim Slater is another personal favourite of mine[11] for his leaning towards smaller companies with high growth potential. His book, *The Zulu Principle*,[12] is a fantastic read and gives you a great insight on what it takes to invest in smaller companies with high growth potential.

If you are inclined to invest in these types of companies, here are some potential set-ups for a screener:

- PEG 0.75 or less (you can relax this to 1 in times where markets are expensive)
- Market cap of less than $250m but more than $10m

- Operating margin 15% or more or Return on equity 12.5% or more
- 3-month momentum higher than the median average (interestingly, this is veering into a technical screen and clearly moving away from the value approach of Graham and Buffett)
- Forecast growth of more than 10% but less than 50%
- ROCE greater than 12%.

Technical Analysis

Technical analysis is the art (or science, depending on how you look at it!) of looking at price charts and interpreting things about the future price action of a stock based on the chart.

You will find that some in the investing world dismiss technical analysis altogether; you will find others who only look at technical analysis. Our time in the market has led us to the viewpoint that the sensible approach is somewhere in the middle. That there is definitely value to looking at company fundamentals away from price, but that there is also great value in being able to read a chart and understand if there is a trend against a particular stock or market which makes it better to wait before buying that stock.

We have been fortunate enough to exchange ideas with one of the best in the business and his advice to us when starting out was to read Stan Weinstein's *Secrets for Profit in Bull and Bear Markets*[13] and *How to Make Money in Stocks*[14] by William O'Neil.

We do not propose to make this section a how-to manual on technical analysis, but if you are serious about stock investing for capital gain and you want to pick those stocks yourselves, it is just as important that you get comfortable on the technical analysis side as you are on the commercial analysis.

Like fundamental analysis, there is no one-size-fits-all. The best traders tend to advocate a simple strategy and become very good at seeing the charts through that lens.

In the Weinstein book mentioned above, he favours an approach whereby you can identify a stock as being in any one of four stages at any given time. That is, basing (stage 1), advancing (stage 2), top (stage 3), declining (stage 4) (Figure 12.1). The idea is that you want to buy stocks ideally at the cusp between stage 1 and stage 2 in order to ride the upwards wave.

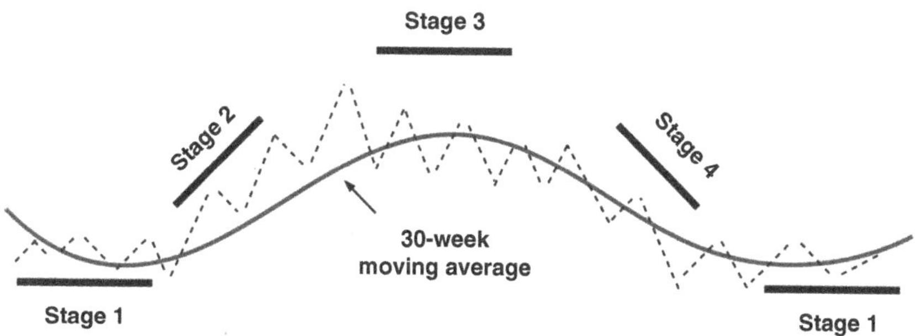

Figure 12.1 Stock stages.

Source: www.Islamicfinanceguru.com.

The Trend Is Your Friend Perhaps one of the biggest arguments for taking technical analysis seriously is that the trend of a stock will undeniably determine where the stock goes in the near term. If you can identify stocks which are in a negative trend and learn not to go near them, the chances are that you will avoid having your capital tied up in stocks that are in the stage 1 or stage 4 phase.

You can use technical indicators to understand where the trend is for a particular stock. For instance, Weinstein has a golden rule of simply never touching a stock which is trading below its 30-week moving average (i.e. 150-day moving average).

Other indicators include the RSI and MACD. However, it is important that you find your own style and set-ups that work for you. As you delve into some of the recommended reading in this area, and you practise, you will find that your approach will evolve.

Chart Patterns Another very popular form of analysis is to look at patterns in a chart. At the simplest level, understanding the historic highs and lows of a stock will help you to understand what technical traders know as support and resistance.

These are the levels at which historically a stock may never have fallen below, and therefore acts as a good indicator of a price reversal when the price reaches that low. Similarly, if a stock is reaching its all-time high, this can be a good indicator that things may be about to cool off. Of course, this is not to say that stocks never go above their all-time highs (that would be a paradox to the term itself!), nor that stocks never go below their historic lows either. However, being aware of these areas can help you to define your strategy: for instance, if a stock is approaching its all-time high, you may choose to wait until there is a clear break-out above that all-time high before you invest in that momentum.

The books we have recommended will shed much light on chart patterns and help you to understand how to incorporate these into your strategy. We also recommend using the plethora of information available online: in particular, YouTube and Twitter are home to some incredibly good resources.

Stocks vs Funds

When you invest in the stock market, there are two routes you can go down. The first route is that you pick the companies yourself according to the criteria that you have. This is investing directly into stocks. The other route is that you invest in funds that are traded on the stock market. These are often referred to as exchange-traded funds and you may have heard its common abbreviation, ETF.

An ETF consists of a pool of money from various investors allocated for a specific investing purpose. This purpose will be defined by the investment manager and can be as simple as getting exposure to specific commodities (e.g. gold ETFs), specific geographies (e.g. emerging markets ETFs), specific types of companies (e.g. smaller companies ETFs) and essentially any kind of exposure you could possibly want. The benefit of an ETF is that you get a basket of underlying stocks that somewhat de-risk your investment, while giving you the exposure to the overall theme of that ETF.

As ETFs are traded openly on exchanges, they are more accessible to investors than regular funds. Combined with the fact that you get exposure to many different companies, it is easy to see why they are recommended as an easy and convenient choice for most investors.

If you recall our earlier discussion on how hands-on should you be, this is exactly the kind of place where the very hands-on folks will prefer to pick stocks themselves. In our experience, this tends to be a minority of people. Even for the people who start off in this camp, many eventually move over to ETFs as life catches up with them and things start getting in the way.

For those who prefer a slightly more hands-off approach right from the start, ETFs can be a great option to invest in the stock market without getting too hands-on by picking individual stocks and not getting too distant and just handing it off to a financial advisor.

Here are some key benefits of ETFs:

1. They save you time. Finding and tracking investments are a time-consuming process. Investing in ETFs allows you to focus on the things that really matter to you.
2. They are easily accessible and liquid as they are traded on exchanges.
3. They are less risky than individual stock picking. This is because generally there are many different assets in an ETF. This offers you protection from bad performance from any single stock in the fund, as it won't have much impact on the overall value of the fund.
4. They give you diversification at a low cost. Investing in many companies yourself can end up costing you a lot through brokerage fees or exchange-rate fees.[15]
5. They provide broad exposure to wider investment themes. Let's say you want to invest in clean energy companies as you believe there is a lucrative opportunity there. Instead of trying to pick individual companies in an area that may not be your area of expertise, you could simply buy a clean-energy-focused ETF.
6. You gain access to otherwise inaccessible investments. ETFs have a sizeable pot of money. This allows them to access investments that may not otherwise be open to you as a small everyday investor. For example, investing in unlisted companies.
7. You leverage the expertise of the fund manager. For ETFs that don't track an index, a fund manager will select companies to invest in, using their expertise.

Naturally, ETFs are not all roses and there are some key drawbacks which are important to be aware of too:

1. DIY stock picking can be more lucrative. You will rarely make astronomical returns through ETF investing. They tend to offer steady returns over the long run. Talented individual investors can outperform by picking stocks themselves.
2. They are not as fun as finding companies yourself. This is for those who are really passionate about investing and finding exciting companies.
3. You may be over-diversifying. The strong-performing assets/companies in an ETF could be held back by the weaker investments. If you

are focused on pure growth of your portfolio, it may be a smarter strategy to focus on a smaller number of holdings. However, with this, comes more risk. The trick with diversification is to have enough diversification to avoid a blow-up of your portfolio but not have *too much* diversification such that it dilutes your performance. Or, as the famous Peter Lynch coined it: "diworsification".

4. They follow the market in down times. ETFs provide you with broad exposure to an index, sector, or market. If any of those experience a downturn, the ETF will likely follow it.
5. They have additional management fees compared to individual stocks. You do not pay management or admin fees for holding stocks yourself directly. However, in return for these ETF fees, you do get the ease and simplicity that come with a ready-made solution.

Like most investments, ETFs have historically performed better when held for a longer period of time and don't typically increase sharply in price. The reason is because ETFs generally track a group of companies. This means for short-term spikes in the price, you would need the price to spike for a significant proportion of those companies. This rarely happens at the same time. What tends to happen is for companies' share prices to increase steadily over time.

While it is rare for the price of an ETF to spike suddenly, they can crash heavily in a day. This can happen when there is a market-wide crash that affects a large proportion of the ETF's holdings.

ETFs have a net asset value (NAV), which gives you the value of the fund when you take all its assets and subtract its liabilities. This can be found on the issuer's website. You want to compare the net asset value per share with the share price. If there's a mismatch, then this could be quite informative. If the share price is larger than the NAV, then this is a good indicator that the ETF may be overvalued.

Conversely, if the share price is less than the NAV, this could be an indicator of it being undervalued. You should also look deeper to understand why there is such a deviation in the first place.

For ETFs that track an index, a tracking error between the two prices is common. You just need to make sure it's not excessive.

When comparing ETFs, do take into account the fees they charge. Ideally you would look at both the current share price and the fees.

As ETFs tend to be more passively managed than normal funds, they usually charge less fees. There are two main fee types you want to look out for:

1. **Total Expense Ratio (TER):** This covers all annual management, trading, and admin costs. These tend to vary between 0.3% and 0.7%.
2. **Foreign exchange fees:** These are levied if you buy an ETF that is in a different currency.

If you do decide to invest in an ETF, the same principles apply that we mentioned when thinking about investing generally.

You need to make sure an ETF investment aligns with your investing goals. For many people, ETF investing is the medium-risk long-term investment they make. If that is you, then have a think about potentially investing a regular amount per month in a particular ETF. Many stock brokers facilitate this for you.

Understanding your own risk profile is also key. Ask yourself whether you would be comfortable investing in high-risk, high-reward investments, where declines of over 30% are quite common. You may be better suited to more stable investments that aim for around 8–10% a year (like many passive ETFs). In general, not investing in line with your risk tolerance can lead to poor investment decisions.

For example, you may not have a high-risk tolerance and if you then choose to invest in a high-risk asset, things can go wrong. Let's assume there is a 30% drop. As you are not ready for such volatility, you may panic and sell and then miss the 70% gain the fund might make over the next year.

After that, your own personal tastes as well as time horizons come in. You may want to focus on certain high growth areas, such as clean energy or emerging markets. These funds are typically cyclical and better for longer-term hold periods. Or you might just want to keep things simple and invest in funds that track an index.

Some ETFs will also pay dividends. ETFs generally have two options for dealing with dividends:

1. **Reinvest the dividends on behalf of each investor:** Reinvesting dividends has historically led to better returns. A study looking at the performance of the S&P 500 between 1980 and 2019 found that 75% of the returns came from reinvested dividends.[16]

2. **Distribute the dividends to each investor:** This will diminish your long-term returns. However, your investing strategy may be oriented to receive a regular income stream to supplement your income. In this case, opting for ETFs that pay out dividends will be the right option.

To find out how an ETF deals with dividends, either check its full title or the issuer's website. ETFs that reinvest dividends tend to have "Acc." in the name. ETFs that pay out dividends have either "Inc" or "Dist." in their name.

ETFs come in different shapes and sizes. While ETFs are generally known for being passively managed, recently actively managed ETFs have become more popular. The most famous example is the ARK ETFs managed by Cathie Wood. She actively picks stocks to invest in that tie in with her investing theme of disruptive innovation. However, with this comes higher fees as the fund manager has a greater involvement. Another thing to keep in mind is that many active ETFs are US-listed and are inaccessible to UK investors for the most part.

Buying Other Traded Investments

Continuing with this idea of there being different types of ETFs, you can also buy ETFs where the underlying investments are not companies, but other assets such as sukuk (a type of Islamic bond), a commodity (such as nickel, gold, uranium, etc.).

How Much Should You Start with in the Stock Market?

It is clear that investing in the stock market is not as simple as taking your money and buying some shares with it. There are costs associated with you buying those shares and you should understand that they eat into your profits before your stock has even had a chance to grow – putting you at an immediate loss. So a £1000 investment in reality is not a £1000 investment when you take fees into account. This can leave beginners with an underwhelming feeling once they make their first investment as they see that their £1000 investment has now turned into £980 due to fees and the bid/ask (more on that below).

For this reason, it does not make that much sense to start with a very small amount of capital. For instance, let's say you have a broker who charges a £10 commission per trade. If a person invested as little as, say, £100, that investment is actually only £90 (not accounting for ongoing custody charges) due to the commission. So for that person to even start breaking even, they would need to see an 11% increase in the share price (!).

Bearing in mind that a good investment property tends to yield around 5–8%, the best savings account normally gives you a percentage point or two above the Bank of England base rate (NB: savings accounts are usually haram[17] due to the interest element, but this is purely for context-setting purposes), and the FTSE100 as a whole has returned 0–2% from 2017–2022 (depending on which starting and ending points you take), and you can quickly see how impressive an 11% return would be. And that would only just be getting you back to the £100 you had in the first place.

You must also remember that besides companies listed on the AIM, a 0.5% stamp duty will also be applicable on share purchases. It isn't much, but it is another fee to factor in.

However, if you started with let's say £1000 instead of £100 and paid the £10 commission (plus stamp duty of 0.5% – £5), your initial fee as a proportion of the investment is much less at 1.5%. The more money you invest, the less you lose in relative terms to the commission and other fees like stamp duty. So with £10,000 using the same fees, you would only be paying 0.6% in fees initially. And so on. So, while there is no theoretical minimum to investment amount, you will need to factor in the above and ensure that it is worth your while to actually invest.

There are also low-cost brokers out there such as DeGiro, FreeTrade, Robinhood, M1 Finance, and Trading212 that will help you save fees. But beware – many of these brokers still make their money off you – just it is hidden in foreign exchange costs.

Is My Money Safe?

Buying stocks is an extremely well-trodden path. The safety of your money needs to be considered from two angles: (1) the investment provider, and (2) the actual investment itself.

Since buying stocks is such a well-known investment type, there are plenty of online stock brokers which make your life very easy.

The Investment Provider

There are a plethora of brokers out there. Here is a list of things to look for when choosing a broker:

Reputation In the same way that you should not trust a bank that is not very well established and does not have the trust of the general public, so too you ought to avoid brokers who are quite new to the industry or who do not have an established track record. Ultimately, your hard-earned money will be sitting with these guys, so you need to have full confidence in them. Seek out brokers who are fully regulated by the local regulator and, if you are in the UK, seek out brokers who offer FSCS (Financial Services Compensation Scheme) protection, meaning that if they go bust, your money is covered by the FSCS scheme for up to £85,000.

Charges There are two things to look out for under charges. The first is the actual commission that the broker takes per trade. So let's say you want to buy £1000 of a particular company's shares, the commission fee will be the fee that is taken to actually execute that trade. Typically, these fees tend to be around the £10 mark for most reputable brokers, but this figure will vary and some take it as a percentage cost of the overall investment amount. Most brokers will have separate fees if you are looking to buy into a fund, so you should look at this too if you think you want to do this.

The second thing to look out for is whether the broker charges a fee for you to actually hold a particular account type. Typically, this will be classed as an administration charge or custody charge and will depend on the account type you hold.

For instance, if you have a stocks and shares ISA or an SIPP in the UK, we have seen some brokers taking a quarterly administration fee simply for that account to exist. It will usually be a certain percentage of the total account value, often with an upper limit in £ terms. For instance, it might say 0.2% of account value up to a maximum of £8. Thus, if you held £20,000 in a stocks and shares ISA, a 0.2% quarterly admin fee would be £40 but since they stipulate a maximum of £8, that is what you would be charged. Of course, these figures will vary and you should check the service charges for the broker you are thinking of opening an account with to see what your running costs will be.

In recent years, many low-cost brokers have appeared that charge either very low trading fees or none at all. How exactly do these low-cost brokers make money? Historically, brokers have attracted customers by undercutting their rivals when it comes to trading fees or offering certain perks. Brokers that charge higher fees, such as Hargreaves Lansdown, justify their fees by claiming to offer a more "premium" experience, from better customer service to a larger variety of stocks.

In 2014, Robinhood came along and disrupted the US brokerage industry by not charging any fees for trading shares. Sensing the threat, many brokers followed this trend.

However, a broker is in the business to make money, and there are a few ways zero-fee brokers make money:

- Fees for a premium account (e.g. an ISA or SIPP account, or an account that allows overseas investing too).
- Withdrawal or deposit fees.
- Foreign currency exchange fees.
- Interest on cash you hold in your account (this traditionally accounts for around half of the revenues of larger brokers).
- Margin lending. This is not halal for Muslims to do, so if you are offered the option of opting in or out, you should opt out. The reason is short-selling involves buying and selling that which you don't own, and profiting from that would be impermissible.
- Rehypothecation.
- Payment for order flow.

Rehypothecation and payment for order flow (PFOF) are all the rage in zero-fee broker business models so it's important you understand them if you choose these brokers.

Rehypothecation sounds complicated, but all it means is that a broker uses the stocks you own as a collateral for their own market activities. An example of rehypothecation is when a broker participates in share lending by allowing short sellers to borrow your stock. It's your stock that is being used, but the broker gets the "rent" for it.

Then we have PFOF, which has become the de facto stable revenue stream for a lot of brokers. The Securities and Exchange Commission (SEC) in the USA defines it as: "Payment for order flow is a method of transferring some of the trading profits from market making to the brokers that route customer orders to specialists for execution." What this means is that brokers will make deals with specific market makers and agree to route your buy and sell orders to them. In exchange for this special deal, your broker receives a small compensation.

Why does the market maker pay for your order? Because they make money on the spread between the bid and ask price, the more orders they receive, the more money they make. It's also interesting to note that in this age of quants and algorithms, order data is very valuable for computers to keep track of the market. And with free trade apps now making significant volume in the market, having that order data ahead of everyone else is really worth paying for.

Depending on who the broker is, it is likely they are making their money from one or more of the following means as well:[18]

- **CFD costs:** Trading212 has a CFD account which functions differently to the usual stock trading in their ISA and "Invest" accounts. CFDs are derivative instruments which are not Islamically permissible.[19] The CFD account has costs associated with CFD losses and holding positions overnight and over the weekends. Also the counterparty to your CFD trade is often the broker itself, and as most retail investors lose money when investing in CFD, the broker makes a nice profit here too.
- **Spreads:** Most brokers in this category will make money through the spread between the bid and ask price. The bid price is the price you get offered by the market for selling a stock and the ask price is the price the market asks of you when buying a stock. At any given moment there is a difference in these prices depending on which side of the table you are on. The broker makes money here.
- **Currency conversion fees:** Most brokers will charge a fee when you convert your currency to buy stocks which are denominated in a different currency.

- **Deposit fees:** Some brokers will charge you for depositing money into your account via certain means, e.g. if paying by debit card.

Product Range If you know that you only wish to invest in, say, the London Stock Exchange, you should check if your broker has access to stocks within the LSE (it almost certainly will). However, if you wish to invest in other countries, you should check beforehand and you should check what the costs associated with investing in these other countries is as it will very likely be different to UK investment charges.

Ease of Use We all like things to be intuitive and nice to use, so it is worth opening an account and playing with a demo account before going live with your own proper account with real money involved. That way, you can get a feel for the interface and see if you like it as each online broker very much has its own feel.

Investment Safety The safety of your money is of course ultimately tied to how your investments perform. The key thing with the stock market is that it can be volatile. So although your money could be safe in the sense that it is with a solid broker through whom you have invested in a fund, that fund could be -20% compared to when you bought it. If you are in it for the long haul, this is not so much an issue as you should expect prices to smooth out over time and give you that return.

But if you need your money at that point, then you would unfortunately have to sell at a loss just to get your money out. This is in contrast to other investment options explained below, like a savings account, where the volatility is pretty much non-existent.

Figure 12.2 is a chart of the S&P 500 since 1927 to December 2022 and shows how, when investing for a longer period of time, you are almost certain to be in the positive compared to when you invested. However, as you can see from the ups and downs in the chart, it is rarely plain sailing. Thus, safety in the stock market is really tied to a long-term investing mentality.

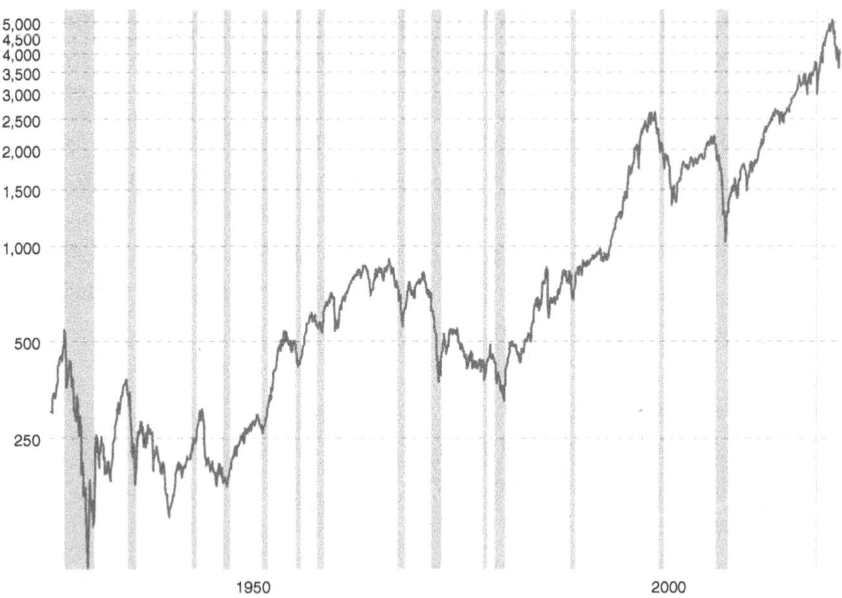

Figure 12.2 S&P 500 Index: 90-Year Historical Chart (December 2022).

Source: Macrotrends LLC.

Can I Get My Money Back Easily?

Getting your money back easily is one of the key plus points about investing in the stock market. The stock market is literally a market which has opening times and closing times and as long as the market is open, you can place a trade (either buy or sell) and have your order fulfilled.

If you want to sell out of an investment, it is as easy as going to your online broker (most of whom have great mobile apps these days too), select your investment and hit sell. You will get the market price at the time, and the cash will land in your online account. There is usually a lag of a couple of days in between you exiting an investment and receiving the cash in your bank account. All in all, this two-day lag (this may differ from broker to broker and country to country) is a minor inconvenience but it is worth bearing in mind in case you do, for whatever reason, need the money absolutely instantly and you are unable to wait two days.

All of this assumes that you will be investing in well-traded stocks or funds. If you invest in less well-known stocks or funds which do not have as much investment volume (this might occur on less well-known stock exchanges, for example), you might struggle to buy or sell that particular product.[20] The chances of this happening on the vast majority of stocks should be relatively slim though, so this is more a point for education rather than a genuine concern.

Sharia Considerations

Investing in the stock market is a bit like going meat shopping. Shares themselves are inherently permissible, just like most meat, but there are some parameters to be aware of.

There are five commonly accepted sharia standards when it comes to screening stocks for sharia-compliance. They are the following: AAOIFI, DJIM, FTSE, S&P, and MSCI. We will focus on the AAOIFI[21] standard here as it is well documented and easy to follow. You can research the other methodologies too and decide for yourself which standard you prefer to follow.

Websites such as www.muslimxchange.com offer the ability to screen stocks against all the standards and apps like Musaffa, Zoya, Muslimxchange, and Islamicly are also well worth checking out.

Here are the AAOIFI criteria when considering whether or not a stock is permissible to invest in.

The Business

Your average Muslim, or even non-Muslim, in today's wonderfully diverse environment, can tell you that it is haram to invest in a company whose main business is alcohol, gambling, pork, night club activities, etc. These are things that we can unequivocally say are haram to invest in without the need for detailed analysis. So the main business of the company cannot violate Islamic law, which rules out many companies immediately.

There is a slightly greyer area of companies in the financial services sector, such as banks and insurers or even, say, stock brokers themselves. These are probably best judged on a case-by-case basis rather than having a blanket policy, but the safest option with grey areas is to avoid them or at least to do a deeper dive and, if necessary, consult with experts on it. Most experts would typically screen these out as standard though.

For instance, take a company like Amazon. On the face of it, they're just a seller of goods and there is not much wrong with that. However, if you consider the range of things they actually sell and note that many of them would actually be haram, there is a judgement call to be made as to whether Amazon would be permissible. This brings us nicely on to the second criterion.

Impermissible Income

Often a business is halal in its activities, but the company also has haram elements involved in the running of it. This can be because they have an element of interest-based income or they are borrowing on interest, for example. This is known as income from non-sharia-compliant investments. The rule of thumb is that the income from these haram investments cannot exceed 5% of the gross revenue of the company. So there are two figures to check here: (1) income from non-sharia-compliant investments; and (2) gross revenue.

The investor has to check the annual reports to determine what percentage of haram income was received and consequently give away that same percentage of their profits to charity. The final encouragement scholars give is that the investor must voice their opposition to these haram activities, either written or orally – perhaps at the annual shareholder meeting.[22]

It is important to note that the annual reports will not neatly tell you things like "4% of our income was from alcohol, 2% was from betting, etc.". It may give clues as to this kind of thing, but this is very much an educated guess unless you have very clear knowledge on this somehow.

The process we just mentioned of an investor giving away a portion of their profits to charity is known as purification. It is important to define what we mean by "profits". In this scenario, we are describing it as both dividends that the stock yields, and also capital gain, which is the price of the share increasing. The reason we highlight this is that there is some difference of opinion among scholars as to whether purification is done solely on dividends or also on capital gain.

The case for purification on capital gain is because some contend that the market price of the share reflects an element of the benefit from haram activities of a company. However, the fact that we even bought the shares shows that the majority of the company assets are halal, which means that the share price is based on the large proportion of halal assets and not on the negligible quantity of assets from haram income. Thus purification on capital gain is arguably not needed, and this is our view. However, the cautious view is just to purify both dividends and your capital gain on a sale.

Debt Ratio

The third criterion is interest-bearing debt to total assets of the company. The total interest-bearing debt should not exceed 30% of market capitalisation. This metric is quite simple to remember, but what is interesting about this one is that extremely successful (non-Muslim) investors also apply similar criteria to their stock screens.

The likes of Benjamin Graham, widely considered as one of the greatest investors of the twentieth century, emphasised this low leverage metric very strongly in his famous book, *The Intelligent Investor.*[23] The same principles regarding debt financing were emulated by his student, the famous Warren Buffett, who is still alive today.

The specific amount of interest-bearing debt might not always be made explicitly clear on the accounts. Sometimes, for instance, "borrowings" as listed on the accounts might be interest-free loans from directors. It is therefore vital to check the supplemental notes to the accounts which will break things down further and tell you specifically.

ETFs

You may recall that we spoke about investing into ETFs earlier. The big question is: are they halal to invest in or not? This depends on what the fund consists of. The easiest way to find this out is to look for ETFs that have been certified as sharia-compliant by scholars. Otherwise you will have to do a manual check.

When doing a manual check, you first make sure that the ETF actually holds the underlying assets. ETFs that synthetically create the same effect using derivative instruments are not permissible to invest in.

You then need to determine whether all the companies or assets in a fund are halal. If so, then, yes, the entire ETF is halal. However, if any company within the ETF is haram, that renders the ETF haram.

If the fund contains impure income from one or some of the companies (less than 5%), then the ETF is still halal to invest in but you should purify your profits by giving that percentage away in charity.

In practice, it is quite difficult for the average investor to manually screen a stock's ETF. This is because ETFs generally tend to have anywhere from 30 to hundreds of different active holdings. For this reason, it might be best to stick to the certified halal ETFs – at least until some automated solution can be developed that can speed up the screening process.[24]

Zakat

Zakat on stocks is reasonably straightforward but naturally needs some figuring out. First, we need to make a distinction between your intentions when buying shares. Are you buying them as a long-term investment for dividends or are you buying them with the sole intention of reselling them for a higher price in the short term? In the latter case, it is generally accepted that your entire shareholding is subject to 2.5% zakat.

This is because your shares themselves are assets you want to sell for profit. So if you bought £1000 of shares and the market value at the time your zakat is due is £1250, you will pay zakat on the £1250 even if you have not sold. So here, you would pay 2.5% of £1250 which is £31.25.

In the former case, i.e. you are purchasing shares as a long-term investment, you can actually go ahead and work out zakatable business assets, to lower the amount of zakat paid each year. These assets include cash, inventories, strong debts (money owed to the business which is likely to be repaid), and raw materials.

There is no need to overly worry about calculating this figure exactly. In most cases, it suffices to simply go to the balance sheet, add all current assets (i.e. liquid parts of the business that are cash or similar to cash in that they can be converted to cash) and some of the non-current assets. The non-current assets which you might pick out are inventories, deferred tax assets, trade and other receivables, tax recoverables, other financial assets and assets of disposal groups held for sale. To summarise: current assets + some non-current assets + assets of disposal groups held for sale. The latter may not apply to all companies so don't worry if you don't see it. The logic here is that just as in our personal lives we pay zakat on things which are generally quite liquid such as cash, the same applies in a business.

So if you do this calculation and you work out that a company has £50m of assets which are zakatable, you should then check what that is as a percentage of all assets. That gives you a zakatable assets percentage, e.g. 30%. You then take 30% of the value of your shareholding, and pay 2.5% on that. So if your shares are worth £1000 and the zakatable assets are 30%, you are paying zakat on £300, which is £7.50.

Slightly confusing? Not to worry; if you don't want to get bogged down with balance sheet calculations, it is also permissible to simply take roughly a 25% of the market value of your share holdings,[25] and pay 2.5% on that. So to continue the above example, your £1000 would have 25% zakatable assets and you therefore pay 2.5% on £250, which is £6.25.

If you are invested in a fund, it is easiest to take this 25% figure for that too. You can use the IFG zakat calculator to painlessly automate these calculations for you.[26]

How Can I Get Access to Stocks?

With stocks, there are a variety of ways to get access depending on what type of investor you are.

DIY

If you are a DIY investor, then you will want to find out the most trustworthy stock brokers for your jurisdiction. In the UK, popular and reputable stock brokers include the likes of AJ Bell, Hargreaves Lansdown, Trading212, Interactive Brokers, and IG. In the US, similarly popular and reputable stock brokers are Fidelity, Charles Schwaab, TD Ameritrade, and Robinhood.

A range of underlying investments exists to get exposure to and a number of ways to get them. Whether that's directly investing in stocks or going the fund route, you should have a world of opportunities to explore once you have opened your account with your stock broker.

Hands-Off

If you are in the camp of people who does not want to pick your own stocks but you are comfortable enough opening your own account and picking some funds, that is thankfully relatively straightforward.

To help you, here is a list of sharia-compliant funds that we are aware of. It may also help if you search terms such as "Islamic" and "sharia" and other variations of these words:

- iShares MSCI World Islamic UCITS ETF
- iShares MSCI EM Islamic UCITS ETF
- iShares MSCI USA Islamic UCITS ETF
- SP Funds Dow Jones Global Sukuk ETF
- SP Funds S&P 500 Sharia Industry Exclusions ETF
- Wealthsimple Shariah World Equity Index ETF
- SP Funds S&P Global REIT Sharia ETF
- Almalia Sanlam Active Shariah Global Equity UCITS ETF.

Super Hands-Off

If you are really not willing to do anything like the above two options, you still have a couple of options open to you. One is to open an account with one of the roboadvisors that exist out there. In the US, these include the likes of Aghaz Investments, the UK has Wahed Invest, and others exist in South East Asia such as Algebra. When you open an account with a roboadvisor, they will pre-package a portfolio for you depending on your risk appetite. This can be a nice way of getting off the fence without having to overthink things too much.

We have found that for many people, a roboadvisor is a great first step to force you to become more active in investing. Many people then decide they want to do something more active than just having a roboadvisor account and they then get stuck into other parts of investing as we have discussed throughout this book.

The other route, if you really want to be hands-off, is to pay a financial advisor. A quality financial advisor will meet with you, listen to your financial goals and needs, and develop a totally bespoke portfolio for you. You will of course need to make sure that if you go down this route, the advisor you choose has some experience catering for sharia-sensitive clients.

Remember that this is a regulated industry, so you should make sure that whoever you go with has the requisite qualifications and licences. It is always a good idea to seek out people who come with the personal recommendation of other people in your network who have had a successful experience with that individual.

Summary

- Stocks are historically a strong performer and can average around 10% per annum.
- You can invest in different areas of the stock market according to your risk appetite.
- You can get an income by investing in quality dividend-yielding stocks.
- Both fundamental and technical analysis are important when choosing stocks.
- There are multiple ways to get exposure to the stock market, you don't just need to be a stock picker.

13 Fixed Income

Fixed return investing is the bread and butter of most mainstream investment portfolios – but for Muslims, it is extremely difficult to find fixed income products as bonds are haram and sukuk are not plentiful.

This chapter outlines the various options still available to Muslims to take advantage of fixed yield returns.

Property: What Is It?

Bricks and mortar. Something you can touch and feel, show off to somebody and which can both generate income and appreciate in value. And every piece is unique too.

The investment that every uncle from the masjid will sagely opine on as the best investment out there. During the height of the crypto boom this uncle is scoffed at by young men with the FTX app on their phone and gel in their hair, but come 2022, those same pretenders are queuing up wanting to chat to the uncle on his HMO strategies.

It's hard not to like property and there's a good reason why it is the staple investment for so many people. For communities like the ones we come from (South Asian), property is adored. Growing up, all we ever heard on the investment front was property. And to be frank, it has stood the test of time with the returns to show its worth in the upper echelons of investing fame.

No doubt we have all heard stories of a distant or close relative who made a tremendous amount of money from property. Whether that's somebody who has a crazy portfolio of income-generating properties, someone who developed properties and sold them on or someone with a more niche strategy like getting planning permission on land and selling the land, the evidence is there to show that there is certainly money to be made in property.

Sadly, not all of these folks will have made their money in a halal way though. Property is particularly attractive because of the leverage aspect; that is, you can get exposure to a £500,000 asset by putting down around 20–25% of that (depending on the bank). If you have put down £100,000 and you are making £35,000 rental income off this £500,000 asset, you can nicely pay off the mortgage over the next 15–20 years and end up with an asset that is probably worth around 2x what it was 20 years ago (so in this case around £1m – on the basis that property prices on average increase by around 3–4% per year[1]), all while having only put down £100,000 initially.

Multiply this by several properties and you can see why that distant relative has a portfolio worth tens of millions and a very tidy income that he or she is making off the portfolio in the meantime.

The same leverage effect is true of property development too and any other way of making money in property. As long as you have something banks are willing to lend against (it typically gets harder and more expensive the further you go backwards from a fully built property to a shell, to land, to land without planning permission, etc.), you can magnify your returns through leverage.

But that does not change the fact that much of this leverage is impermissible, depending on the source. And since you are reading this book, haram leverage is likely to be a red line for you.

In this chapter, we will analyse the different ways that you can make money in property in a halal way.

Returns on Offer

The returns in property very much depend on the kind of property investing you do. As we mentioned in Chapter 12 on the stock market, there are sub-categories even within this asset class. The riskier property investing (such as land or property development) will garner better returns than very safe offerings such as commercial property which is let out on long leases to publicly traded, large companies.

The following are the types of property investing that we will discuss:

1. Buy-to-let.
2. Buying to flip.
3. Property development.
4. Land development.

We will also discuss at the end of this chapter how you can get access to these flavours of property investing if you do not want to do all the work yourself.

Buy-to-Let

For investors who want a stable income from the money they invest as well as the opportunity for the asset they invest in to grow, buying a property in order to let it out is an ideal choice.

There are several choices to make when going down this route: the type of property and the mode of investment. The type of property really does come in many shapes and sizes. The most fundamental choice you should decide on is whether you want to make an investment into a residential property or a commercial property.

Residential properties tend to be the default choice for many investors but our view is that this need not be the case. Residential property can feel safer as it is more familiar, but residential property can also come with its own headache. If you are undertaking the investment yourself, you will become responsible for all tenant issues, including broken boilers at midnight and other such day-to-day issues that can come up.[2]

Contrast that with commercial properties where the nature of the leases tend to be much more landlord-friendly. For example, you can require properties to be refurbished and brought up to scratch every 5 years by the tenant and you can negotiate upwards-only rent reviews. On top of that, businesses are just generally easier to deal with. They aren't as *human* or *emotional* as that family that lives in the terraced house you let out. They behave in a predictable, professional way. Taking all that in the round, you might want to reconsider making residential property your default.

The other important choice to make is the type of property and area that you go for. For residential, you have a choice that ranges from city centre apartments to sleepy-town detached houses. Whatever you choose, the key things to bear in mind are (1) what kind of rent you can charge, and (2) the occupancy rate of your property.

If you are investing in a city centre apartment, for example, you might initially be underwhelmed by the rent you might receive. But when you factor in that the occupancy rate will be very high across the year with a waiting list of potential tenants ready to replace your existing one, not to mention the superior capital appreciation, it suddenly becomes quite attractive.

On the flip side, you might be attracted by the potential yield on a detached house in a small town, but when you factor in the potential for months going by without a tenant and the stagnant property prices, it becomes less appealing. As we have said throughout this book, returns are generally linked to the risk you take.

The hallmarks of a good buy-to-let property are:

- Potential for capital appreciation in the property itself.
- Certainty or near-certainty that you will get your desired yield by being able to get enough rent and enough occupancy.
- Low-fuss tenants.
- Optional to unlock better yield: do some development work to the property to unlock more rental income, for example, add a bedroom, change the layout, convert it to a HMO,[3] etc. Naturally this means more work but that is the *quid pro quo* of unlocking better yield. We will discuss property development fully in Chapter 14.

There are some interesting alternative ways to get exposure to buy-to-let properties that require far less input from you, which we will discuss in the "How Can I Get Access?" section.

Property Development/Flipping

Developing properties is an extremely popular investing method and, for many, a profitable business. We have heard of people who have had very successful careers who have moved into developing properties or simply flipping them as they are once they had their first taste and saw the riches on offer.

"Flipping" a property simply means reselling a property, often in a short timescale. It is undoubtedly a higher-risk approach than buying a property which is ready to let out or sell, because you are by definition trying to polish something which is rough and unlock some gain by doing that.

Property development comes in many shapes and sizes. The most popular option is a refurbishment. These are properties which people buy which have some area for improvement. This could simply be that the property looks tired and dated and a simple refresh of carpets, a few licks of paint, perhaps some new doors or other minor work could lead to a healthy uplift in the resale price.

The human mind is a funny thing and, in our experience, if you show people a nice-looking, modern, fresh property, there is a natural tendency to associate value with that property and pay a certain amount of money for it. Show the same property to them, however, when it is not looking its best or even when it is unfurnished, and many people simply get tunnel vision and cannot see the potential in a property. As such, they completely undervalue the house, not realising that simply spending a few thousand pounds or dollars on that house would add tens of thousands of pounds of value back to it.

There is actually a new startup that specialises in doing exactly this for people looking to sell houses. Flyp.co uses their property renovation expertise to make cosmetic and other touch-ups to a house and add tens of thousands to the asking price within days. See Figure 13.1.

It is in this arena that many property developers play, spotting badly-taken photos that look unattractive or envisaging something great in that tired old inherited house that the family just wants to encash.

You may even have seen properties on the market where a few months ago you saw the old version of the house and less than a year later you are seeing the same house looking totally brand new after a refurbishment, now being sold with a £20,000–£30,000 mark-up on what is was being sold for last time.

Other times, value is attributed in doing something additional to the property beyond superficial improvements. These might be things like a loft conversion to get in an extra bedroom or two, a single-storey extension, a re-arrangement of internal walls to make things more functional, and so on. Unlocking this kind of value is somewhat harder than the first type of improvement that we talked about, simply because it requires more experience and vision.

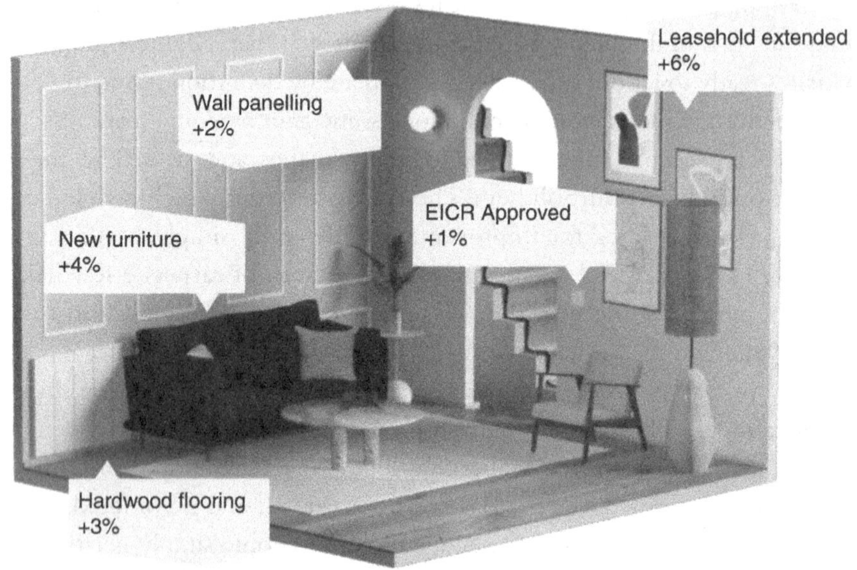

Figure 13.1 Home transformation.

Source: Fly homes / https://www.flyp.co/how-it-works / last accessed January 03, 2023.

Again, this is where it is helpful to visit properties with someone who is experienced. Once you have visited enough properties and done a certain amount of refurbishment yourself, you too will start seeing the potential for single-storey extensions out into the garden and very quickly be able to price that up, figure out how long it will take, understand how much value it will add on to the property, and factor all of that in to your bidding price.

Adding this kind of value to properties is helpful not just for when you are buying properties for resell, but even if you are a buy-to-let investor looking to build a portfolio of income-generating assets, one way to unlock more yield is by buying these kinds of properties and then renting them out.

In this analysis, instead of thinking about how much money you could gain by reselling, you think about how much rent the property could give you once you have done the work. The rental market and the purchase market work very differently, and it is entirely possible that whereas in a resale scenario a single-storey kitchen extension might add on £10,000 to the resale price, it adds very little to the potential rental amount that you could get.

As a result, refurbishment or improvement works should always be undertaken through the lens of: *what is in it for me?* You should not simply improve a property for the sake of it if you could have left it as it is and got the same amount of money for it either in a resale or renting scenario. That is a monumental waste of time, effort, and money – three very precious resources.

For the above reasons, particularly when renting out, a common method of analysis is to think about how much rent you could get for every square metre or foot of property. After all, the higher this number, the more value you are squeezing out of your property.

So in the above example, if extending the property does not get you any more rent or very minimal rent, that ratio of rent to square foot is actually going to decrease. For this reason, something known as HMOs (house in multiple occupation) have become a very popular method of property investing. This is where a single house is rented by multiple people. The reason it has become so popular is because you can unlock very strong yields by renting out a house this way.

Let's say you have a three-storey house with plenty of rooms. There is a market ceiling as to how much you can rent out that property for under the traditional method of simply finding a family that wants to live there. However, as soon as you start splitting that house up into bedrooms and renting individual spaces in the house with access to what then become communal areas like living rooms and kitchens, you can unlock more total rent.

For instance, the market may be £1,000 rent per month for a large 5-bedroom house in a certain area, but if you can instead rent out a bedroom at £250 per month, you are unlocking 25% extra yield. Over a year, you are getting £15,000 instead of £12,000 which has a massive difference on your overall yield. Assuming a £250,000 purchase price, that's 6% yield versus 4.8%. In the long term, these numbers make a difference.

In short, property development offers something for both flippers and holders – either turning a (hopefully quick) profit or ending up with a better yield on your buy-to-let. Be prepared, however, for lots of hard work and lots of being let down.

In our conversations with people working in the property development game, one consistent theme is that the development itself always takes longer than you anticipate because of how difficult it is to get builders and other tradespeople you need for your development. These people will typically have several jobs on the go at any one time and they are notoriously difficult to pin down.

The other thing to keep in mind is that when you first get into the industry, you won't know what a good builder looks like, and so you will inevitably end up kissing a few frogs or overpaying. Our recommendation would be to overpay in the early days rather than go for the cheaper but unknown option. The amount of money it takes to fix mistakes and the amount of money badly done work shaves off your exit price is almost always going to be significantly more than the savings you might make in the short term. Trust us, we've been there.[4]

You should not let this put you off if you want to get into property development, but it is important that you go into it with your eyes open.[5]

For anyone feeling rather put off by the difficulties of property development at this point – doing it yourself is not the only way, and the options that we will discuss shortly in the "How do I get access?" section are potentially more suitable for you.

Land Development

Through your time reading this book, you will have hopefully learned by now that different types of investments come with different risk profiles. And that even within a single asset class, there is a range of risk. We discussed this at length in Chapter 12 on the stock market and the same applies in property.

Land development is at the riskier end of the spectrum within the asset class of property itself. The safest is undoubtedly the straightforward buy-to-let, the medium point would likely be property development, and the riskiest would be land development.

The reason why land development carries a very high risk (and higher upside) is because it is a specialist area that, if done badly, leaves you with a useless piece of land. At least if you get property wrong, you still ultimately end up with something tangible.

The upside in land comes where you can identify and purchase plots of land without any planning permission on it and then get planning permission for it. With this planning permission, that land becomes more valuable overnight, as then property developers are happy to take this off your hand to build property on it for them to sell into the market as well.

Done well, land development offers incredible returns and the opportunity for you not just to flip the land, but also then to build on it having acquired that land cheaply instead of having to pay higher prices for land which already has planning permission, which makes our overall return fantastic. Doing something like this would fit the increasingly popular "build-to-rent" model of property investing, whereby you build properties from scratch in order to then let them out. Similar to what we discussed in the property development section, you can unlock great yield this way if you are willing to undertake the time investment and expense.

Land investing does come with its risks though. There can be all kinds of troubles with land which might prevent you from ever getting permission to build on it and subsequently it becomes very difficult to shift that land.

Although we have advised this with all the property sections, this is an area where having an experienced hand alongside you is not just a recommended action, but is a must.

Is My Money Safe?

The asset itself is a safe one. There is a good reason for the saying "safe as houses" to mean that something is incredibly safe. That is because property is a tangible and finite asset with real utility and value and also enjoys a long track record of being a good investment.

When purchasing a property it is important to do your due diligence. Our advice here is to make sure you do two things: first, when you are thinking about buying a property, take someone experienced along with you to view the place. There are often tell-tale signs of problems in a house which an inexperienced eye will miss.

When I[6] was buying my first property to live in, I came across a great off-market property. It ticked all our boxes: two lovely spacious living rooms, ample space upstairs for the kids' bedrooms, and the cherry on top was a fantastic attic space that I had claimed as my own and where I was already working out where my desk would sit and my armchair would rest.

I got as far as verbally agreeing a price with the seller and it was only later when my father and father-in-law visited the property that they noticed one of the rooms had a sloping floor: a danger sign for structural issues which can be extremely costly to fix. Perhaps there was nothing in it and maybe it would have all been fine, but I did not really fancy taking the chance and I pulled out of the purchase.

So definitely take someone experienced with you if you have not yet got a trained eye when it comes to properties.

Second, make sure you give ample time for the legal due diligence and do not be afraid to raise enquiries with the sellers' solicitors for anything you are unsure of. The legal process after prices have been agreed is often seen as something to get through or an unnecessary delay, but you should pay attention during this period. Read the enquiries that your solicitor will send over and add to them as you see fit based on what you saw when you visited the property.

Every property is unique, and there are all kinds of weird and wonderful tales that every property has. The property I mentioned above had a private road by the side of it which I definitely would have been investigating if the process had gone further, to fully understand my potential rights and obligations. The last thing you want as a property owner is something like that which could have you on the hook for repair costs when the road falls into disrepair or anything out of the ordinary happens.

Rights of way also tend to be a popular spanner in the works. Your solicitor will, as standard, ask about whether there are any rights of way over your potential property but you should spend some time observing this stuff in reality to really work out whether it will be a hindrance. I have heard of examples where people unknowingly bought houses where their back garden was a right of way for the whole street of houses. This meant occasionally looking out of your window and seeing random people traipsing through. Or worse, your children playing in the garden and random people going through.

None of this is unsolvable and very rarely will something cause a property sale to fall through. But you must not just see the legal stage as a tick box – make sure you are paying attention.

By and large, though, given how stable and solid property is, your money will be safe although it is important to recognise that property is not something that is very liquid.

Things get a bit more complex if you use sharia-compliant financing on a property. There, the risk ratchets up a few notches as you now need to meet the payments every month. If you don't, you're in trouble and could see the property being taken to auction and sold off for a loss.

The planning permission strategies on land that we discussed above are also a little higher risk too, given there is no property actually on the site, and if you've tried and failed to get permission, it will make selling the land that much harder.

The other important safety element to consider goes beyond just the asset itself. If you are buying a property yourself, then the above applies. However, if you are simply getting exposure to a property via another provider, then the same levels of due diligence apply to that provider as they would to any investment provider. See Chapter 9 on "How to Do Basic Due Diligence into an Investment Company".

Can I Get My Money Back Easily?

Although property is regarded as a safe asset class, it is not generally regarded as a liquid asset class. So the answer to this question very much depends on how you are getting exposure to property.

If you are getting exposure to property by buying property yourself, then you will know from being on the buyer side that selling a property is not straightforward and takes some time. If you find yourself in a situation where you simply have to sell your assets in order to raise cash, property is not the kind of thing you can get rid of overnight.

So while you will be able to get your money back as long as the market has not turned against you, it will take some time.

If you have exposure to property through some other means, you must examine the liquidity options with that particular investment provider. We will discuss the various options in the later sections, but, for instance, if you access property through a REIT, that could actually be very liquid indeed.

Sharia Considerations

When it comes to property, there is plenty to consider from a sharia angle. No matter which route you are taking to actually get exposure to property, you fundamentally need to make sure that the way that the property is being invested in is sharia-compliant, i.e. that there is no impermissible leverage.

In addition, once you have got over that hurdle, you should also make sure that particularly for buy-to-let properties, that you are not tenanting properties out to companies which are doing obvious haram. While there is some debate on the technicalities of whether rental income is permissible from, say, a gambling company, our view is that it is better to steer clear of any tenants which openly do immoral things, particularly when you have easy alternatives.

Zakat

Let's assess the zakat considerations when it comes to property. As you probably know, zakat is never due on the home you live in. But if you are investing in property, then the zakat you need to pay will depend on what kind of property investing you are doing.

If you have invested in a property with the sole intention of reselling, then you will owe zakat on the entire value of the property. If you have an Islamic mortgage on this, you should find out whether it is a *musharaka*-based mortgage or a *murabaha*-based mortgage.

If it is a *musharaka*-based mortgage, you should only pay zakat on your portion of the property. If it is a *murabaha*-based mortgage, then zakat is due on the entire property. The reason for this is that in the *murabaha*-based mortgage, you are the ultimate owner.

You may deduct a year's worth of any non-interest portion of your mortgage payments if there is difficulty in meeting the zakat, but it is safer to pay zakat on the full amount.[7]

Where you have bought a property and you let it out, no zakat is due on the property itself. Instead, you will only owe zakat on the rental income which you have taken in and which remains as cash in your possession. However, if you have spent your rental income before your zakat is due, then you will not owe any zakat.

Where you invest in property with the intention of reselling but then change your mind, your zakat also changes accordingly (and vice versa).

Now let's consider a few worked examples.

Example 1

You buy a property with a sharia-compliant buy-to-let mortgage. You intend to rent out the property and benefit from the annual income which is £15,000.

On your zakat date when you come to calculate the zakat on this property, you realise that of the £15,000 rental income:

£12,000 went on repaying the mortgage.
£2,000 was spent on refurbishment costs.
£1,000 remains and it is sitting in your bank.

You will pay zakat on the remaining £1,000 if your overall wealth on the zakat date is above *nisab*.

Example 2

You invest £10,000 with Cur8 Capital. After taking out any fees that are due, you have £600 for the annual income from this investment. You still have the full amount in your bank on the zakat calculation date.

Zakat will be due on the £600 if your overall wealth on the zakat date is above *nisab*.

Example 3

You bought a house with the intention of reselling in 2018. For three years, you paid zakat on the full amount while you were trying to sell the property.

After your 2021 zakat payment but before your 2022 zakat became due, you decided in the interim that because the house was too difficult to sell, you would simply rent this out for the long term.

In 2022, you will therefore only pay zakat on the rental income in the same way you did in Example 1.

How Can I Get Access?

When it comes to property investing there are plenty of options nowadays. Going direct and hands-on will generally get you the best returns if you know what you are doing. However if you are inexperienced, there are a few other smart ways.

The method you choose of getting exposure to property will have an impact on what kind of returns you can make.

DIY

The most obvious way is the way we have discussed throughout this chapter which is to simply buy the property yourself. This is a very hands-on approach. The benefits here are that if you are an advanced investor, you have the ability to make your investments completely bespoke according to your wishes. You will probably know what you want, have a team that you can get in for refurbishments, solicitors that you regularly use, and so on.

However, even if you are a beginner, as long as you are prepared to embrace the learning curve and make some mistakes in the process, the DIY route can still work.

REITs

Another option is to invest in a property through a REIT – a real estate investment trust. These are professionally managed pooled vehicles whereby the fund manager will invest in certain types of real estate according to the mandate for that particular REIT.

For instance, you may have a commercial storage REIT that only invests into commercial storage properties, a data centre REIT that only invests in data centres, or a REIT that only invests in a certain geography, and so on. The advantage here is that while you get exposure to a certain property type, you get the expertise of the fund manager and all their capabilities of sourcing quality property deals.

REITs are publicly listed on stock exchanges, meaning that they are very accessible and act like a stock in the sense that you can buy it through a broker and get liquidity. And since you are not buying property directly, rather a slice of a property trust, you can get started with much lower investment amounts.

When it comes to the sharia-compliance of REITs, it can be somewhat of a minefield. That is because most REITs will use leverage which will invariably be conventional rather than Islamic.

If you come across a REIT which does not use leverage, that would be a good candidate to get sharia-compliant REIT exposure in your portfolio.

Here is a two-step checklist for analysing whether a REIT is sharia-compliant or not. A word of warning though: during both our research for this book and direct conversations with scholars, as well as our day-to-day investing activities, we are aware of a growing number of scholarly voices who call for screening of REITs and ETFs (and other funds) to be reimagined. The argument is that applying the same screening analysis on a holding vehicle as you do for a trading business is inequitable.

From a personal standpoint, our preference on REITs is zero debt. Unlike a trading business where any leverage has an indirect impact on profits, in a REIT, your leverage directly affects how much return you make and therefore how well you do as an investor.

Step 1: Check the REIT's Revenue You want to make sure that the REIT is only making money from rent rather than any other income sources. In addition, it is worth at this point checking what kinds of properties the REIT is making money from. From a sharia angle, it is better to avoid REITs where the money is coming from investments in properties which are then being let out to companies operating in haram sectors, such as gambling.

If the revenue source is mixed, ensure that the non-compliant revenue does not exceed 5% of the total. If it exceeds this, it is not permissible to invest in. If it is 5% or below, you may invest in it but you should purify that amount of your income from the REIT and give it away to charity.

Step 2: Check the Total Debt Similar to stocks, the debt in a REIT should not exceed 30%. However, if the debt is Islamic debt, this limit does not apply. Our preference is for zero-debt REITs from an Islamic standpoint (or REITs with Islamic debt).

For those of you living in Muslim-majority countries, the options are somewhat better when it comes to finding sharia-compliant REITs. Here are some sample ones to get you started. Note, we have not reviewed these REITs from an investing perspective so you should undertake this due diligence.

- Emirates REIT (UAE)
- Al-'Aqar Healthcare REIT (Malaysia)
- KFH Capital REIT (Kuwait)
- Axis Real Estate Investment Trust (Malaysia)
- Sabana REIT (Singapore)
- Inovest REIT (Bahrain)
- KLCC REIT (Malaysia)
- Al-Salam REIT (Bahrain)

This is by no means an exhaustive list but provides a good starting point for you to conduct your own research. Each of these REITs will invest in different things. For example KLCC invests in commercial and office buildings (including the famous Petronas Twin Towers in Kuala Lumpur). Meanwhile the Al-'Aqar Healthcare REIT primarily owns medical centres, hospitals, and other similar health-related properties.

As such, you can build up your own blend of REITs and gain hands-off real estate exposure left in the hands of experts and make great returns off the back of it.

REITs are common for buy-to-let exposure and possibly even some property development, but less common for land development. You may need to seek out private investment companies doing land investing who are willing to take on your capital – although please ensure you do your due diligence on any investment company you put your money with.

Stocks

Similar to publicly listed REITs, you can get exposure to property by buying stocks in listed companies whose business means that they are exposed to the property market themselves.

House-builders are very popular options and will generally correlate with the state of the wider housing market. As the price and demand for new builds increase, the better the performance for the house-builders. However, these can be affected by wider macro issues such as interest rates, mortgage availability, and so on. And since you are buying an individual company, there can be company-specific issues holding it back.

Another less direct option is to buy stock in companies whose main clients are house-builders and other similar players in the property market. For instance, you might want to research bricks manufacturers, cement manufacturers, and so on. Because their business relies on the overall state of the property market and for property developers to be buying from them, their share price will generally move in line with the wider property market.

So the stock market can be a nice, liquid way to get a general exposure to property. But remember – investments in property companies is not like investing in property itself, and adds a significant layer of volatility and company-specific risk to your investment.

Private Funds

Another option when it comes to property investing is to invest with a private provider. This is similar to the REIT option whereby you are buying into a fund manager's expertise and their ability to source excellent deals, given their expertise and also their large investment pot.

However, unlike the REIT option, private real estate investing is slightly more opaque. Since these vehicles are not listed on any stock exchanges, you might have to work a little harder to get access to them.

The advantage of private vehicles is that you will sometimes find something that you cannot get access to in a REIT. This could be a particular type of property exposure you want, or it could simply be the fact that a private fund is offering better returns that it can generate.

If you are investing in a private fund, you should do the usual due diligence as if you were investing in a REIT from a commercial and a sharia perspective, and you should probably also do some extra due to the fact that a publicly listed REIT already has a layer of diligence due to the fact that it has been listed on a stock exchange.

The key things to check with a private real estate fund are:

- Its fees.
- Who is the fund manager and what is their experience?
- What types of real estate is the fund investing in?
- Is there any liquidity window for you to withdraw money if you want to?
- What is the tax treatment for you?

If you are satisfied with all of this, then investing in a private real estate fund can be a fantastic option to get real estate exposure. It means that you get all the advantages we discussed with a REIT with potentially more favourable returns or tax treatment.

Getting access to quality private real estate funds can be tricky though, as most quality funds generally have very high minimum tickets (typically seven or eight figures). If you are able to meet these minimum limits directly, then you can invest in these high quality private real estate funds. These will typically be available through top-tier investment banks who will be sensitive to your sharia needs.

If you are unable to meet these minimum limits, you can still get exposure to quality private real estate funds. There are several players in the market looking to democratise real estate investing, either at the fund level, or by allowing investment in individual properties.

Depending on the jurisdiction you are located in, you can do a search for real estate crowdfunding platforms that are done without any debt involved. This is much easier again in Muslim-majority countries.

Summary

- Property investing comes in many shapes and sizes but has proven itself to be a quality and resilient asset class.
- There are multiple ways beyond just paying cash and getting exposure to property, to actually get exposure to real estate.
- Leverage (sharia-compliant) makes property almost unique in that you can get exposure to a much bigger asset than you would otherwise afford.

This concept of democratising private fund investing is also exactly what we are doing in our own lives running the Cur8 Capital platform.

SME Financing: What Is It?

SME financing is the lifeblood of any economy. "SME" stands for small and medium-sized enterprises and includes essentially all companies other than the big blue chips and the technology startups that get venture capital backing (more on those in Chapter 14 on alternative assets).

An SME is typically a bricks and mortar business that scales linearly rather than exponentially. A chain of petrol stations scales linearly for example.[8] Each new petrol station requires a capital expenditure, but once it is made, it makes a relatively predictable return.

So if you are the owner of a petrol station you max out with that petrol station at a certain point. After that, the only way to expand is by opening multiple petrol stations or by reducing your capital expenditure on stock somehow.

This is where SME financing can come in. SME financing helps businesses by giving them short-term and medium-term loans in order to accelerate on key areas and reduce their capital expenditure.

SME financing has become more popular as an investment with the advent of crowdfunding platforms, favourable regulation, and technology and the historic lack of higher yielding assets. The SME financing investment platform sits in the middle and connects investors with money on the one side with those who are looking to receive financing, on the other. You are effectively lending money to a cash-generating business and getting back a fixed return.

There are a few different forms of SME financing – and consequently investments in that – that are available to investors. First, you have a typical loan that is designed to finance general cash flows. Next, you have financing available against specific assets, such as heavy machinery or property. Finally, you have invoice financing, where the investor effectively buys the incoming (but deferred) payment due as per an invoice to the business at slightly less than face value. The investor profits once the invoice is paid in full.

There are also interesting new forms of revenue financing and subscription financing entering the market that are particularly designed for technology and digital-first businesses.

Your "sharia alarm bells" may be ringing at this point. All of these financing products have conventional equivalents and certainly need to be structured carefully. Unlike equity-based instruments, these products do look a lot more like interest. We'll cover this in more detail in the "Sharia Considerations" section below.

Returns on Offer

Returns will vary based on the type of product, the length of the term, and who the underlying company is that the monies are being given to.

As a rough rule of thumb, you are typically looking at a range of somewhere between 6–15% per annum with a typical time horizon of an investment roughly in the 12–36 months range.

Is My Money Safe?

Ultimately the safety of your money depends on the creditworthiness of the underlying business. Therefore, the critical thing in this whole transaction is the ability of the platform to do high quality credit checks and due diligence on the recipient SME.

Ultimately there will always be a risk of the SME defaulting, and the type of entities that you are dealing with here will not be as creditworthy as, say, the government or a blue chip corporation. However, that is also why you are getting the above-average returns.

A vital way of reducing your risk when investing in SME financing products is to diversify your pot of SME financings across a range of different companies from different sectors and geographies. That way you spread the risk of default across multiple companies – and the chances of all of them defaulting at the same time is very low.

Can I Get My Money Back Easily?

You cannot get your money back at all in most SME financing investments. This is because the money is now with the SME and there is no way of getting it back. Second, due to sharia reasons, it is difficult to buy and sell "debts" at anything other than par value.

On the bright side, you are getting regular payments every month, and the term of an investment is typically relatively short.

Sharia Considerations

An SME finance investment is usually structured via a commodity *murabaha* structure. This is approved by leading Islamic scholars and its usage is widespread in the market. However, we note that a number of other scholars advise that, where possible, if another product structure is possible, it is better to use that. The reasoning behind this is that commodity *murabaha* can, from some perspective, seem too synthetic a way of transforming a loan contract into a sale contract.

Ultimately, for the average investor, you should check that the platform you are using is signed off by an Islamic scholar and that should suffice.

In the longer term, our view is that if we can move on from commodity *murabaha* models to other uncontroversial models, that is for the best. We discuss this further in the "How halal should you go" section in Chapter 14.

Zakat

Investing in SME finance is usually through a commodity *murabaha* structure and so, if we look through to the underlying investment, ultimately there is a debt that is owed to the investor and paid back to them slowly over time. Zakat is due on the full amount of a debt that is due to you (and you are reasonably confident it will be paid back). Therefore, zakat would be due on the full amount of the investment.

How Can I Get Access?

There are a raft of startups out there today who operate in this space. These include Lendo, Funding Souq, Qardus, Ethis, Erad, and others. Each of these platforms allows you to invest with them in the SMEs they finance. The largest number of them can be found in the Middle East, though there are some operating in the UK and Malaysia as well.

The other route to invest in SME finance is through a diversified fund that invests across a range of these types of products. We are not currently aware of any such product live in the market today, though we would love to offer such a product to the market through our platform, Cur8 Capital, at some point.

Property Financing (Savings Accounts): What Is It?

Property financing comes in many forms but at the heart of every financing there is the same process that takes place:

Source of capital => finance provider => property-backed finance

What one has to do as a finance provider is to match up between the type of financing you offer and the sources of capital you should tap into. If you are financing a very low risk, long-term property mortgage, the kind of returns you can offer to investors will be very stable but not high.

The typical type of investment product that services such a financing, will be people holding monies in savings accounts with an Islamic bank.

However, if you're looking to raise money for a property development project, your financing has a much higher chance of delays, defaults, and other issues. Consequently, the financier will charge you a higher rate. This also means that the kind of investor you attract will be those who are seeking out higher returns. We'll address this type of investment in the next section.

But for now, let's focus on one of the best-known and popular investment products across the world – the savings account.

Islamic savings accounts are as competitive – if not market-leading – in most countries across the world. The reason for this is simple: conventional banks have other sources of financing they can dip into that Islamic banks – particularly those in the West – do not have access to.

A conventional bank can lend off other banks whereas an Islamic bank typically does not have that luxury. They are much more reliant on savings accounts as their source of investment and as a result they offer the best returns relative to conventional banks.

In Muslim-majority countries however, Islamic banks are roughly on par with conventional banks as Islamic banking is not a niche specialist banking service in those countries – it is a mainstream offering.

Returns on Offer

Savings accounts rates will vary based on interest rates. Interest rates are set by central banks across the world. Central banks use interest rates to control money supply across the economy and to control inflation rates. The higher the inflation rate, the more likely interest rates are to be higher as well.

The Federal Reserve is the United States of America's central bank and its rates are particularly important for the world. This is because the dollar is the currency of international trade, the currency oil is bought and sold in, and the currency that a number of other countries peg their currency to – particularly those in the Middle East.

As we write this book, in the UK, the Bank of England has raised interest rates to 3%, the highest it has ever jumped up in 33 years. The strong likelihood is that in the following decade we will see interest rates remain higher than we have seen them over the last decade and a half.

If interest rates are so high and savings rates are offering the best returns they have ever, that means you should invest in savings accounts right?

Not necessarily.

The key thing to remember with savings accounts is that they do not usually protect your capital against inflation, which, today, stands at around 10%. That means that even if you are making 4% per annum in returns, you are losing 6% when adjusting for inflation.

The key reason is that the "capital" you are using here is just your cash. There isn't an actual asset you are holding. Contrast this to a property. If you buy a £100,000 house and make a 6% rental return on it per annum, your £100,000 "capital" is actually much better protected against inflation as property prices have historically increased in line with inflation.

Is My Money Safe?

Savings accounts are probably the safest kind of investment. Indeed, in certain countries the governments actually guarantee protection in case of a loss caused by, say, a bank collapse, up to a certain threshold. In the UK, for example, this threshold is £85,000.

So, at a basic level, a savings account is about as safe as it gets. However, as we discussed, when accounting for inflation, a savings account is probably not the best place to store all your money in the long term – as you'll end up losing money due to inflation.

Can I Get My Money Back Easily?

One of the biggest selling points of a savings account is how easy it is to withdraw your money. Most banks offer standard rates for their easy access accounts where it is possible to extract your savings within the day. You can also access higher rates on savings accounts where you agree to lock away your money for longer periods of time. These are also referred to as "notice" accounts as you have to notify the bank that you would like to withdraw the money ahead of the time you actually need the money.

So the answer depends on what type of product and duration you ultimately choose to invest in, but, relatively speaking, extracting money from a savings account is pretty straightforward.

We are advocates of using savings accounts for this precise reason. Whenever you know you are likely to have a short-term cash requirement over the next 18 months, holding the money in a savings account makes sense because you can benefit from the profit return and not lose as much as you would otherwise due to inflation, and at the same time you are safe in the knowledge that you can easily withdraw the money when the need arises.

If you are holding for longer than 18 months it is time to start thinking about making investments other than savings accounts. The longer the period you are holding for, the better you are able to withstand volatility in the price of your asset and the longer you give for the asset to generate income and trend upwards in terms of price.

Sharia Considerations

Islamic savings accounts come, in many structures. They commonly use either a *wakalah* (agency) arrangement, or a commodity *murabaha* arrangement, or a *mudaraba* (joint venture) arrangement to structure the investment.

A *wakalah* or a *mudaraba* model is usually expected to return a variable rate of return not a fixed return – and if you read the fine print of an Islamic savings account – that is also what is happening as well. However, in practice, Islamic banks give you the precise amount you were told would be the "expected profit rate" with nearly the same certainty that a conventional bank offers on its savings accounts.

Our view for this product is, so long as an Islamic savings account provider has confirmed with reputable scholars that their product is halal, then we would have few qualms using an Islamic savings account.

Zakat

Investing in savings accounts usually takes place either through a *mudarabah* structure, a *wakalah* structure or a commodity *murabaha* structure.

Given the underlying activity will, in all these cases, ultimately generate a debt that is owed to the investor and paid back to them slowly over time, zakat would be due on the full amount of the investment.

How Can I Get Access?

Nearly every Islamic bank across the world will offer a savings account. Use the most popular comparison websites in your country to do your research, and make sure you go for an Islamic bank – not a conventional one. Their savings accounts are not sharia-compliant.

Property Financing (Bridge and Development Finance): What Is It?

Investing in bridge and development financing is higher risk but higher reward. But when we say "higher risk" that is all relative. Ultimately, your money will be invested in financing transactions where the financier still has a security over the property. So if things went south, the financier would still be able to claw back some or all of the capital by repossessing the property.

This type of investment product is not usually offered by Islamic banks. Instead you will have to seek out specialist bridge financing and development finance lenders.

Returns on Offer

Instead of a 2–5% rate of return you are looking at with a savings account, with development and bridge finance you can expect a 5–12% rate of return per annum.

Bridge finance on blue chip, liquid, well-priced properties is likely to yield at the lower end of that range, while development finance on a site that is still half-finished is likely to be at the upper end of that range. It all ultimately comes down to the risk the lender is taking in these transactions and where they sit in the pecking order if things unravel and there is a line of creditors at the door.

For people at the front of the queue, they will be happy to take a slightly lower return for that additional security, while people who are towards the middle or back of the queue will want a higher return.

Is My Money Safe?

If you invest in these sorts of financing deals, you do benefit from the ultimate safety of having some sort of recourse to the property itself should things go wrong – but you don't really want to get to that position. Repossessing a property, going through the legal process, and going through the selling process all take time and money and eat away at the investment.

You can significantly decrease your exposure to default risk by spreading your investments across a basket of such investments or investing through a fund that invests in these sorts of deals.

Can I Get My Money Back Easily?

The investment periods for these sorts of financings are usually between 6–24 months and you are unable to withdraw early once you have invested.

Sharia Considerations

A similar sharia analysis applies here as to savings accounts.

Zakat

Investing in bridge and development financing usually takes place either through a *mudarabah* structure, a *wakalah* structure, or a commodity *murabaha* structure.

Given the underlying activity will, in all these cases, ultimately generate a debt that is owed to the investor and paid back to them slowly over time, zakat would be due on the full amount of the investment.

How Can I Get Access?

It is pretty difficult to get exposure to this type of financing as an investor. Typically, the type of investors that are involved in this sector are corporates, institutions, and ultra-high-net-worth investors.

In the UK, there are two main players of note: Nester and Offa. The former has a digital platform to cater for affluent everyday investors, while the latter deals primarily with high-net-worth investors. Both platforms have credible teams behind them as well as institutional investors who invest with them.

Sukuk: What Is It?

Sukuk are often called Islamic bonds and serve that purpose in the portfolio of Muslim investors.

A quick glance at nearly any institutional wealth manager's portfolios will show that they have allocated many of their clients' portfolios to hold some bonds. Bonds are usually issued by governments, blue chip corporates, and quasi-governmental institutions to raise some money for their ongoing activities. In return, these debtors agree to pay a fixed interest payment on an ongoing basis. Bonds are impermissible, of course, because they are just a simple interest-based loan.

This is where a sukuk comes in. A sukuk is similar to a bond in that its issuers are also governments, blue-chip corporates, and quasi-governmental institutions. However, rather than paying back interest on a loan, a sukuk gives investors ownership over some kind of asset which is now being leased out by the debtor. So rather than generating a fixed return through interest, a sukuk-holder gets a fixed return through rent.

There are multiple types of sukuk in the market – *ijarah* (lease) sukuk, *musharakah* and *mudarabah* (joint venture) sukuk and *murabaha* (mark up) sukuk – but for our purposes we'll treat them as a single thing.

Table 13.1 summarises the key similarities and differences between sukuk and a bond.

A key thing to be aware of is that sukuk are not to be confused with SME financing or higher risk property financing, because although those types are also sharia-compliant debt financing with a fixed return, the nature of a sukuk is very different.

Table 13.1 Comparison of sukuk and a bond

Similarities	Differences
• Both provide investors with payment streams • Bonds and sukuk are issued to investors and may be used to raise capital for a firm or government • Both are considered to be safer investments than equities • Sukuk investors receive profit generated by the underlying asset on a periodic basis while bond investors receive periodic interest payments	• Sukuk involve asset ownership while bonds are debt obligations • In theory, if the asset backing a sukuk appreciates, then the sukuk can appreciate whereas bond yield is strictly due to its interest rate • Assets that back sukuk are halal whereas bonds often involve *riba* and may finance non sharia-compliant businesses • Sukuk require sign-off by Islamic scholars • Sukuk valuation is based on the value of the assets backing them while a bond's price is largely determined by its credit rating • Certain types of sukuk are more illiquid, due to sharia rulings around the sale of debt and the impermissibility of selling debt at less than face value

Sukuk are typically a lot less risky because only large corporations or sovereigns, i.e. governments, would issue them, making it safer and low-risk, low-return. If one were to draw a continuum of risk and reward for the various fixed income instruments we have covered in this section it would look something like Figure 13.2.

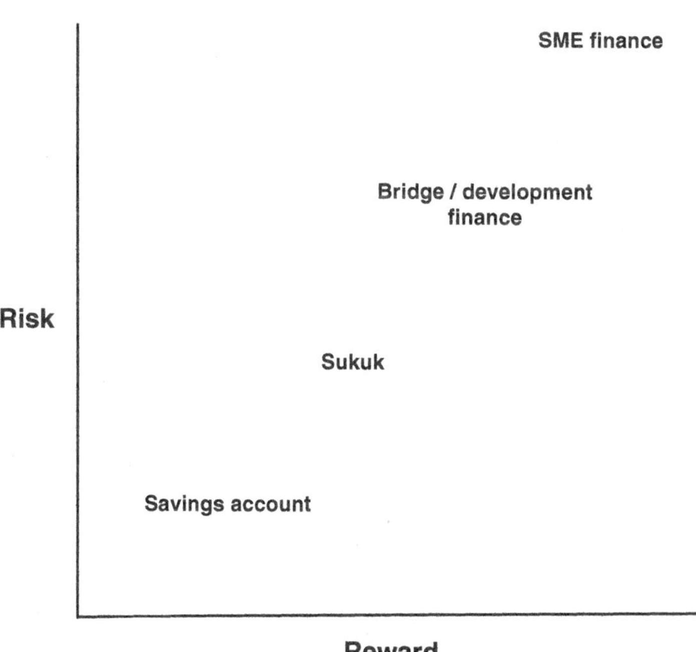

Figure 13.2 Continuum of risk and reward.

Source: www.Islamicfinanceguru.com.

Returns on Offer

Sukuk are an interesting investment class because out of the four fixed income categories we have covered, they probably offer the best risk-adjusted returns. Note, that doesn't mean they will offer the highest returns, but that, relative to the risk exposure you agree to, they offer the best returns.

Sukuk typically yield somewhere between 2–8% today and can provide a nice counterpoint to the stock market. Usually when the stock market is down, bonds are up, and vice versa.

However, as was the case during 2022, in rare situations both stocks and bonds can suffer. In the case of 2022, it was due to the roaring inflation that swept the globe. In response to that, central banks raised interest rates. However, higher interest rates typically drive down bond prices (because the fixed return offered by a bond now looks less appealing), and that is what we saw happen in 2022.

Conversely, if you think that interest rates are unlikely to rise much further, and that inflation is now broadly under control, such a market can present some very interesting buying opportunities. As an example, a US Treasury bond that previously yielded you 0.5% is now offering up to 4.5%. Note though that US Treasury bonds are impermissible, we just use it by way of example.

Is My Money Safe?

The biggest and most obvious risk when it comes to fixed income investing – is default, and that's no different with sukuk. Whoever is taking your money – whether it is a company or a government – if they're not doing well enough in terms of profit or economic growth to keep up with payment schedules, you're in trouble.

Is it common for governments and large corporations to default on the payment schedules of their sukuk? No. But it is not unheard of either. There have been a handful of corporate sukuk defaults across the Middle East and Southeast Asia. Sovereign sukuk defaults have not yet happened, as it would mean that a government is unable to meet payments, but they can also happen in rare and extreme circumstances. The easiest way to sidestep this whole minefield is by investing in a sukuk fund that spreads your exposure across a basket of sukuk.

Currency risk is the other risk that global investors should be conscious of. Sukuk are typically denominated in dollars or in a local currency. This means that if you are buying in pounds sterling and after your investment the pound rose against the underlying currency of the sukuk, you would end up getting back less than you should have.

One way to protect yourself from this currency risk is to hold your returned capital as dollars or the local currency, and only convert it back to your home currency when the rate is favourable. In the meantime you can continue investing in other dollar-denominated investments, of which there are many.

The third risk, which is again applicable to all fixed income products, is that your capital is not typically safe in a sukuk. You will receive a profit rate during the life of the sukuk and at the end you will get back your original capital investment. However, a number of years may have passed since you first invested, and the capital amount, while numerically identical to what you initially invested, will not be worth as much due to inflation.

Can I Get My Money Back Easily?

Sukuk are very liquid and can easily be exited in the most part. Of course, for most of us, we will never be holding an individual sukuk given the high buy-ins, so the question of exit is really a question of "how liquid is the sukuk fund that I am investing in?"

Publicly listed sukuk funds are very liquid and can be exited and entered at the click of a button. Even private sukuk funds are typically much more liquid than your average private fund. In the private sukuk funds we have historically partnered with on Cur8 Capital, we have seen quarterly redemption windows offered.

Sharia Considerations

The sukuk market has been the scene of some intense sharia debates over the last two decades. Mufti Taqi Usmani caused a significant rumble in the market back in 2007 with his comments that up to 85% of the sukuk market may not be structured in a way that is sharia-compliant.

There are two issues at the heart of these debates:

1. Is the sukuk truly asset-backed or is it just "asset-based"?
2. Does the sukuk structure guarantee the repayment of the original capital?

The second of those issues particularly applies to the use of *musharakah* and *mudarabah* sukuk as those structures are seen as joint venture structures by the sharia, and yet in the context of a sukuk, one party ends up always receiving the original capital at the original price.

Since 2007, there has been a slow trend in the industry and sharia governance standards set by central banks to emphasise that sukuk should be asset-backed and that the type of sukuk structure used should not abuse the joint venture structures of the sharia. The AAOIFI also reviewed and tightened its guidelines further. In light of that, the *ijarah* (rental) sukuk has become very popular, as that structure does not suffer from the same restrictions placed on joint venture structures.

The upshot for you, as an ordinary investor in sukuk, is that you should ensure that any sukuk fund you invest in, has been signed off by a reputable scholar or scholars' board and today it will be pretty uncontroversial.

Zakat

Sukuk are typically offered through an *ijarah* structure where the principal amount is invested in a rental property, while the profit on top is rent.

In this scenario, zakat would only be due on the profit and any cash amounts associated with the sukuk. This is because if you were to own a property directly and rent it out with the intention of holding it for the long-term, zakat would not be due on the value of the property; it would only be due on the rents you make from it annually.

How Can I Get Access?

There are three main routes to get exposure to sukuk.

The first way is through investing in publicly listed sukuk funds. The Franklin Templeton Sukuk fund is probably the most prominent and accessible public fund out there. though there are others.

You can find this fund on your usual brokerage platform by searching its name. Two things to note though:

1. Franklin Templeton's fees are relatively high in comparison to your typical bond fund. It charges a 5.75% initial charge, and ongoing charges of 1.5% as at the date of writing.[9]
2. Over each of the last five years it has underperformed against the Dow Jones Sukuk Index (though, admittedly not by very much).

The second route is for those who are more affluent. They can go ahead and directly buy a sukuk via their private bank or high-end broker that can facilitate the purchase of less well-known and well-traded sukuk. Typical entry tickets for sukuk can range in the millions, and certainly will start in the hundreds of thousands of dollars.

A third route is to use a provider like Cur8 Capital where we give access to institutional private sukuk funds at affordable minimums by clubbing lots of investors together. Of course, the slight downside here is that you have to pay Cur8 a platform fee, which you wouldn't have to do if you went directly.

Summary

- Fixed income comes with different risk profiles depending on what kind of thing you are financing – with sukuk probably offering the best risk-adjusted.
- Financing is generally an illiquid investment.
- You may lose all your money if the underlying business goes bust. You would have some recourse to things like charges over land, etc. but these might be difficult to actually recover in reality.

14 Alternative Assets

Alternative assets comprise the "everything else" apart from fixed income and stocks investing. They are typically a little bit higher risk and less liquid – but not always. There are a number of very safe and very liquid alternative assets out there too.

Pound for pound, alternative assets are where you'll find the highest long-term returns and our view is that alternatives should form an important part of most people's portfolios – especially those people with long-term investment objectives. We'll cover how to structure portfolios in the next section, but for now, let's unpack the various different alternative assets out there.

Crypto: What Is It?

Cryptocurrency has been one of the breakout asset classes for the last decade. As Figure 14.1 shows, the crypto market as a whole attracted huge amounts of money from 2020 through to the end of 2021. Thereafter there has been a significant fall, but overall volumes still remain higher than the previous highs seen in January 2018.

An early investor in bitcoin who got in when bitcoin launched at $0.0008 and invested $100 would today be worth around $2.6 billion if they had been brave enough to hold it without selling till today. Indeed, late last year they would have been worth closer to $8 billion. In other words, Forbes would be including someone like this on their annual rich lists.

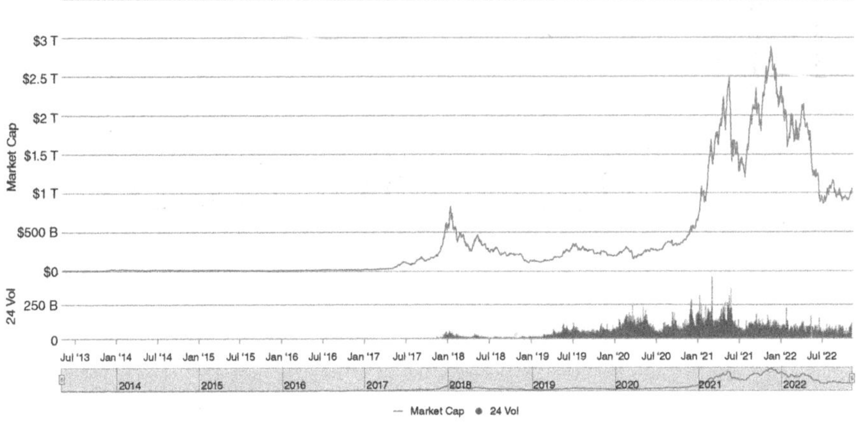

Figure 14.1 Performance of the crypto market.
Source: CoinMarketCap.

These numbers alone mean that cryptocurrency is an important asset class to consider and understand. This is particularly important if the Muslim community is to level up with the rest of the world. For that levelling up to happen, it will be important to invest in outsize-returning investments – and cryptocurrency could be a good candidate.

Cryptocurrency relies on blockchain technology or similar alternatives. This is a new type of technology that allows the decentralisation of the "ledger".

We appreciate that probably means very little to the uninitiated, so let's explain how things are done today in a simplified way. When you make a transaction or a trade, that trade is run through an established and regulated bank, both on the side of the buyer and the seller. In the background the banks then talk to each other and settle the transfer of monies.

The crucial players in this transaction are the banks. The reason why the buyer and seller trust each other and their ability to pay is because we trust the banks that they bank at and their ability to competently, accurately, and honestly handle these transactions. If we did not trust them, we simply wouldn't transact.

At the heart of the bank therefore, you will find that a ledger (or, in truth, many interconnected ledgers) records these transactions to make sure everything is completely accounted for.

Blockchain technology allows you to do this without the two banks. Decentralised networks of computers all maintain a single ledger that is completely transparent and perfectly open to examination. The technology is incredibly hard to hack (as you would simultaneously need to hack all the nodes in the network) and because there isn't the overhead of two entire banks in this setup, you end up with much lower transaction fees (at least in theory!).

With regard to cryptocurrency itself, it is usually the lubrication that makes each blockchain project work – and there are many of them. One analogy that we found very useful was between a cryptocurrency and a casino chip, or cryptocurrency and the token you buy at theme parks for use on rides. These plastic tokens are intrinsically worthless, however, they are worth a certain amount of money within a certain context. In Alton Towers, or in the casino where they are used, they are worth pretty much the same as currency. But outside of Alton Towers and the casino, their value depends on how easily exchangeable they are in other locations, whether the person you are offering them to regularly goes to Alton Towers/the casino, and whether enough people know about Alton Towers/the casino for them to value the tokens anyway.

The value of cryptocurrencies is linked to the network within which they operate. The more people join the network, the more acceptance it has as a tradable asset, the more the value the coin has. Lately though, people have noted the similarities between this and your classic Ponzi scheme. So now the most reputable new crypto offerings seek to create a network where they are actually trying to do something valuable in the real world, and where the coins that they will accept in their network gain value to the extent people join the network to benefit from whatever thing that network is known for.

For example, certain cryptocurrencies are linked to education, where students pay and are rewarded in the token of the network, and where hirers can come and buy the best students judging from their results, using the network's tokens. Here, one can see that if such a network becomes massive, those tokens will have value even where they are not being directly used on the network itself to buy and sell education.

Returns on Offer

There are three broad styles of crypto investing. First, there is crypto trading, where you are entering and exiting cryptocurrencies rapidly with a view to make returns based on chart and price analysis more than anything else. Returns here are dependent on the trader and the best can make triple-digit returns per annum while the worst end up losing all their money.

Then you have crypto value investors. These investors are looking for a capital gain and are willing to hold the currency for a while. We have already trailered some of the returns possible in cryptocurrency above. These days, the market is much more mature, so those kinds of incredible returns are much rarer. However, crypto adoption is still only around 10% of the world's population,[1] so we are early in the crypto journey (if indeed you believe that cryptocurrency will ultimately become as widely used as mainstream finance) and that means a lot of profit is unrealised to date. Consequently, double, triple and even quadruple digit returns are still quite common in this space.

Finally, you have the slightly lower risk and more fixed-income-like investment: crypto staking.

Crypto Staking

The bulk of crypto investors are long-term investors hoping for a rise in the value of the coins they hold. There are, therefore, a lot of assets lying around doing nothing. So if you can figure out a way to put them to work without risking them, that sounds like a useful endeavour. The analogous financial product in mainstream finance would be the savings account. It takes advantage of stagnant money by giving you a small return in exchange for using your money to lend out and make a higher return themselves.

Crypto staking – not to be confused with crypto lending – is a facility that uses people's coins to offer liquidity on a platform, or to provide the mechanism through which new coins are minted, or some other such facility that happens to be useful to that blockchain project and its long-term success.

Crypto these days is offering serious annualised returns anywhere between 3–40% (and we've seen even as high as 90% before). Of course, usually, the higher the annualised return, the more speculative it is. But even at the lower end, those kinds of returns are about 3–4× what the best mainstream savings accounts are offering (though of course they are *much* safer).

Let's give some hard numbers to clarify things. Let's assume you invest in bitcoin. Right now the markets are choppy but let's assume that things will resolve themselves and bitcoin will continue to grow over the next 4 years to return 3x. If you invest £5000 at a 10% compounding return for 4 years, without any capital appreciation it returns around £7,500, and with capital appreciation you're probably looking at closer to £20,000–£25,000. Without any yield activity your return would be closer to £15,000. So that's an improvement of 40–60% on the total return.

Therefore, if you're investing in crypto for the long-term anyway, it is worth exploring the safer types of yield-generation, simply because it'll add to your bottom line quite significantly.

The crucial points to examine when reviewing a staking investment opportunity are:

1. What is the coin that is being staked? *If this is a volatile coin, you should recognise that even if the yields are great, the value of your investment could well halve or go to nothing.*
2. How is your coin going to be used? *Is this a safe use of your coins and what kind of worst case scenarios could you envisage?*
3. Is there any lending involved? *Often the terminology is all jumbled up and actively uses the types of phrases seen in mainstream banking. However, usually, there is not any lending going on in crypto staking. However, there is another investment strategy called crypto lending which does involve lending, so make sure you steer clear of that.*
4. Is there a lock-in period? *There is usually a lock-in period, and the longer periods offer the better returns.*

You may also come across a term called "cryptocurrency mining". This is very different to crypto staking. Crypto miners are the owners of the various decentralised computers that are responsible for maintaining different blockchain projects and they get a payment from the network for providing that service. Usually this is getting the right to print some of that particular coin. Getting into crypto mining is a bit like starting a side hustle or starting a business – so we wouldn't consider it an investment in the traditional sense and won't expand on it further here.

Is My Money Safe?

Cryptocurrency investing is a very high-risk investment and you should only put in as much you are willing to lose. There are arguably some safer cryptocurrencies that are fully pegged to the dollar or gold, and these are generally less volatile than other currencies, however, here too there are a number of untested hypotheses about what happens in high-stress scenarios and we have recently seen the collapse of some of these projects as well.

The other key risk with cryptocurrency is also the exchange that you use. Today, Binance is the largest crypto broker globally, and there are some others out there like Coinbase and Kraken. There have been some recent well-publicised and spectacular collapses of some of the other exchanges, so it is better to go with the more-established players, in our view. They are usually better set up to deal with safe custody of your assets and withstand hacks. If you are a little more tech-savvy and a little more paranoid, you may well want to extract all your cryptocurrencies and keep them in a "cold" wallet, i.e. one that is not connected to the internet.

Can I Get My Money Back?

One of the major appeals of cryptocurrencies is that they are incredibly liquid and you can buy and sell your coins day or night almost instantaneously. It will take you about 3–5 working days to get the money back into your bank account off whatever exchange you are using.

Crypto staking is of course different. There you are locked in for whatever period you agree to be locked in for.

Sharia Considerations

One of the core tenets of Islamic contractual law is that a transaction must have something called "*Māl*" as consideration. An accepted definition of a transaction among Islamic scholarship is an exchange of *Māl* in consideration of *Māl*'.[2] If the consideration is not *Māl*, then the contract is rendered void.

Māl literally means something that can be possessed or acquired and it can be corporeal (e.g. a car) or usufruct (e.g. the right to exclusively occupy a property, or a tenancy as we usually call it). According to a prominent school of Islamic jurisprudence (the Hanafi School), *Māl* is "what is normally desired and can be stored up for the time of need". Desirability and storability are therefore key considerations for something to be deemed *Māl*. Thus, birds in the sky, or a scent, or a passing thought in one's mind, are variously not *Māl* as they are either (1) not in anyone's possession, or (2) too temporal for there to be effective storage. The key initial debate is therefore whether cryptocurrencies/blockchain tokens constitute *Māl*.

There are three main *fiqhi* positions that scholars have adopted on cryptocurrencies:

1. Cryptocurrency is not *Māl* and is purely speculative and is not a sharia-compliant investment.
2. Cryptocurrency is a digital asset but not a currency.
3. Cryptocurrency (of certain kinds) is currency.

Our view is that position 1 is wrong as cryptocurrencies are worth at least something. It is clearly worth something to all those people willing to pay a lot of money for it, and it is clearly worth something to all those businesses who are willing to accept it as a means of payment.

It is true that when it is all stripped away, a "bitcoin" is essentially an entry on a ledger that is not intrinsically very valuable. However, the pound coins and notes in our pockets are very similar in this regard, and yet we still uncontroversially understand them as *Māl*. Ultimately value derives from the meaning we imbue into things, and if many people do in fact value bitcoin, then, well, it's valuable!

We would suggest that position 2 is probably about right at this moment in time and it is a view shared by prominent Islamic finance scholars today, such as Mufti Faraz Adam.

We would suggest that position 3 is probably a bit punchy, given the current state of play in the cryptocurrency industry. It is very obvious that a currency that is prone to crashes, online heists of millions, huge fluctuations in price, is one that is not an effective means of payment.

In particular, at times of high transaction volume, the transaction cost of each transaction can go up enormously, and one can end up having to either wait a long time for one's transaction to be processed, or one pays through the nose for it to be processed. That is not what we look for in a currency as we want instantaneous execution – not high and unpredictable transaction costs.

However, if a cryptocurrency emerges out of this present phase which gains credence and acceptance because it is secure, quick, low in transaction cost, etc., and it subsequently becomes a very readily accepted currency, then we see no reason why it cannot sit alongside fiat money.[3]

Once we have concluded that conceptually cryptocurrencies can be sharia-compliant, then we need to consider which projects are in fact sharia-compliant. We have been slowly screening and compiling crypto projects over the years and have an active list on our website[4] – this should give you a head start.

For other crypto projects, the key things to think about are:

1. Does the White Paper talk about any particularly challenging concepts at the heart of the project that would make it non-compliant, e.g. does it rely on any gambling or uncertainty as part of the architecture of the project itself?
2. Does the coin specifically target illicit sectors, such as gambling, interest-based lending, or adult entertainment?

For most tokens this analysis is pretty straightforward as most tokens are effectively clones of one another architecturally. However, for novel structures it usually does require someone with sharia knowledge to screen them.

Crypto Staking Sharia Analysis

Crypto staking has a slightly separate sharia analysis. The field is muddied by the complicated and contradictory usage of terminology, so let's set aside the terms "yield farming", "liquidity mining", "staking" and "lending" and just look at how you will be remunerated as an investor:

1. **Get money for being a broker:** You get remunerated because you provide liquidity to an Automated Market Maker ("AMM") such as Uniswap or Pancake. These are automated brokers (think AJ Bell, or Hargreaves Lansdown, but for crypto and completely automated so that the crypto protocol itself does the brokerage work without any need for human brokers) and make their money by keeping a small cut on every transaction that happens.
2. **Get money for being part of a PoS project:** Most crypto projects need a way to generate new tokens. Bitcoin's method involved mining – but this is a relatively expensive and non-carbon-friendly method. There are now alternatives where just by you holding a coin means that you get a portion of new coins minted. This approach is called a Proof of Stake ("PoS") crypto project. You earn simply through holding that coin.
3. **Get money for lending your coins for interest:** You get remunerated as you are lending your coins to a broker or exchange (such as Binance) who then uses those coins to lend out to others and earn an interest rate – and then pass a portion of that interest back over to you.

Yield farming is typically associated with either (1) or (3).
Liquidity mining usually means (1) but can also mean (2).
Crypto staking usually means (1) or (2).
Crypto lending usually means (3).

Our view is that (1) and (2) are *generally* permissible, while (3) generally is not. (1) is permissible as you are engaging in what is fundamentally a halal activity of brokerage, while (2) is permissible as you are simply benefiting contractually from the holding of a coin. The way those new coins are minted is not an "interest" payment to you as the project is not lending your staked coins in any way. The new coins are just issued as the mechanism designed to issue new coins for the project.

The reason for the "generally" is that each crypto project can vary in its mechanics and crypto is a rapidly changing landscape, so it isn't really possible to give a definitive answer at this stage.

Zakat

Most cryptocurrencies are best modelled as digital assets in our view. Under this conception, zakat would not be due if you are a long-term holder of that token. However, zakat would be due if you are a trader in that token and have bought it for the sole purpose of reselling it shortly.

Certain cryptocurrencies are now being used as currencies – with bitcoin probably the most prominent among them. It is arguable that, because such tokens are actually being used as currencies, they should be given the zakat treatment of a currency as well, i.e. to charge zakat on the full amount.

Our personal view in this respect remains that we do not think that cryptocurrencies have got to anywhere near the level of liquidity and seamless transfer that is needed to properly label a cryptocurrency a "currency". The irony of that statement is not lost on us.

How Can I Get Access?

You can access cryptocurrencies widely today through both specialist crypto brokers such as Coinbase, Binance, Kraken, Fasset, Rain, and through stockbrokers who are also offering a limited range of crypto tokens that you can purchase. For the technically savvy, you can also just hold your coins directly through a digital wallet and transact directly through that with people or platforms buying or selling crypto. For the vast majority of people though, going through a crypto broker is the easiest solution and gives you the most choice with the best rates.

There are three main strategies we think about when it comes to directly investing in crypto:

1. **Buy bitcoin and ethereum:** These are the two largest and most established cryptocurrencies today and are heavily used as well. It is difficult to see their value collapsing to nothing – unless of course crypto as a whole comes tumbling down. Their prices are very closely linked to the fortunes of the entire crypto ecosystem and so buying them is similar to buying a tracker fund on the crypto industry as a whole. For the new crypto investor looking to just gain some exposure to crypto without necessarily risking large amounts of money or spending a lot of time doing research, this is a good route to go down. By you buying this you are effectively saying "I think there's something there, and I want to be exposed to it at least to some extent."
2. **Buy a basket of alternative cryptocurrencies ("alts").** Alts are everything else in the crypto world. They are much more volatile with strong price movements both up and down. The smaller you go in terms of alts, the more the risk and the reward and the harder the due diligence. So one strategy that people adopt is buying a large basket of alts – at least 30, and possibly over 100. The thinking is that a few of those alts will succeed enormously and you have exposure to that, but all the ones that fail don't drag down your portfolio.
3. **Trade cryptocurrencies.** Trading involves buying and selling cryptocurrencies for very short periods to exploit price movements. Trading anything is time-consuming and highly technical and comes with a tremendous amount of risk. It should not be taken on lightly and you should be prepared to lose much of, or even all of, the allocated sums you put into trading. This is only suitable for advanced traders.

Aside from the above, there are also two indirect ways you can invest in crypto:

1. Invest through the stock market.
2. Invest in early-stage crypto startups.

Crypto Exposure Through the Stock Market

Going directly into crypto can seem daunting for the uninitiated, but there are ways to gain exposure to crypto through the stock market. We'll run through a few here.

Crypto Mining Stocks Akin to gold miners, these companies primarily generate their revenue from the transaction fees they get from mining crypto and by selling the mined crypto itself. Many crypto miners have recently pivoted to holding (or "HODLing") their mined crypto.

Keep in mind that with crypto miners you are also exposed to the business risk of the company itself which you wouldn't otherwise be exposed to if you were simply holding bitcoin. A number of crypto miners have recently struggled because they have been overleveraged and the methods of mining they deploy are no longer cost-effective as cryptocurrencies like bitcoin have taken a plunge in price.

Key things to watch out for here are the total mining power of the miner which dictates how much crypto they mine, their margins on each newly minted coin, and the amount of crypto that they hold on their balance sheet.

You should give bonus points for companies that mine and hold other cryptocurrencies apart from bitcoin, diversifying their operations. Although you should still get comfortable that the other coins have been chosen with some thought and are likely to be worth something in the future.

Funds/Trusts This is where you invest in funds/trusts that directly hold bitcoin, ethereum, and, sometimes, other cryptocurrencies. Funds/trusts also look after the custody aspect of holding crypto and for this they charge management fees which can be substantial. There aren't many options available at the moment through this route but we can expect more options in the future as crypto becomes more mainstream.

Given the high management fee and premium price, in our view this option is only suitable for those who want a completely hands-off approach and can't wait for the adoption of low-cost bitcoin ETFs – more on these shortly.

Crypto ETFs Crypto ETFs (exchange-traded funds) are funds listed on the stock market that specifically invest in the theme of crypto. More details on ETFs can be found in the stocks section above. Crypto ETFs are still in their infancy as they have faced pushback from regulators in the past but there are positive signs that regulators are warming to the concept.

Last year saw the launch of the Purpose Bitcoin ETF in Canada, which was the first Western-traded Bitcoin ETF. They charge a management fee of 1% which compares favourably versus the 2% fee for the Grayscale Bitcoin Trust. Since then, a number of crypto-related ETFs have been approved. They include:

- ProShares Bitcoin Strategy
- Grayscale Bitcoin Trust
- Valkyrie Bitcoin Strategy
- VanEck Bitcoin Strategy
- Purpose Bitcoin ETF
- Bitwise Crypto Industry Innovators ETF
- Global X Blockchain ETF
- Invesco Alerian Galaxy Crypto Economy ETF
- The Bitcoin Fund.

A crypto-focused ETF can be a great low-cost way to gain exposure to crypto without much work required on your part. The only downside of this option is that it is pretty rare to find ETFs that are completely sharia-compliant.

The two issues here are, first, that not all cryptocurrencies are sharia-compliant – and so inevitably these ETFs will be including certain projects that Muslims would not want to invest in. Second, a number of these ETFs have structured their fund so that they don't actually directly hold the cryptocurrency. Instead, they hold a derivative instrument that synthetically creates the same effect of them holding that currency. This is problematic – as we discussed previously in the stocks section – because the sharia does not permit Muslims to buy and sell derivatives.

ETFs that primarily hold crypto themselves should be fine, provided the underlying crypto is compliant.

Picks-and-Shovel Plays "Pick-and-shovel" is an investment strategy where you invest in the supplier of a certain product rather than the product itself. This strategy was coined back in the nineteenth century during the California Gold Rush, where the businesses selling supplies to the miners outperformed the gold miners themselves.

For this strategy, you need to understand what makes crypto tick and look for the companies that provide these services. Examples include the likes of AMD and NVIDIA, two very strong semiconductor companies in their own right. They supply the GPUs that power the machines that mine crypto and thus can expect demand for their products to increase with the increased adoption of crypto.

Other lines to explore could be around cybersecurity, quantum computing, developer tools, and financial rails companies. These are the modern "picks" and "shovels" for crypto-related companies.

Early Adopters The early adopters of crypto and blockchain technology will put themselves in pole position to benefit from this growing market. From payment processors such as Visa and Mastercard facilitating the use of crypto for everyday payments to companies that build products on the blockchain.

A great recent example is IBM using blockchain technology to develop COVID-19 vaccination passports. Using blockchain will enable efficient data tracking of vaccination records across countries and could bring in a lot of revenue for the firms that provide this service.

DocuSign is a leading e-signature company that addresses the full lifecycle of contract management online. They have enhanced their offering with a blockchain solution based on ethereum to facilitate smart contracts – contracts that use code to enable the automatic execution of clauses if certain conditions are met.

Facebook famously rebranded as Meta and is now doubling down on its metaverse and virtual reality equipment. The jury remains out on how this will play out, but if it does well, Facebook has a clear lead on the rest of big tech.

Initiatives like these could help companies such as DocuSign, Meta, and IBM dominate the market for years to come if these technologies provide a genuine competitive advantage and as demand for these types of products increase.

It is consequently worth researching and understanding which of the big mainstream technology companies is delivering compelling projects in crypto.

Investing in Crypto Through Startups

Crypto venture capital funds have raised over $121 billion as of 2022,[5] and these institutional fund managers deploy into crypto startups at the very early stages. Typically, these funds deploy their money into a crypto project 1–2 years before any tokens or coins are made publicly available. In other words, these investors get in very early and are already marking up their investment by the time the world finds out about that particular crypto project for the first time.

The second big attraction for investing early alongside venture capital (VC) funds is that investors can navigate the terrain a little better. Usually (but not always!) institutional investors conduct rigorous due diligence and have deep experience in the fields they are investing in. In almost all cases, it takes a very credible team to raise a funding round from a top VC fund.

Through our own VC fund at Cur8 Capital we have invested in a handful of crypto startups and our preference has been to invest in those projects that have a deeper underlying utility that outlasts any temporary price movements or hype. We particularly like the "picks-and-shovels" startups that are coming up with key technologies that other crypto companies will need to use in the coming years.

For example, we invested in Anything World a couple of years ago, a company that automates the rigging and animation of 3D objects in a metaverse or gaming environment. With the explosion of developers working on these technologies, automation tools like Anything World can significantly speed up work and reduce the labour needed to achieve the same result. Anything World has subsequently raised another larger round earlier this year in which we again participated.

The additional bonus that comes from investing in crypto through venture capital is that most of these startups are EIS-eligible, meaning significant tax rebates for UK taxpayers.

For more about startup investing, see Chapter 15.

Honourable Mentions

No analysis of crypto investing would be quite complete without spending some time explaining NFTs and the metaverse.

NFTs Non-fungible tokens (NFTs) are any digital assets that are stored on the blockchain, with their ownership represented not by a title deed but a digital certificate that is publicly available for anyone to inspect. NFTs have found initial traction in the artwork space, with a huge spate of digital art mushrooming up over the course of the last two years.

However, the application of NFTs goes much further than this and can extend to anything that gives access to something – e.g. a ticket or access pass – all the way to digital records of physical assets such as real estate, cars, jewellery, diamonds, and more. This market is incredibly early and it is not yet fully clear if it will remain a cottage industry or mushroom up into something enormous.

The likelihood is that if a use case of NFTs finds real product-market fit, and that use case happens to be an enormous market, the NFT industry as a whole will ride on its coat-tails. This is similar to Facebook "cracking" it and the subsequent spawning of an entire industry called "performance marketing".

As an intrepid and hands-on investor, if you are curious about this corner of the internet, you should get involved in the community and learn more. However, if you're the average investor without as much appetite for the more niche assets, you should probably sit this one out for the time being.

We leave you with the slightly horrific NFT that Ibrahim first bought. Say hello to Figure 14.2, Psychonaut Ape Division #3619.

The Metaverse The metaverse is the name given to any virtual reality environment that is constantly persisting (you can login to it at any time), where you can meet with other individuals in a live context and where you share with others socially and spatially.

Metaverses have actually existed for quite a while – take many online gaming environments, for example – but it is only today that the virtual reality headset technology is getting us to the point where a truly immersive experience is becoming possible.

Figure 14.2 NFT #3619.

Source: Ibrahim Khan.

If we fast forward to 40 years in the future where many of us could be spending hours every day in our workplace metaverse environment, one can quickly see the implications of this. Metaverse "real estate" becomes valuable; advertising completely changes given the shift in eyeballs into the metaverse; how we socialise would also have an added metaverse dimension to it. With that in mind, intrepid investors have been buying up metaverse "real estate" aggressively in recent months and years. The challenge is that no one quite knows which of the competing metaverses will be the "one" that really takes off.

Right now, our humble view is that things are a little too embryonic for the average investor to be dabbling here. But if you are an investor that happens to be interested in this space, then you should feel free to dig into the area and it is people like you who will be best placed to unearth some gems.

Summary

- Crypto is a highly risky environment where you could lose all your money.
- Crypto also offers the opportunity to invest in the technology of tomorrow – this comes with significant potential reward.
- Many popular exchanges have gone bust. You have the option of taking all your coins off any online exchange and going for a completely offline wallet. Operate carefully.
- There are several crypto strategies to make money, including crypto staking. You are not limited to just investing in crypto projects.
- Be careful to make sure you understand the crypto project that you are investing in from a sharia perspective – ensure you read the White Paper and fully understand what the project aims to achieve.

Startups: What Is It?

A startup is quite literally any new business starting up. But when we talk about startup investing, we are actually referring to a small subset of new businesses that are formed. There are normally three main principles which differentiates this group from other small businesses:

1. Startups are designed to scale very quickly.
2. The objective of a startup is to become an industry leader (or create an entirely new industry) and quickly grow to monopolise their sector.
3. A startup is targeting a big potential market and there is a path to eventually making hundreds of millions in revenue.

This has three implications:

1. **Startups care less about short-term profitability and a lot more about long-term growth:** That is why the majority of startups will be loss-making in their first few years and spend the majority of their cash flow on increasing user growth. In fact, you still have companies like Twilio who are loss-making up till today based on this principle. While this is an extreme case and startups do look to reach profitability within at least 5 years, it shows how startups are willing to put off short-term profits for much larger profits in the future. It is also why some loss-making startups have much higher share valuations than their profit-making peers because investors are looking forward to the large potential future growth.
2. **The majority of startups are internet-based, and almost always tech-based. They always have some form of leverage:** There are very few products and industries that allow startups to scale very rapidly with minimal amounts of capital. The internet is one such place.

   A startup can scale to millions of users across the world at very little cost. There is no need to build more factories or set up foreign offices. Everything can be done from the company's main headquarters at a very small marginal cost. This business model point is critical in identifying a "true" startup. The thing that an investor wants to see is magnification of returns and leverage. Leverage can be of many kinds:
   (a) Technology
   (b) Capital
   (c) Brand and content

   Microsoft doesn't need to hire one more person for each new download of Windows or each new subscription of Office 365 it sells. Its tech and software have leverage. Similarly, with £100,000 to invest we can either buy one house or three houses with leverage from a bank loan (Islamic of course!).

   Brand and content also have a power far more than money used to create it. We buy Coca-Cola and not Tesco Cola because Coca-Cola has a powerful brand. So for each £1 of marketing, Coca-Cola secures potentially hundreds of pounds of sales.

   A good rule of thumb to figure out if you have a startup that could potentially get to a scale that is worthwhile is to work backwards and ask yourself, "Can I see this company making at least

£100 million in annualised revenue in a decade's time?" If the answer to that is "yes", then you have a potential investment. Even if your answer to that is "yes, but it is very unlikely", then you have a potential investment. This is because, necessarily, it is very unlikely that a new company will ever get to those kinds of revenue numbers – but the point is you're playing at least the right game.

The reason why the £100 million annualised revenue number is so important is because usually company valuations are based on a multiple of annual revenues, with 10× annualised revenue being seen as a generous-but-ballpark multiple often used. At £100 million revenue, that company is now worth £1 billion. A company with a £1 billion valuation is often referred to as a "unicorn" in the startup ecosystem owing to its rarity. As angel investors (investors in the very early rounds), we like unicorns because they are, on average, the size of company we need to invest in in order to make a 30x or more return.[6] More on this in the "Returns on Offer" section below.

3. **Startups solve new problems or old problems in novel ways:** Another key trait of startups is that they are working on hard problems where the solution is not obviously known. The best kind of startups are working on a problem where there is an underlying industry or cultural shift. Think Google in the 1990s when the internet was just taking off and we needed a good way to sort through all this new information being generated. Or Facebook in 2006, when interacting online in a social context was a novel but growing trend.

   A recent example is Beyond Meat where there is an underlying cultural shift towards more ethical forms of protein, but we still desire the taste and texture of meat. Beyond Meat solves this problem and has grown up to a market cap of over a billion dollars in just a few years. All these companies run decent businesses on their own, but what has caused them to explode in scale is the underlying industry shift.

   There are also cases where the startup itself can create an industry shift. Good examples include Uber and Airbnb where these startups completely disrupted old industries and created completely new industries for themselves.

When looking at a good startup to invest in, you need to find the startup's "defensibility". This is what differentiates this startup from the tens of others trying to solve similar problems, and why it is that *this* startup will grow to become the industry leader ahead of others.

In a lot of cases, it is not so much to do with the idea but why it is this startup that will solve the problem better than anyone else. Defensibility could be intellectual property (technology that can be patented), network effects, economies of scale or the passion and background of the founders or a company's unique business model.

Returns on Offer

In 2004, an entrepreneur called Peter Theil became one of the first outside investors in a small but exciting startup led by a Harvard dropout. The startup wasn't the first in its sector – which was teeming with competition – but it had a stellar founder and a great, simple user interface that just seemed to work. The founder was called Mark Zuckerberg and the startup was Facebook.

Theil invested $500,000 for a 10% stake in Facebook at the time. He continued to hold some Facebook – now known as Meta – shares until relatively recently when he cashed out for over $1 billion. All in all, his initial investment back in 2004 has netted him over 2000×. It must be stressed that an investment such as Facebook is incredibly rare and few venture investors are ever lucky enough to get access to a startup like that.

A better way to do venture investing is to have a rigorous understanding of portfolio construction and being incredibly disciplined about your investment strategy once set (and then hope that you stumble upon a Facebook as a nice bonus).

The best people in venture portfolio construction are the elite venture capital funds. They will typically structure their portfolios across 25–40 startups of similar stage. The reason the similar stage is important is so that the risk and reward associated with each startup is roughly equal.

The aim for the average venture capital fund is to return 5x or more of the initial investment. But expert fund managers know that playing it safe doesn't get them there, as unfortunately around 50% of investments will not return even the original capital.

That means that the remaining 50% of investments need to make back significant returns. Given how rare it is to find an outstanding company that does more than 20x, a venture fund would be extremely happy to find just one or two of such companies, with the rest of the profitable companies making 2–5x on average. Figure 14.3 portrays this diagrammatically.

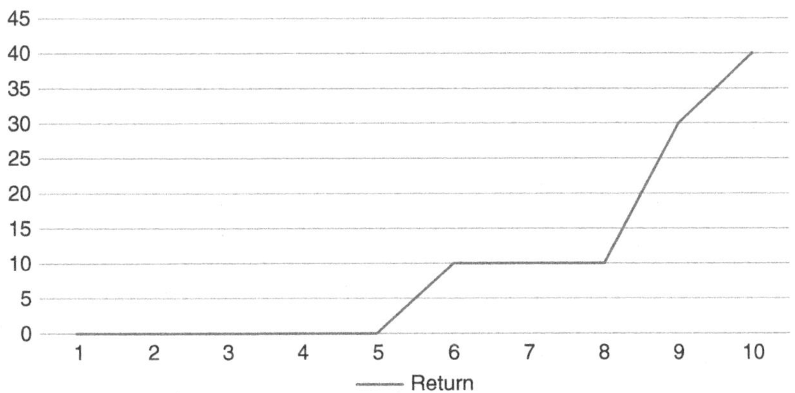

Figure 14.3 Power law distribution.

Source: A. D. Barroso, Power Law in Venture Capital: Why Portfolios Matter. *Medium* (6 October 2019). https://adiezbarroso.medium.com/power-law-in-venture-capital-why-portfolios-matter-8d3fb2afac5e (accessed 13 December 2022). Public Domain.

In Figure 14.3, Barroso sketches out a portfolio of 10 companies with 5 making no returns, 3 companies each making a return equivalent to 10% of the portfolio, 1 company making a return of 30% and the final one making a return equivalent to 40% of the portfolio. In other words, the few big winners need to be so big that they completely outweigh any of the losers.

If all this portfolio construction talk is getting you excited, you're probably an angel investor. If on the other hand, you're struggling to stay awake at this point, you're probably a fund investor. We'll explain more about the ways to invest in venture capital shortly.

Is My Money Safe?

Startup investing is risky business and not suitable for all investors. Your money is frankly not safe if all you invest in is the occasional startup. Your chances of picking even a break-even company is likely about 50% if you are a well-connected tech investor, and around 25% if you're an average investor with poor access to quality deals. Therefore your chances of picking a winner are very slim if you take this unsystematic approach.

If, however, you invest through a professionally managed fund or you build up your own portfolio, you are much better placed to, at the very least, break even and, ideally, make some profit. The key reason for this is that you will have taken many more "swings" of the bat to try to hit the ball out of the park. Logically, the more swings you take, the more likely you are to hit upon a big winner.

But taking enough swings is just one part of the puzzle. You also need to make sure you're playing on the right pitch in the first place. You must ensure that the deals you are getting access to are truly high quality deals that have the potential to make the kind of returns needed to make your portfolio work. This is the stage that most venture investors get wrong as they erroneously believe that not only are they great pickers of startups, but that they have great access to deals. We already know that even the best venture investors are basically not very good at picking a big winner, with even the top-performing VC funds having just a 7% hit rate of finding an outlier company.[7] This is why the access point is so important. Even a mediocre investor with great access to a seam of high quality startups to mine from will make incredible returns.

As professional venture investors ourselves, we have seen how the most competitive deals play out and we can assure you that, as an everyday investor, you do not have access to the best deals.

Here's how it works: Any high quality founder wants to have a high quality fund on their side as they know the fund will bring a wealth of experience and contacts along with their money. Founders are also very conscious of the secret sauce of their company getting circulated too widely and are typically coy about their pitch deck becoming too widely read. Consequently, they will look to run a fast, relatively secretive process, and look to create competition between funds so as to bid up their price.

What gives any startup the premium feel is having top funds fighting over it. That dynamic simply wouldn't happen if that startup decided to raise on a crowdfunding platform. Consequently, a crowdfunding platform is probably the last place a startup ends up when looking to raise money, as by that point they have explored and had rejections from the VC funds they had approached. A crowdfunding platform also charges the startup money for raising capital for them – something no high quality startup (which has no shortage of offers) would ever entertain paying. This is also, by the way, the exact reason why savvy investors steer clear of crowdfunding platforms as a source of deals to invest in.

A great example of access is the recent Twitter takeover by Elon Musk. He pooled together a band of investors for this venture that reads like a who's who of Silicon Valley. They included elite venture funds Sequoia Capital and Andreesen Horowitz, Saudi royalty, the Qatar Investment Authority and the founder of Oracle, Larry Ellison.[8] The particularly incredible aspect of these investments was how the actual due diligence took place and how deals got struck. In a telling screenshot of a Signal message, Marc Andreesen, the co-founder of Andreesen Horowitz, promises Elon, "If you are considering equity partners, my growth fund is in for $250M with no additional work required."[9] See Figure 14.4.

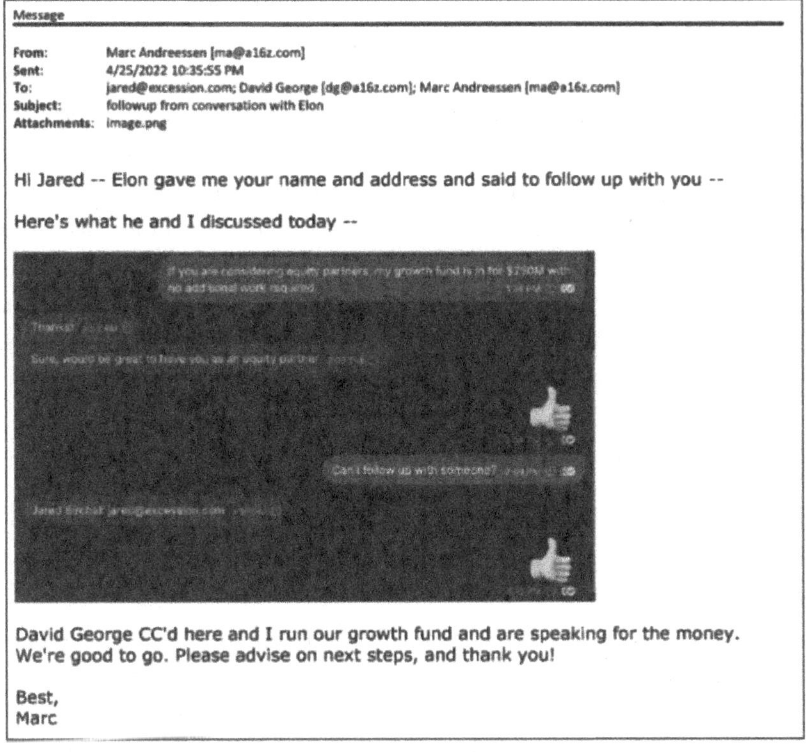

Message

From: Marc Andreessen [ma@a16z.com]
Sent: 4/25/2022 10:35:55 PM
To: jared@excession.com; David George [dg@a16z.com]; Marc Andreessen [ma@a16z.com]
Subject: followup from conversation with Elon
Attachments: image.png

Hi Jared -- Elon gave me your name and address and said to follow up with you --

Here's what he and I discussed today --

David George CC'd here and I run our growth fund and are speaking for the money. We're good to go. Please advise on next steps, and thank you!

Best,
Marc

Figure 14.4 Screenshot of conversation.

Source: Delaware Court of Chancery. Public Domain.

Marc is on phone conversation terms with Elon and this is how the deal was struck. That should speak volumes about why access is far more important than picking ability. You or we did not get access to that deal because we're not in that particular circle.

Can I Get My Money Back?

Startups are a highly illiquid asset class. Startup shares are not publicly traded which means it is very difficult to sell them to someone else. In order to sell your shares, you actively need to find a buyer yourself for those shares, and you both need to come up with a way to price the shares too in order to complete the transaction.

There are now some "secondary" markets available such as on Crowdcube, Seedrs, and Forge Global where you can sell your shares. With Crowdcube and Seedrs, you are restricted to shares you bought with them – which is problematic, as our view is that crowdfunding platforms are not the best place to go hunting for startup investments generally. And with Forge Global, they specialise primarily in later stage private companies such as SpaceX or Stripe. That's great if you have a later stage company in your portfolio, but if you're trying to sell an early-stage company there is likely to be little to no demand for it.

You should go into any startup investment expecting to hold it for somewhere between 5 and 15 years, though with a number of them you will expect to see results (or busts) within the 5-year mark. The long-running ones are actually the better investments because typically only the most durable and robust companies survive longer than 5 years.

Sharia Considerations

Let us forewarn you, this section gets quite technical quite quickly as it is designed to be a reference point for you as investors – both beginners and advanced – going forward.

So before we get into the weeds, here's the TLDR version: venture capital investing is at heart very sharia-compliant as it is just equity investment with pure risk and reward-sharing. Of course, you want to make sure that the business you are investing in is not a gambling technology startup – that would be an issue. But structurally, venture capital is in the right sharia ballpark.

However it's never that simple. There are three key challenges that crop up in venture capital (and most equity-related investments frankly):

1. Venture capitalists (VCs) use preference shares and debt instruments (PS) to invest in their portfolio companies and these are standardly viewed as haram by the majority of scholars.
2. Investing through convertible instruments, such as convertible loan notes (CLN), simple agreements for future equity (SAFE) and advanced subscription agreements (ASA).
3. Preferred return (PR) – this is only relevant for investments through venture capital funds – it doesn't really crop up if you're angel investing.

The very simple ways to side-step these issues are:

1. **Beginner:** Only invest via a sharia-compliant venture capital provider. We'll cover more on what options are out there a bit later on. Avoid investing independently through mainstream platforms where the sharia-compliance analysis is not done for you.
2. **Intermediate:** At this stage you are ready to take some of your own decisions and make individual investments into startups. Make sure you only buy and sell ordinary shares, invest through priced SAFE notes and ASAs, and not charge the interest associated with a CLN. Avoid investing through any VC funds (apart from funds that are labelled as sharia-compliant)
3. **Advanced:** At this stage you are ready to get more into the weeds and potentially deploy larger amounts. All of the guidance for the intermediate stage applies to you. Additionally, you may want to invest in VC funds as well, including ones that are not sharia-compliant out of the box. You would have to negotiate additional terms in a side letter with the fund to address issues such as PR and get the support of a sharia scholar and VC funds expert to deal with ancillary terms that come up in each VC fund agreement.

That said, let's get into the nitty-gritty.

SAFE Notes, *ASAs*, and *CLNs*

SAFEs (or ASAs in the UK) are an equity-like instrument and in practice will convert into equity at the next round (or within a set time frame such as 6 months or 12 months. In effect, a SAFE is an agreement where the founder says to the investor, "Look, let's not worry too much about properly pricing this thing. Right now the important thing is to get a bit of money and just get the ball rolling. So let's kick the *exact* price down the road, but I will give you certainty on the lowest price and for the upper price it will either be an $x million valuation or a 20% discount on whatever the next round's valuation is set by the lead investor (whichever is better for you)."

The investor turns around and says, "Great, that saves me the legal and time cost of having to undertake rigorous due diligence and legal negotiation, and instead we can just get started, knowing that eventually an institutional (professional) VC fund will come in and negotiate and set the price of the next round and I will be getting a discount on that anyway."

Our view, like most scholars who have given this instrument serious thought, is that SAFEs are sharia-compliant. The interest element of a SAFE is of course not permissible, but this is rarely charged in practice – we have never seen someone actually request the interest. And these days most SAFEs don't even have an interest element.

The only thing to watch out for are unpriced SAFEs, because scholars prefer if SAFEs specify the price at which they will convert so that there is certainty as to the share price in an up or down scenario. We personally think that even in an unpriced SAFE there is sufficient certainty, given the wider market dynamics and the discount multiples being clearly stated.

ASAs are even more straightforward as they require conversion within 6 months and therefore have even more certainty baked in.

Similarly a convertible loan note, if it is being used basically to replace the role of an ASA or a SAFE, is fine in our view, as long as no interest is actually charged or paid. Take the interest element out of a CLN and you're basically left with a SAFE so the same analysis would apply.

However, if a CLN does have interest, and it will be charged, that is problematic.

What Are Preference Shares and What Is a Preferred Return?

In order to analyse PS and PR from an Islamic perspective, let's first define what they are.

- **Preference shares:** When you are a shareholder in a company, you get shares. Shares come with standard rights – usually, rights to receive a dividend, vote, and in the event of the company being liquidated, to get paid back on a pro-rata basis with the other shareholders.

But what if you want to give different shareholders different rights? Think of a family company. You might have a father who wants to give shares to his children, but doesn't want them to have any voting rights attached to those shares while he is alive.

In the case of VC, a VC fund will want certain advantages over other shareholders if it is investing into a company. Hence, "preference" shares.

- **Preferred return:** This whole concept centres around an investor in a VC fund (whereas PS is relevant to when the VC fund itself is investing into companies). Under a standard private equity or VC fund, the money is distributed according to a particular order, with the ultimate aim of splitting profits 80/20 in favour of investors. So what happens if an investor puts in £100? (This is going to get slightly complicated, so bear with us.)

  First, investors will receive back their invested capital (£100). Next, investors will receive all profits up to, say, 8% (£8) (this is usually known as a "hurdle"). After that, the fund manager receives all the capital until it has caught up with the investors (who have been taking all the profits up to this point) so it will take the next £2, as then the profit split will be 80/20. Finally, once the fund manager has caught up with the investors, all profits will be split 80/20, in favour of the investors.

  The preferred return is the name given to the "8%" in the above example. This amount is a guarantee for the investor that they will get at least all the profit up to this amount, and will only have to start sharing the profits with the fund manager after they exceed that amount. In other words, the fund manager makes nothing if they don't make a profit above 8%.

What Is the Islamic Issue with Preference Shares and Preferred Return? The first thing to say when discussing PS and PR is that these constructs are modern constructs that are tied up with the invention of the modern limited liability company and as such classical Islamic law doesn't directly address these instruments. However, there is enough broader analysis and scholarship to be able to constructively address these issues – and scholars have done so.

- **Risk-reward sharing:** The basic issue is that under the classic models of an equity contract in Islamic law (*musharakah/mudarabah*), there is an ethos of risk-reward sharing, whereas under the PS or PR set-up, a certain class of shareholders are getting, well, preferential treatment.
- **Similarity with debt:** The other reason why Islamic scholars don't like PS and PR is that they look like debt in many ways. Under a PS you may be due a fixed return every year, regardless of the company's performance, and these returns may even be cumulative and compounded so that, if in a particular year the dividend is not issued, in a subsequent year the dividend due to a PS shareholder will make up for the missed dividend. Preference shares can also be drafted in relation to the interest rate (as opposed to the performance of the company), which further strengthens the debt-like characteristics of this instrument.

  Similarly, a PR too can look like debt in some ways. One can have a compounded PR, for example, and whenever there is a profit, the investor gets the first bite at the cherry. Admittedly though, PR is much less debt-like than PS.
- **Unequal power dynamics:** Ultimately, when you boil it all down, Islamic finance wants to create a system where there is less uncertainty and injustice (as explained in a video we did). So, stripping it all back, the real issue with PR and PS is that some people end up with greater rights and protections than their partners in the business.

  They get preferential treatment in the core ways a stock can be valuable: (1) in obtaining dividends; (2) in liquidation scenarios; and (3) even in selling a stock they get an advantage – they can assess whether or not they should convert their preference share to a common share if that is now worth more (now that the business has grown, proven its model, and become much more valuable). Why do they get that power and why do companies agree to give such PSs? Because the investors are bringing the money.

  But Islamic law does not like financiers taking excessive advantage of their economically stronger position and has these and other rules to balance the risk-reward spread more equally.

Why Do VCs Use Preference Shares and Preferred Return? So we know Islamic scholars and Islamic law don't like the look of PS and PR. But why do VCs use PSs and PR in the first place? Answering that might give us a clue about how we can come up with a sharia-compliant alternative.

Preference Shares Typically, VC investors use PSs for one of three reasons:

1. To get dividends paid first to them before they get paid out to any other shareholder (and so if there's only enough for them, they're the only ones who get dividends that year).
2. They get priority before other shareholders when it comes to liquidating the stock – so if there's not enough money for others to get paid, a PS shareholder will be the only one that gets paid.
3. To get the ability to convert the PS into common stock if the investment's value rises so much that the VC ownership percentage would be more profitable if PSs were converted to common stock.

These are technical reasons that translate roughly into the following two actual real-life motivations of a VC investor.

1. To stop founders of a company selling/liquidating their company immediately after raising the capital from the VC. If a company has £0 in cash terms before investment, and a post-investment bank balance of £1.5m, then, assuming the founders hold onto 80% of the equity, if they were to liquidate/sell at this point, they'd make £1.2m and the VC would get back £0.3m. Not a great outcome for the VC, you'd agree!
2. To try to maximise returns, by protecting downside risk. Most companies a VC will invest in will tank. That's the nature of the business. So VCs want to try to minimise, as much as they can, the losses that accrue from such tanked companies. Let's use the example of £1.5m investment (for 20% equity) into a company and assume that at the point the company has failed and is being liquidated, there is only £500k in the bank account. In such a situation, as the PS has priority over other shareholders, it will take all of that £500k. Yes, it'll still be a £700k loss, but at least the VC has gained an extra £100k that it wouldn't otherwise get if the £500k had been split pro rata to its shareholding.

We have no sympathy for (2) as that is just trying to have your cake and eat it. We have some sympathy for (1), but again, in our view, this does not require a PS structure to achieve. A well-drafted shareholders' agreement (and other ancillary documents) should achieve the same effect. But let's turn now to understand why people use PR, before we explore how Islamic law has some alternatives.

Preferred Return VC funds offer PR on their funds overwhelmingly because investors demand it and it is now established market practice. Part of the reason is risk-mitigation of course: an investor knows it is easier to make less than 8% than it is to make above 8% returns. Therefore, they ask for the first 8% (which is more likely to be achieved) to be given to them.

But another part of the reason is that investors like to compare against other investment options they may have, and they might reasonably consider that 8% is a return they could quite easily achieve in other investments that are more liquid and less risky (e.g. a leveraged return on property). So, if the fund manager will get a profit share on the profits made, they want it only to kick in once they have made above 8%.

Sharia-Compliant Solutions

- Let's address a solution to PR first, because it is the easier of the two to address. **Preferred return:** The AAOIFI Standard states at provision (3/1/5/5): "It is permissible for the partners to agree on any method of allocation of profit, either permanent or variable, for example, by agreeing that the percentages of profit it shares in the first period are one set of percentages and in the second period are another set of percentages, depending on the disparity of the two periods or the magnitude of the realised profit. This is allowed provided that using such a method does not lead to the likelihood of a partner being precluded from participation in profit."[10]

  So fundamentally, a difference in the split is allowed between two different portions of the profit. What the AAOIFI Standard rightly doesn't like though is that the fund manager is entirely cut out of profit in a particular portion of the profit. So applying to the PR context of a VC fund, the Standard requires that at least a small fraction of the first 8% of profits accrues to the fund manager, say, 5–10%.

This solution should get us to sharia-compliance (and also achieves the commercial purpose of the PR). Fundamentally, a PR is part of a wider economic set-up where the profit is split 80–20 – which is perfectly sharia-compliant and pretty fair. So there isn't much tweaking to do here in our view.

- **Preference shares:** The International Islamic Fiqh Academy states: "It is not permissible to issue preference shares with financial characteristics that involve guaranteed payment of the capital or of a certain amount of profit or ensure precedence over other shares at the time of liquidation or distribution of dividends."[11]

  So the Fiqh Academy is saying that preferential treatment with respect to dividends and upon liquidation is the issue. In a VC context, an investor is not typically that bothered about a preferential treatment for dividends. The reason being, most startups won't issue dividends, and the profits will come out upon a sale or IPO, rather than dividends. So a VC investor should be able to get comfortable dropping preference on dividends.

  That leaves us with the preference on liquidation issue, and, though the Fiqh Academy doesn't mention it, the convertibility issue (i.e. the ability to switch from PS to common stock).

So, what are the solutions?

- **The *tanazul* solution:** The literature on PS treatment in Islam consistently does not allow preference in a liquidation scenario. Even some recent attempts by Al-Suhaibani, M. and Naifar[12] to come up with an Islamic PS, do not allow preference on liquidation. However the Malaysians do allow such preference on the basis of *tanazul*. This is the concept of the other shareholders in the company willingly foregoing their automatic right to equal standing with the PS shareholder, and saying "We give up our right in your favour – you go ahead and take preference in a liquidation scenario".
- **The *wa'd* solution:** Another approach you can take, which is inspired by the AAOIFI Standard (3/1/5/4 of the Musharakah Standard (12)), is a *wa'd* (promise) structure. 3/1/5/4 states that it is valid for a partner to bear the responsibility for the loss at the time of the loss, without any prior condition that he would accept such responsibility.

In Islam, a *wa'd* is a unilateral promise from one party to another and is not seen as a binding contract (which is bilateral). However, under English law one can make unilateral and binding commitments. Thus one could get the founder to enter a *wa'd* to take on the loss at the time of the loss, should one arise. This would not cause any sharia issues, and still give English law protections.

- **The negligence solution:** Islamic law also permits the founder to compensate the investor in case of loss that arises out of the founder's negligence. Thus one could set up some paperwork that either (a) made the definition of negligence pretty broad (to be triggered in a liquidation scenario only) – thus triggering a negligence payout for the investor on liquidation; or (b) give the investor sole discretion to decide, in a liquidation scenario, whether the founder has been negligent.
- **The best solution:** Of course, the most sharia-compliant option to deal with the preference on liquidation issue is to reject it and share in the risk just as one shares in the reward.
- **The next-best solution:** The best solution is unfortunately not often commercially palatable/workable so the next-best solution is one of the three solutions just detailed. In practice, *tanazul* is usually the easiest solution to use and why it is the most often used.

Zakat

Zakat on startups is the same as zakat on any private company. You would need to figure out what liquid assets a startup has, and then figure out what percentage of that money you as an investor have an equivalent stake in.

For example, if Company ABC has £1m in cash today in its account, and you are a 2% shareholder in the company, you are liable to pay for £20,000 of that £1m. In other words, you would pay 2.5% of £20,000 as zakat.

We offer a free zakat calculator on the IFG website (through our Cur8 platform) that you can use to easily do any calculations.

How Can I Get Access?

There are four main ways to invest in startups:

1. crowdfunding platforms
2. join an angel syndicate

3. personally find a startup to invest in
4. invest in a VC fund.

Crowdfunding Platforms

The easiest way to get started in startup investing is through crowdfunding platforms where you can often invest in startups from as little as $10. This is a good way to get a feel for startup investing and will help you learn how to differentiate a good startup from a bad startup.

The significant downside of crowdfunding platforms is that most startups can list on the platform, and, because there is a cost associated with raising money on a crowdfunding website and some marketing effort on the side of the startup needed, it is normally a last resort from a startup. For this reason, startups on crowdfunding platforms are not always of the highest quality, there is minimal information on the startup you are able to access, and no further due diligence is done by more experienced eyes.

There is also an underlying conflict of interest between you as an investor and the platform. They are getting paid by the startup for every additional dollar they can raise for the startup. They are effectively the estate agent for the startup.

Additionally, mainstream crowdfunding platforms do not sharia-screen the startups they list, so there is no way of guaranteeing that the various sharia issues we discussed above are being navigated properly.

Having said all of that, there are often interesting startups that do list on these platforms – and you can find some absolute gems as well. If nothing else, these platforms can very quickly help you develop your due diligence muscle by screening hundreds of opportunities.

Mainstream crowdfunding platforms include Republic, Seedrs, Crowdcube, and sharia-compliant platforms include Ethis.

Join an Angel Syndicate

An angel syndicate is a group of angel investors who band together to invest in startups. An angel syndicate could be focused on a certain sector or industry or be sector-agnostic. There are many benefits of being part of an angel syndicate. Because you are investing as a group, you are able to do the following:

- Source a larger number of, and higher quality, startups.
- Invest larger amounts of capital in each startup and therefore have more say in negotiations.

- Get access to more information about that startup, for example, detailed financial accounts and multiple due diligence calls.
- Benefit from the due diligence of a larger number of experienced investors.

The best angel syndicates are the ones with the best deal flow and with the deepest track record. These two factors ensure that they are optimised to receive further great deals in the future.

Angel syndicate leads are usually not full-time investors, and they are usually only remunerated through the profit share, rather than any management fees. Fees are charged upfront though for administrative purposes and deal execution.

Beware of any brokers/crowdfunding platforms masquerading as angel syndicates. The quickest way to check if you're dealing with a genuine angel syndicate is by studying the fee structure. If the startup is the one having to pay any fees, this is probably not the sort of syndicate you want to join as it isn't optimised for the best deals.

There are some very high quality angel syndicates on Angellist, the world's leading angel syndicate platform.

Personally Find and Invest in a Startup Yourself

If you are looking to personally find and invest in a startup yourself, the best way to do this is to plug yourself into your local startup ecosystem. Startup culture is all about collaboration and sharing talent and resources and are therefore normally clustered around the same events and organisations. A good place to start are "demo days". This is where startups who have gone through an accelerator programme pitch to an audience of investors. This is a good place to meet with startups directly as well as to start making a name for yourself in startup circles which naturally improves your deal flow.

Investing in startups yourself gives you the most control over your investment.

The downsides, however, include a lower number of startups you are exposed to, high minimum investments (normally $20,000–$50,000) and no second opinion on which startups to invest in.

Invest in a *VC* Fund

Investing through a good VC fund with a track record and strong deal flow ensures that you achieve three key things:

1. A proper portfolio construction and diversification.
2. Access to a quality deal flow and the ability to close those deals.
3. Benefiting from a fund manager's ongoing management of individual portfolio companies and shepherding them in the right direction.

There are three material downsides though. First, most institutional VC funds are inaccessible, with minimum tickets of $500k–$5m. Second, for those who like doing this. investing through a VC fund isn't as fun as choosing your own deals. Third, because a fund invests in only those things the fund manager chooses, you really can't ensure sharia-compliance unless the fund manager states that they will adhere to those guidelines.

The good news is that there are now a large number of angel-focused VC funds that have popped up where you can invest with much lower amounts. You can find a large number on Angellist. To our knowledge, the only such fund that is sharia-compliant today, however, is the one offered by us on Cur8 Capital.

UK taxpayers should pay particular attention to EIS-compliant VC funds, as they come with significant tax breaks built in. For more on those benefits see our tax-saving strategies section in Part II.

Cur8 Capital are also collaborating on an ongoing basis with the larger institutional VC funds with high minimums, and clubbing together with our entire platform to gain access to these funds as well through minimums of £5,000. So far we have opened up access to a leading Middle East fund and a Pakistan-focused fund. We are seeing this trend develop with other players entering the market – particularly in the Middle East – and expect that access to such institutional funds will become dramatically easier in the next few years.

Summary

- Venture capital is a high-risk, high-reward asset class.
- Diversification is a must in venture capital.
- You must ensure that you are able to get access to the highest-quality deals in order for VC to be a viable investment.
- There are multiple ways of getting exposure to venture capital including investing in funds, angel syndicates, or sourcing deals yourself.

Private Equity: What Is It?

Private equity investing is investing in all the other sorts of businesses other than startups and technology businesses.

What does that cryptic statement mean? Well, another way to understand it is to think about how a private equity investor looks to make money and what kind of money they seek to make.

A private equity investor will look to add value to a traditional business – let's say a chain of pharmacies – by adding further chains, reducing costs, and increasing product lines. They will also look to take on significant debt to finance all this activity. The hope is that the business is worth 2–6× more in 3–5 years' time and the private equity investor can sell the company on.

The kind of returns possible in private equity are usually only possible through using debt – as that magnifies the returns made through the value-add work the investor may have done. This of course raises sharia-compliance issues, but more on that later.

Returns on Offer

Private equity has consistently outperformed the stock market over the last decade. See Figure 14.5. Private equity funds typically target a 20% IRR and seek to return a 3–5x multiple on their fund back to investors.

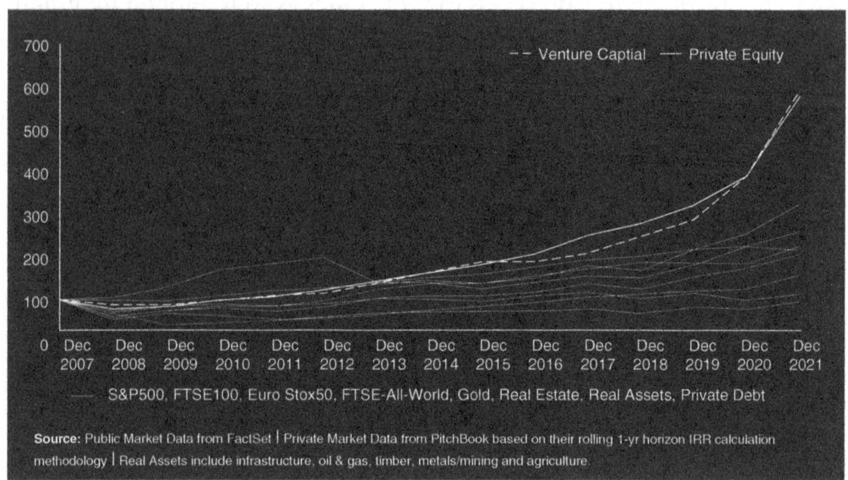

Figure 14.5 Performance of private equity.

Source: FactSet / www.factset.com / last accessed January 03, 2023.

Private equity returns usually come much quicker than venture capital as well. Because we are dealing with businesses generating cash flow here, the distributions can come a little earlier.

Is My Money Safe?

Private equity investing is a highly technical investment class and not for the beginner. That said, if you tool up on your private equity knowledge and ideally get some guidance from books like this and financial advisors, there is no reason to not get involved.

Private equity funds are diversified across a range of assets and so are a lot lower risk than an individual private equity deal. Given we are dealing with larger, more mature, and cash flow-generating businesses, the risk of a business going completely bust is much lower too.

Overall, private equity is definitely lower risk than venture capital investing, but still an investment only suitable for a high net worth or sophisticated investor who understands what they are getting into.

Can I Get My Money Back?

The same analysis applies for private equity as it did for venture capital. You are investing in illiquid private shares of companies, and these take a while for a fund to sell down and then pass through distributions to you. So if you need this money earlier than 5 years, private equity is probably not the thing for you. However, if you can be patient with some of your money – that is where any private equity investment you make should be made from.

Sharia Considerations

At the heart of private equity is getting some kind of leverage. Usually this takes the form of interest-bearing debt. There are therefore three ways of doing private equity in a sharia-compliant way:

1. You don't use interest-bearing debt at all and find opportunities that don't need debt to make great returns.
2. You use sharia-compliant debt.
3. You use something called a "sharia wrapper".

The No-Debt Option

There are still some opportunities out there where it is possible to invest in a business and make a high return over a short duration through just adding value, careful cost-cutting, repackaging a product, and/or selling licences and franchises.

The problem with this route is that there are next to no private equity funds who actively state that this is their strategy. It doesn't economically make sense for your typical fund as it massively decreases the deals they can go for, and the profits they can make overall.

Use Sharia-Compliant Debt

If you can convince an Islamic bank to give you some sharia debt, then you can run the same private equity strategy as usual – just with sharia debt.

However, the challenge is that there aren't actually that many Islamic banks available and not a huge amount who will deal in the kind of lending needed to finance a private equity investment strategy.

Use a Sharia Wrapper

The third and least palatable route is to use something called a "sharia wrapper". Effectively, what this structure does is allow sharia-compliant investors to invest in something that is haram but at a technical level so they are able to say what they are investing in is halal.

Scholars will allow institutional funds to avail themselves of these structures from time to time due to specific circumstances, such as regulatory or tax reasons, however, scholars and the AAOIFI – the global sharia standards authority – really limit the use of such a structure.

There are now some platforms that exist where they offer non-compliant private equity funds through such wrappers to everyday investors. We would advise caution against this. There are plenty of uncontroversial halal alternative investments that an everyday investor can opt for instead.

Zakat on Private Equity

Zakat on private equity is the same as zakat on any private company (and therefore identical to startups). You would need to figure out what liquid assets a company has, and then figure out what percentage of that money you, as an investor, have an equivalent stake in. For example, if Company

ABC has £1m in cash today in its account, and you are a 2% shareholder in the company, you are liable to pay for £20,000 of that £1m. In other words you would pay 2.5% of £20,000 as zakat.

How Can I Get Access?

There are unfortunately very few Islamic private equity players out there. Those that do exist typically tend to limit themselves to institutional investors. Examples include Fajr Capital, Shuaa Capital, Wafra Capital, Arcapita, and Gulf Finance House.

At Cur8 we converse regularly with larger funds like these and will regularly partner up with them to offer everyday (but affluent) investors access to these funds (or even individual deals) through our platform at much smaller tickets. We also plan to develop our own PE fund in due course.

If you're a larger ticket investor looking to invest $10m or more, a few different opportunities open up for you and you should reach out to some of these institutional funds we mentioned above as they may be able to service you directly.

Gold: What Is It?

Gold has increased 51% over the last 5 years, giving approximately 10% returns every year.[13] Those are impressive numbers and on that basis alone it is worth digging further into this asset class.

The actual asset itself is pretty straightforward – it is a piece of metal. But it's a piece of metal that from the start of human history has been ascribed value. Due to its portability, relative chemical stability (it doesn't rust, explode, corrode, dissolve, evaporate, etc.) and rarity, gold has been used as a currency on and off for much of modern human history.

There are a few key benefits to holding gold as an investment:

1. **Diversification:** As a hedge against currency inflation and macroeconomic policies like quantitative easing and debt issuances, gold is a great investment. Gold is also largely uncorrelated to other asset classes. So, for example, if oil prices rise, airlines start struggling. But there's no equivalent causal relationship between gold prices and most other assets.

2. **Good for bear markets:** Gold is seen as a safe asset and so in times of turbulence – which we are very likely to see a lot of in this upcoming decade – investors flock to it as a safe haven.
3. **Very liquid market:** When you invest in an asset you want to be able to exit it quickly and not be stuck with it while you find a buyer. Gold is very much that sort of asset. You can buy and sell it online within minutes, or in person with a local gold dealer. This makes it a nice low risk investment that you can store some value in that won't get eroded by inflation.

There are, however, a few important downsides to investing in gold too:

1. **It doesn't earn anything:** If you held £100 of gold for 20 years, after 20 years you would have roughly the equivalent of £100 of gold after adjusting for inflation. The capital increase is driven in large part by the inflation rates. However, if you invested £100 in a property with a 5% yield, you would have ended up earning £200 in the yield, and most likely much more than that, as your yield will increase as inflation increases, and as you reinvest your rental profits back into other property investments. In addition, your £100 would have kept its value in line with inflation too – just like gold.
2. **Storage:** Gold storage costs a lot if done properly, and is best left to the professionals. Insuring for gold is also expensive business – as insurers know how much burglars like to go after it. But you can avoid this cost (or reduce it dramatically) by not actually taking delivery of the gold and letting the gold broker hold it for you.
3. **High premiums on spot price:** Gold brokers will sell to you at a mark-up of 5–10% above the spot price. You will then also lose roughly that much when selling it too. So in order to break even you need the gold price to go up by about 15–20%. That is a significant amount of movement you are relying on. Gold prices have been rising on average around 15% over the last 5 years to be fair, but this won't go on forever.

Is This a Good Time to Invest in Gold?

In order to decide if now is a good time to invest in gold, we should consider the following factors:

1. Will gold go higher? (i.e. do we think governments will print more money and that stocks will take a pounding and uncertainty will continue?)
2. What are the alternatives?
3. Ease of purchase, transaction cost, and storage cost.

On point 1, while we are no experts on gold prices, we are fairly confident that we will see further macro instabilities, supply chain disruptions, energy crises, and uncertainty in the markets to continue for a year or two at least. Based on that, we would expect gold prices to at least hold their value.

On point 2, we think there are a whole range of alternative investments to consider but in order for there to be a truly effective comparison to gold, the investment class should be safe and easy to exit from. The only true alternative to that is a savings account. Savings accounts are actually yielding a decent amount right now in the high interest environment we find ourselves in. They are unlikely to fully hedge you against all inflation though, so probably worse than gold overall in terms of return. However, in terms of certainty of getting back exactly what you put in – you can't beat a savings account.

The other option is property – but property is usually harder to price accurately and usually more illiquid. Even property investing in its more liquid forms – e.g. through a REIT or through a platform like Cur8 – is still not as liquid as the gold market.

Finally, on point 3, there are now ways to sidestep at least some of this cost by not buying and holding gold directly. If we did buy gold, we would buy it via an online broker such as Bullion Vault and Minted, where you typically get the best price and can save money in storage cost by choosing to just leave the gold with them. Alternatively, we would buy via a gold ETF where you can significantly reduce purchase cost (as the ETF will be buying in bulk). We would not buy physical gold and take actual delivery if we were looking to buy gold as an investment due to the security issues.

Our Preferred Gold Investment Strategy

Our preferred approach is to hold a steady 5% or so of our portfolio in gold and just maintain that, regardless of price. So if gold prices rise and our gold holding becomes 10% of our portfolio, we would sell it to get back to 5%. And if gold prices fall and our holding is worth 3%, we would buy more gold to get to 5% of our overall portfolio again. The reason we take this approach is, we think of gold as essentially an equivalent to cash, but one where there is a potential for a little growth.

But we don't like putting too much in gold as we don't consider it a productive asset – and we like to invest in productive assets as they are going to make much more money in the long term.

Returns on Offer

Gold has generally been on an uptrend during the course of the last two decades, peaking around periods of market turbulence or the excessive printing of money. See Figure 14.6.

Figure 14.6 Performance of the gold market.

Source: Jewellery Quarter Bullion Ltd./ https://www.bullionbypost.co.uk/gold-price/20-year-gold-price-history-pound-sterling-ounce / Last accessed 29 December 2022.

Broadly speaking, holding gold will protect your wealth from the ravages of inflation and even increase above that for certain durations such as the last 5 years.

Is My Money Safe?

Gold is a pretty safe investment, but where you might actually end up losing money is if your gold got stolen. If you are investing in gold through an ETF or an online broker, as long as you are confident as to the storage and security provision of the gold itself, your gold should be safe.

Care should also be taken when investing in any type of gold derivative. Quite aside from the fact that such an investment would be haram, it also means that your investment in gold is not direct and could therefore significantly magnify up positively or negatively. Online platforms sometimes are not as explicit as they could be when the gold investing they are offering is in fact a derivative instrument.

Can I Get My Money Back?

Gold is a highly liquid investment and so you can very easily get your money back. However, what type of gold you hold and on which venue will determine how practically easy it is to sell your gold.

For example, if you decide to own gold through a piece of jewellery, the gold would need to be processed in order to be reusable, or if you bought through a platform, the gold will usually only be sellable via the platform you bought it. So make sure you understand your exit options before you commit to buying gold through any avenue.

Sharia Considerations

Gold itself is clearly halal to invest and trade in, however, there are a few important guidelines to adhere to when you interact with the various different ways you could invest in gold.

First, gold is seen as a currency by the sharia and, as such, exchanges of gold must be on the spot and without deferment of either delivery or payment. This is because if deferment enters into the transaction, there is likely to be a fluctuation of value, which means that £100 is now potentially going to be exchanged for £99 of gold – and that is the essence of *riba*.

Second, you need not always take delivery of the gold, but you should ideally have a way to potentially get hold of it if needed. This is because the sharia is keen for you to trade goods that you own and possess, and while it is acceptable to store your gold with someone, if the gold is not even theoretically capable of being delivered to you, then doubts are raised as to the validity of the contract under Islamic law.

Third, you must actually buy and sell gold, not derivatives representative of gold. This is because there is a famous hadith that clarifies ownership and possession as key requirements for a sale:

> Narrated on the authority of Hakim bin Hizam, "I said: 'O Messenger of Allah, a man is asking me to sell him something that I do not possess; Shall I sell it to him?' He said: 'Do not sell what is not with you.'"[14]

Based on the above principles, Table 14.1 shows the sharia analyses of each of the common ways of accessing gold today.

Table 14.1 Sharia analyses of accessing gold

Method of buying gold	Sharia analysis
Physical gold via bullion or coin websites	Halal, but do make sure you're actually buying a physical asset and there is clarity over ownership records and when ownership transfers to you. Ideally you should also be able to take delivery even if you don't ever exercise it
Physical gold via debt securities	Objectionable because you don't own the gold, you just have a claim to the value you have invested in, which can either be traded for gold or cash when redeeming
Physical gold via jewellery	Halal
ETFs that hold physical gold	Halal
ETFs that hold gold futures and options	Haram
Gold stocks and shares	Halal (but do check for debt levels)
Futures or options	Generally seen as haram
CFDs, spread betting, and other derivatives	Haram

Zakat on Gold

Gold is viewed as a currency by the sharia and, as such, 2.5% of the value of your gold would need to be donated every year. For example, if you own £1000 worth of gold as of the date on which your zakat is due, you will need to pay £25 in zakat. It doesn't matter if you bought the gold many years ago at a much lower price; you will need to pay zakat annually on the value at the time.

Zakat is another reason why gold doesn't necessarily make sense as a big chunk of your portfolio, as each year that amount will be eroded. And there is wisdom in that – the sharia doesn't want wealth sitting in non-useful places just collecting dust. The sharia encourages us to invest that money into productive things where the zakat burden is significantly lower (as there are less liquid assets).

How Can I Get Access?

There are seven main ways to invest in gold for an everyday investor:

1. Physical gold via bullion or coin websites.
2. Physical gold via jewellery.
3. Exchange-traded funds (ETFs) that buy gold.
4. ETFs that trade in gold futures or options.
5. Gold mining companies.
6. Futures or options.
7. CFDs, spread betting, or other derivative products.

Let's take each of these in turn.

Investing in Gold Bullion and Gold Coins

The first and most ancient way of investing is by holding actual chunks of gold. The standardised two forms of this are either gold bullion or gold coins (or shares in these). A gold bullion is a rectangular chunk of gold worth around $750,000 these days, so probably not an investment most people can make or should make unless you are confident of being able to safely store that gold bullion effectively. Gold coin is a much smaller and more affordable size of gold in the shape of – you've guessed it – a coin.

You can also buy percentage shares in both of these types of gold shapes via a gold dealer or online. You can also buy gold by weight too.

There are a whole range of gold brokers online but three that we've particularly interacted with and found to be decent are Bullion Vault, Bullion by Post, and Minted.

Investing in Gold via Jewellery

Investing in gold jewellery is a popular way of investing in gold and the positives are you get to actually use the gold, it looks nice, and you know the gold is safe if you literally have it around your neck, for example.

The downsides are considerable though – especially if you look at it from a pure investment lens:

- You will likely be paying for the workmanship of the piece, not just the gold price.
- You will likely be buying a less than completely pure 24 carat gold piece – as 24 carat is very soft and easily scratches so is not usually used for jewellery. Given this, make sure you are not paying 24 carat prices for the jewellery.
- To safely store and insure the gold are an absolute nightmare. Here in London we've had so many Asian households targeted, as burglars know that we like to keep gold in the house.
- When you wear gold, it has the potential to get lost. If you left it in storage, on the other hand, it is less likely to get lost – but then it's not much use as jewellery!
- When you come to sell it, because each piece of jewellery is different, you won't get a standardised price, you'll spend time shopping around and bargaining, and you will likely not get as good a price as a pure gold coin or the like. This is because the buyer knows they will need to melt the gold down to remake something – so they pass that cost on to you.

All in all, if you are buying gold jewellery for jewellery – that's great. If for investment only, then there are probably better ways to invest in gold.

Investing in Gold *ETFs*

- US Gold ETFs: Here is a list of gold ETFs available in the USA. The two italicised ETFs in the list below are not sharia-compliant as they do not actually hold gold. Rather they create the same effect via holding gold futures and options. Everything else is fine. We have included their ticker code in brackets:
  - *Invesco DB Precious Metals Fund (DBP)*
  - GraniteShares Gold Trust (BAR)
  - iShares Gold Trust (IAU)
  - Aberdeen Standard Physical Gold Shares ETF (SGOL)
  - SPDR Gold MiniShares Trust (GLDM)
  - Perth Mint Physical Gold ETF (AAAU)
  - Van Eck Merk Gold Trust (OUNZ)
  - SPDR Gold Trust (GLD)
  - *Invesco DB Gold Fund (DGL)*

- UK Gold ETFs: All of the below ETFs are a way to invest directly in physical gold in the UK:

  - Xetra-Gold (OGLD)
  - WisdomTree Physical Swiss Gold (SGBX)
  - Invesco Physical Gold A (SGLP)
  - iShares Physical Gold ETC (SGLN)
  - WisdomTree Physical Swiss Gold (OGZU)
  - Xtrackers Physical Gold ETC (EUR) (OXA5)
  - Xtrackers Physical Gold ETC (XGLD)
  - WisdomTree Physical Gold (PHGP)
  - Gold Bullion Securities (OGG9)
  - Gold Bullion Securities (GBSS)
  - HANetf The Royal Mint Physical Gold ETC Securities (RMAP)
  - Xtrackers IE Physical Gold ETC Securities (XGDU)

To compare directly between the fee structures for each of these ETFs/ETCs use platforms like www.justetf.com.

Investing in Gold ETFs That Trade in Futures or Options As mentioned above, under Islamic law, most scholars opine that futures or options trading is not permissible (though a small minority disagree). And when it comes to gold and precious commodities in particular, scholars are particularly careful about any deferment in delivery or payment. This is because gold has historically been seen as a currency even if it is not used like that as much these days.

As such, any ETFs or ETCs (Exchange Trade Commodities) are best avoided where they link their return to gold via futures or options holding, and an individual investor certainly shouldn't engage in it.

How to Invest in Gold Mining Stocks and Shares

The other way to invest in gold is to invest in gold mining stocks. This is relatively effective as gold mining stocks naturally rise in price when gold prices rise (as what they are mining is now worth more).

However, if you choose to invest in gold mining stocks, understand that you are buying a company with all its complications and subtleties. You are buying a business and no two businesses are alike. Just like buying Shell or BP isn't the equivalent to buying oil directly, buying gold miners isn't equivalent to buying gold directly.

For each of the below stocks you should check that it is sharia-compliant from a debt perspective. Here's a list of some companies in the FTSE 100 that mine gold:

- Polymetal International
- Antofagasta (does only a little gold mining)
- Fresnillo (does only a little gold mining)
- FTSE 250 Gold Stocks.

Here's a list of companies from the FTSE 250 that mine gold:

- Centamin
- Petropavlovsk
- Highland Gold Mining
- Hochschild Mining (only does a little bit of gold mining)
- Small Cap Gold Stocks.

Finally, you have some smaller companies that also mine gold. Typically, smaller companies are higher risk and higher reward:

- SolGold
- Greatland Gold
- Pan African Resources
- Chaarat Gold Holdings
- Shanta Gold
- Trans-Siberian Gold.

Investing in Gold via *CFDs*, Spread Betting or Other Derivative Products

Investing in CFDs and spread betting is unambiguously haram. This is because there is no real gold trading taking place and the economic effect is exactly symmetrical to that of gambling.

- There's a reason why spread betting has "betting" in the name.

A Note on Other Assets

We have covered a blizzard of different assets and you might be feeling spoilt for choice – but there is more!

So far we have covered the mainstream asset classes, but there are now a number of very compelling alternative asset classes out there that weren't traditionally even considered an investment until recently.

Here is a list of the most prominent ones from among them:

- forestry
- watches
- artwork.

Forestry

Forestry investing has seen a spectacular run over the last decade, generating 10–14% returns year on year. The concept is a really simple one – you own a forest and you harvest the trees in a controlled way every year and plant new trees to replace them. Over time, the value of the underlying land increases and every year your harvest is sold to make profit.

Gresham House is probably the most prominent European forestry fund, with over $6 billion in assets under management today. We recently partnered up with them to offer Cur8 investors access to this unique asset class.

Forestry fund investing in the UK is also really interesting from a tax perspective as, just like investing in startups, the government wants to encourage it. There is no inheritance tax (after holding it for 2 years) or capital gains tax on forestry investing, among other benefits.

Watches

Rolexes, Omegas, and Patek Philippes don't just look good, they are a potentially great investment. The best watches from the best watch companies hold their value and increase yearly. According to expert watch market analysts, the best watches in the market consistently have outperformed the stock market over the last few years, see Figure 14.7.

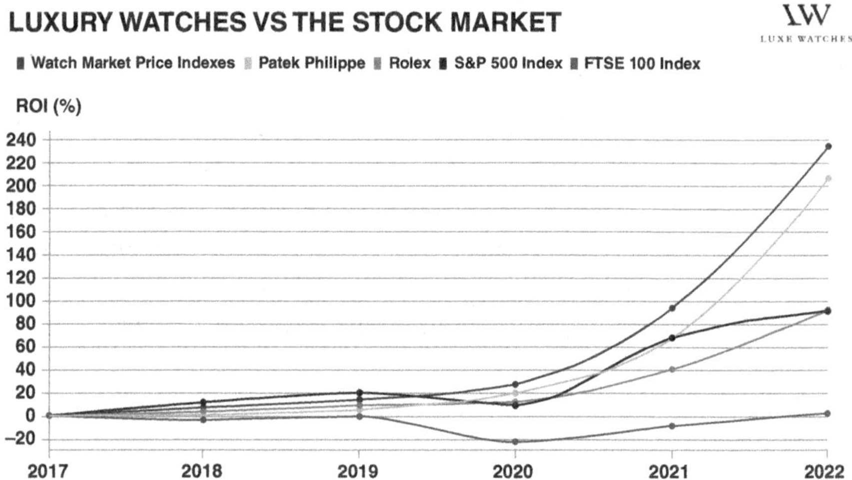

Figure 14.7 The best luxury watch brands to invest in.

Source: Luxe Watches.

The challenge with this asset class is that entry tickets can be pretty high (£50,000 up to £1m or more for the best watches, though entry-level watches can be obtained for around £5,000), the market isn't as liquid and transparent as others (you can't just log in to a broker account and sell your watch), and watches don't "yield" anything like a property or a bond or a stock.

Our view is that watch investing is still a very nascent investment landscape so only enter it if you have a passion for watches and are willing to put the time and money in to navigate this complex world.

Artwork

According to Masterworks analysis in Figure 14.8, contemporary art has outperformed the S&P 500, real estate and gold by a considerable margin over the last few decades. Artwork is a wonderfully uncorrelated asset, i.e. it doesn't get affected by choppiness in other asset class price, and it is a relatively deep market, with over $65 billion transacted in 2021.[15]

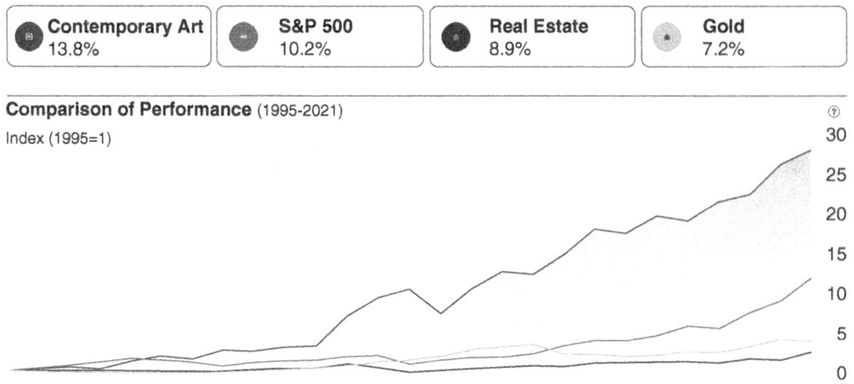

Figure 14.8 Masterworks: comparison of performance, 1995–2021.

Source: Masterworks, Comparison of Performance (1995–2021). https://www.masterworks.com (accessed 23 November 2022). Public Domain.

Masterworks are the clear leader in this space, and have become the largest art buyer globally over the last few years. They are an online platform that gives access to artwork from a $15,000 minimum investment amount and are open to global investors.

A lot of care needs to be taken around the sharia screening of artwork though, both to ensure that immoral scenes are not being depicted and also to understand what the message of the artwork is. Sometimes you can have artwork that is an abstract painting, but then you read into the background and it turns out it is actually a nude painting. Go figure!

How Halal Should You Go?

Having covered a number of asset classes, where there is a clear spectrum of sharia views, the question that arises is: how halal should one go?

Let's identify the salient issues here:

1. In stock investing, there is a range of views on what is acceptable in terms of conventional debt in a business – from 33% debt/market cap ratio, all the way down to 0%.
2. In property investing, there is a question over whether it is permissible to use an Islamic mortgage or not.
3. Also in property, there is the question of whether it should be permissible to use conventional debt when acquiring property in countries where there is no Islamic debt available.
4. In private equity there is the question of "sharia wrappers".

Our view on navigating these issues is to consult three key sources:

1. The AAOIFI standards.
2. Islamic finance scholars we trust.
3. Our conscience.

Stocks

When it comes to stock investing, the AAOIFI very clearly sets out the guidelines and the consensus of Islamic finance scholars in line with those standards. Our personal views are also in line with the aforementioned authorities.

There are certain people who are uncomfortable allowing *any* conventional debt to be held within a company or *any* haram income sources. We have some sympathy for this view – it is after all unambiguously halal if you invest in such companies.

However, scholars have allowed some leeway in order for Muslims to have a sufficiently broad number of companies to invest in such that it is possible to have an investment portfolio at all. If you just screened for zero debt companies that are in halal sectors, you end up with approximately 1500–2000 companies out of a total universe of over 100,000 companies. These zero debt companies tend to be over-weighted with technology and health stocks – both sectors that usually do not take on debt capital due to the long and uncertain maturation cycles of their products.

Property

Ibrahim once went to a dinner and a stranger walked up to him and said: "Aren't Islamic mortgages just like conventional mortgages?"

The man was joking – he'd seen us on TikTok and had decided to introduce himself to us this way to get our attention. We guess it worked – here he is getting a mention in this book.

The topic of Islamic mortgages has been the single most hotly debated subject in Islamic finance over the last two decades. There are two firm camps that are particularly entrenched.

This is a book on halal investing so we won't go through the Islamic mortgage arguments in detail.[16] Our view, in summary, is that Islamic mortgages are permissible and should be used – though there are clearly improvements that can be made to the product from a commercial and sharia perspective.

Running the analysis we outlined above, Islamic mortgages are in line with the AAOIFI standards and are approved by senior Islamic finance scholars globally. Our own consciences are very clear on the subject too. Sh. Qaradawi and the European Council for Fatwa and Research issued their famous fatwa a couple of decades ago opining on the permissibility of taking out a conventional mortgage to buy one house to live in.[17] The shaykh explained that he initially did not view mortgages to be allowed in any instance, however, given the repeated nature of this question from his audience across Western countries, he came to change his position as he concluded that for Muslims in the West, owning at least one home amounted to a necessity or, at the very least, an urgent and persistent need.

The very same fatwa highly encouraged Muslims in the West to work with European banks to quickly come up with a solution to the problem that was in line with the sharia so that conventional mortgages were not needed. Islamic mortgages were the culmination of a long effort by a number of Muslims to do exactly that.

To then critique and abandon them due to debatable *fiqhi* disputes to our mind is not in the broader interest of the Muslim community. What it ultimately does is set the community back. Where we see the market today is that there are two main Islamic banks – Al Rayan and Gatehouse have exited the market (for the foreseeable future it would seem in the case of Al Rayan) – meaning that Muslims suddenly have very few credible options to get their homes financed. The banks have undoubtedly been informed, at least in part, by the continued conflicted perspectives of Muslims with respect to their product and the backlash they consequently face from certain quarters.

There are smaller providers such as Wayhome, Heylo Housing, Primary Finance, and Strideup, but their capacity to meet the demand of Muslim home-buyers is just not there yet.

So, counter-intuitively, those that so vehemently opposed Islamic mortgages for not being Islamic enough, have potentially caused an environment where Muslims are once more faced with the unpalatable option of a conventional mortgage or renting. For us, that is reason alone to support Islamic mortgages.

Sharia Wrappers

The second property issue we identified – namely the taking of conventional debt when investing in countries where there are no Islamic options – is closely tied with the analysis of sharia wrappers for private equity and other non-compliant investments.

The AAOIFI is very cautious about the use of commodity *murabaha* structures and with the use of sharia wrappers generally. Islamic scholars are similarly cautious but do allow it in certain situations. Our conscience suggests to us that to stay away from these matters is the better path – certainly for an everyday investor.

Overarching Impact Considerations

Sharia-compliant investing has historically been seen too much as a tick-box exercise rather than something that should bring us spiritually closer to God. If we want to achieve the latter, then thinking about not just the form of the investment but the substance of it as well becomes imperative.

The first four decades of halal investing and Islamic finance have taken us from having no modern Islamic institutions and financial products to having version one and version two products across the board.

In the next two decades, however, we need to strive to take Islamic investment and financial products to embody the spirit of the sharia, not just the form. *Impact investing* is the term given to this type of investment in the mainstream investment world. It comprises investors taking into consideration environmental, social, and governance (ESG) factors within each investment they make.

An impact fund would typically avoid investing into the following industries:

- Aerospace – due to the carbon footprint brought by flying.
- Defence, and security – due to the moral and political costs associated with creating weapons.
- Alcohol – due to the health and societal harms.
- Recreational drugs – due to the health and societal harms.
- Cigarettes and addictive substance manufacture – due to the health and societal harms.
- Pornographic or illicit materials – due to societal harm and moral considerations.
- Automotive (other than electric).
- Gambling – due to societal harm and moral considerations.
- Construction (other than construction companies with clear carbon-neutral policies).
- Consumer goods.
- Mining.
- Oil and Gas.
- Packaging (due to the pollution and landfill contributions this sector makes).
- Power (other than clean energy).
- Retail – particularly those that pay below minimum wage in developing country factories and encourage "fast fashion".

Sharia-compliant investments can often overlap naturally with impact investing. Muslims do not invest in alcohol or tobacco or illicit industries either, for example. However, the vast majority of sharia funds do not adhere to ESG standards explicitly and so would be comfortable investing in a sharia-compliant oil company, for example.

There are three key ways Muslim investors should be factoring in impact into their investments:

- investing in ESG;
- investing in Muslim countries;
- investing to create the most growth in a country.

Investing in *ESG*

There is now a small, but growing, wave of ESG sentiment within the Islamic finance world, with stocks funds offered by providers such as BIMB Investment Management in Malaysia, Wahed Invest, Arabesque, and Jupiter that adhere to both sharia and ESG standards.

Our expectation is that we will continue to see a steady growth of ESG-compliant sharia funds as customer expectations demand that. All other things being equal, we as Muslim consumers should be demanding that from our sharia fund managers. Looking after the planet, protecting the rights of employees, stamping out corruption and fraud are all values that we do and should aspire to protect.

Investing in Muslim Countries

Foreign investment into a country is one of the key ingredients to a growing economy, and Muslim countries are no different. All too often Muslim investors end up placing the bulk of our investments in Western markets. Whether that is property investments across Europe, the UK, or the USA, stock markets in the same regions and Japan, or private market investments via UK, European or US fund managers, it all ends up growing the pot of already hugely prosperous and developed countries.

It is a crying shame in our opinion that the largest Islamic stock market funds managed by iShares or HSBC are heavily concentrated in the US market and end up solely growing the pot of companies and countries that the rest of the market already funds.

It is far more impactful in our view for Muslim investments to be going into emerging markets and Muslim-majority countries, really leading the development of these ecosystems. The reason for the higher impact is because there just isn't as much general investment going into these countries and ecosystems otherwise. In the developed world the Muslim investment pot is a small drop in the ocean, in a Muslim country Muslim investment is the entire lake.

That is easy for us to say and it is true that the infrastructure is not really there for investors all over the world to be able to easily access Turkish, GCC, Pakistani, African, Malaysian, and Indonesian stock markets. We are hopeful this will get built over time.

In the private markets space, things are a little better with significant emphasis in Pakistan, the GCC, and Turkey to retain local investment monies within the region, and efforts by Western investment managers like Cur8 Capital and Wahed Invest and others to drive part of their offerings towards the direction of Muslim countries. As consumers we should be aware of these issues when it comes to our investment decisions and we should be vocal about our preferences whenever we are asked for our feedback from investment providers.

And entrepreneurs looking for something to work on? The gauntlet has been thrown.

Investing in Investments That Create the Most Growth in an Economy

Investing in a particular geography and within certain constraints can be impactful as we've just discussed, but there are things investors can do that super-charge the impact of any investment. If we revisit our core goal for writing this book and all that we do at Islamic Finance Guru and Cur8 Capital – it is to help Muslims level up financially.

If we are realistic about doing that quickly, then it is necessary to focus investment in those sectors that are likely to grow over the next few decades and to ride that wave and become leaders in that space. There are multiple examples before us. South Korea rode the wave of technology and electrical appliances. Israel rode the wave of cybersecurity, tech, and software. Germany rode the wave of heavy industry, health technology, and automotives. India focused on the software industry. The list goes on.

Similarly, the Muslim community should identify key areas of growth over the next decade and systematically invest into these sectors. These could include:

- Biotechnology
- Web 3.0 and the Metaverse
- Open banking and Banking as a Service
- Clean energy and climate tech
- Quantum computing
- Artificial intelligence and machine learning.

The most high impact ways to invest in these areas in our view are:

1. To actually become an entrepreneur and look to materially progress innovation directly.
2. To back the startups and entrepreneurs working on groundbreaking projects at an early stage.

The first option requires an enormous amount of sacrifice and isn't right for everyone, while the second is higher risk, given the higher risk associated with startup investing.

Whether the entrepreneurial route is right for you is a question for you to decide. Whether startup investing is right for you and how much you should invest in startups is a question of weighing up life goals, timelines, risk appetites, and portfolio construction, which brings us nicely on to Part IV!

PART IV

How to Construct a Robust Portfolio

15 Portfolio Theory

It is time to return to Figure 8.6, which we shared in Chapter 8, where we outlined three basic types of portfolio you could end up constructing. In this chapter we will cover:

1. Why having a goal for your investments is key to portfolio construction.
2. What kind of goals you should have and the particular considerations for each of these goals.
3. The role time horizons play in your asset selection.

Having a Goal Is 80% of the Solution

Jemima was a friend of my sister's[1] and was introduced to me to have a chat about her investments.

"Jemima", I said, "you're keen to invest now clearly, as you've asked to have a chat with me."

"Yes."

"What are you investing for? Is there anything particular you are saving up for?"

Jemima made a noncommittal noise. "Nothing in particular, I just want to park my money somewhere."

"The problem with that, Jemima, is that if you don't know *what* you are investing for, it is very hard to create a portfolio that achieves that thing."

Jemima shrugged. "I guess I want to save for my two kids. They're both under five right now, but that would definitely be something I want to do for at least some of my money. I'd rather not have university fees wipe me out at the time."

I smiled: "Now we're talking. With that single statement you have told me some very important things. First, that you want to save a portion of your money (not all) for university for two children in roughly 15 years' time. Second, how much you will require to invest now in order to have the kinds of amounts you need at the time your kids go to university. Third, the liquidity levels and risk levels that you would be willing to tolerate with your investments."

Having a goal for your investments is really important because it gives you a North Star to aim at with your money. Absent this North Star, you really don't have anything to guide you in terms of your risk profile, your time horizons, which country you should invest in, and the mix of investments you should make.

But with a tangible goal in mind, things become a lot clearer, like they did for Jemima. And, like Jemima, you can even have multiple goals for your portfolio if you like.

What Goals Should You Have for Your Money?

We do two hours every Friday of 10-minute calls that anyone can book in. Over the years we have spoken to literally thousands of people about their investments and the surprising thing is that there are actually very few practical goals that most of us share when it comes to our money. They are:

1. Saving for a rainy day fund.
2. Saving for retirement.
3. Saving for children's university fees.
4. Saving for a house.
5. Saving to buy a particular luxury (e.g. a holiday).
6. Saving for an additional income.

There will certainly be others that some people will have that are unique to them, but those are much less common.

Let's talk through the salient factors for each of these goals.

Saving for a Rainy Day Fund

A rainy day fund must be on-hand and available when unforeseen circumstances crop up. That means that it must be invested into liquid and safe investments such as savings accounts with very low volatility investments such as REITs.[2]

For a detailed breakdown on rainy day funds, see Chapter 5.

Saving for Retirement

For almost everyone, this goal will be a consideration, however, it will manifest itself differently for each person based on:

1. How many years you have left till retirement:
   (a) The longer you have, the more risk you can take.
2. What government schemes are available for you to invest in:
   (a) Government schemes often come with significant benefits but typically restrict your access to retirement money until a certain age.
3. How much you already have in your retirement pot:
   (a) The more you have, the less aggressive you need to be going forward to get to your goal.
4. How much you need to live off during retirement:
   (a) Rather obviously, the more you need, the more you'll need to save now.
5. What you plan to do during your retirement:
   (a) If you plan to do a lot of travelling, that needs to be factored in.

For those who are just starting to engage with this goal and have plenty of years ahead of you, here are the key factors you should think about now:

- Be aggressive early on in your investments as you will have time to recover if things don't pan out, while if things do pan out, you could end up sitting on some spectacular returns.
- Take advantage of government schemes as much as possible but leave some of your savings aside to invest in things that are more easily accessible too.
- Run a calculation using any of the plethora of online calculators to figure out how much you should be investing every month in order to hit your goals.

For those who are much closer to retirement and perhaps coming to the game a bit late, here are the key considerations for you:

- Try to make up for lost time with government schemes and get onto them as soon as possible.
- Save aggressively – especially if you are below your target numbers. You are still earning and that will become harder the older you get.
- Ensure that your housing circumstances are as risk-free and budgeted as possible. Ideally you will have cleared your mortgage by the time you retire and have the necessary budget to maintain your household going forward.

Retirement is a complex topic with many other factors to consider. For more reading on this go to Chapter 4 where we cover retirement in a lot of detail.

Saving for Your Children's University Fees

A decade of investing is roughly the length of one full economic cycle (or the time between one crisis and the next, the cynic might say).

When saving for your children, you have the distinct advantage of knowing exactly how long you need to save for and how much you will need to save. Assuming you start investing the month your child is born, you have roughly 18 years – or two economic cycles – to get around £100k that you will need to pay for your child's university fees.

In the first decade, you can afford to be more aggressive – investing in illiquid assets that are higher return. In the second decade, you should slowly dial it down into safer and more liquid investments until your child hits 18 and you need to make your first payments.

The other thing to bear in mind when saving for children is that there are often government schemes to contribute towards investments, or at least not pay tax on. In the UK there is a saving and investment account called a JISA, or a Junior ISA This is like the ISA that each individual adult has, but a JISA has a tax-free limit of £9000, rather than the £20,000 for an ISA.

Saving for a House

There are three distinct phases to buying a house: aspirational, attainable, and within reach.

When you start your house-saving journey you might be so far off having enough to buy a house that this goal is just an aspiration at this point. In this state, you should run the numbers and figure out if you can realistically save money every year and be in a position to buy a house in ten years' time. If the answer to that analysis is "yes", and you are happy to put in a decade's worth of saving, then do so.

If the answer is "no" – or you want to get to the goal faster, then the next consideration is weighing up which of the more risky investments you would be willing to make in order to speed up the achievement of this goal.

If, on the other hand, you have now less than 5 years of saving to get to your goal, it is fair to say that your goal is now "attainable". In this scenario we would not make high-risk investments or foolhardy decisions. We would look to slowly shepherd your wealth from aggressive to moderate risk all the way up to having the money to buy your house.

Finally, you are now a year or two out from buying your own home. At this point you should be holding cash or a savings account and taking no risks whatsoever. This is because you can't afford the market volatility to wipe out the savings you have made just when you have enough to pay for the home.

Saving for a Luxury

Luxuries manifest themselves differently for different people. Some people like cars, others pianos, and yet others like watches. Whatever your luxury of choice, the investment strategy to get there remains simple.

First, you need to make sure you can actually afford the purchase. There is no point starting to save for a Bugatti Veyron when you barely save £10k a year. You will die before you have enough money to pay for that car.

Second, you need to set yourself a date on which you'd like to make your purchase. Working back from this will give you both your timeline and the risk profile you will need to go for in order to secure the kind of returns you need to hit your goal.

Saving for Additional Income

A client at Cur8 Capital uses one of our historic investments to fund 50% of his retirement. The investment in question yields him approximately 11% per annum and pays out every two years. Our client knows he only needs £40,000 to live off, and he gets £20,000 through his pension. The remaining £20,000 per annum is generated through his investment into the 11%-yield investment.

Our client can do this because he has already saved £200k. An 11% annual return on that gives you £22k – the amount he is looking for.

Like our client, when saving for additional income, you will be looking to invest into low- or medium-risk investments that give a regular cash yield. How much income you settle for will depend on your risk appetite. In the case of our client, he is willing to be quite aggressive so that we can unlock a higher return – but he can do that because he knows he already has a wider portfolio that will more than carry him along anyway.

The Role Time Horizons Play in Battle Plans

As the more discerning among our readers will have surmised, hitting your goals is all a matter of matching the right timelines with the right risk appetites and the sought-after return profiles.

Figure 11.1 nicely illustrates how two of those factors interplay for the most common asset classes. The higher the risk, the higher the reward.

Now, if we factor in liquidity and time horizons too, we get something like Table 15.1.

Table 15.1 Overall risk and return profile

Risk	Return	Liquidity	Time horizons
Low	Low	Very liquid	Short-term (a few months to a couple of years)
Medium	Medium	Somewhat liquid	Medium-term (2–5 years of expected hold period)
High	High	Not liquid	Long-term (5+ years expected hold period)

The highest-risk investments are the hardest to extricate yourself from and will take the longest to bear fruit. An example of this would be investing in venture capital. Startups are hard to exit and will take years to grow.

At the other end of the spectrum you have saving accounts. They don't return very much, but are low risk and you can withdraw out of them whenever you like.

Going back now to Figure 8.6. Another way to characterise any portfolio is one made up of multiple goals working in tandem. The average person will simultaneously be going for multiple things at any point. For example, they could have the following mix of goals:

- saving for a house (in the next 5 years);
- saving for kids' university fees (15 years left);
- an emergency fund (need to add in 3 more months of runway);
- going on hajj (next 5 years).

Now if we are to apply the learnings from this chapter to those goals, we might end up with something like Table 15.2.

Table 15.2 Goals and investment decisions

Goal	Investment decision
Saving for a house	Medium-risk, medium-term
Kids' university fees	High-risk, long-term
Emergency fund	Low-risk, short-term
Going on hajj	Medium-risk, medium-term

Next, we put the precise numbers for each of the goals and what it'll take to achieve them. Where there isn't enough money to hit all the goals, we will need to weigh up which of the goals are most important to us. With this particular mix of goals, it is likely we'll end up with a medium-risk portfolio as outlined above.

Now that we have considered portfolio construction theory, let's now move into application.

16 Case Study: Conservative

Let's now take some example personas and work through constructing their portfolios together. Remember, there is never a magic bullet or exact formula when constructing a portfolio. As we discussed at the outset of the book, portfolios are wonderfully individual in that they are a unique blend of your goals, risk appetite, and, to a certain extent, your personal preferences.

Let's start with Martin. Martin is a high-earning expat with significant savings. He's 40 and wants to retire by the time he's 50. He manages to save around £50k per year and his key focus is becoming financially independent so he can retire.

There are a few key facts that are important to establish in order to construct this portfolio.

- Martin estimates that he needs £60,000 (after any fees or taxes) to live on every single year.
- He already has around £200,000 saved up.
- He has no short-term needs for any money.

Take some time to have a think yourself on how you would go about constructing this portfolio taking everything you have learned into consideration. As a reminder, here are some key mantras to remember:

- Risk is proportionate to reward.
- Never lock yourself into an investment when you know you need the cash sooner than the investment will mature.
- Managing risk does not mean avoiding risk altogether.

Go ahead and write down how you would construct a portfolio for Martin without looking at our version. Then come back and compare our thoughts with yours.

What We Would Advise

There are vital bits of information in this case study that mean a high-risk approach here would be pointless. Martin is on track to save £500,000 over the next ten years anyway, and is already sitting on a good pot of money.

The goal is clear: build up an investment stream that safely and passively generates the £60,000 per year that Martin needs to live. That being said, another key bit of information is that Martin is 40 and likely still has 40–50 years of his life to fund. It's vital therefore that his investments keep up with inflation.

Our suggestion for this portfolio would be a property-heavy approach. If Martin can invest in property over the next decade, he can enjoy retired life living off the rental income.

If he allocated 50% of his portfolio to property, he would have around £350,000 worth of cash to gradually drip in over the next 10 years (£250k in savings over ten years plus half of his existing £200k savings is equal to £350k). This could be deposit money each time and use leverage, e.g. 4 deposits of £87,500 purchasing properties each around the £500,000 mark. Assuming Martin could get 6% net yield from his properties, he would be getting £120,000 per year (£30,000 from each property) once this is in full flow.

If, for instance, Martin decided to buy a property every 2.5 years, he would end up with properties with £2m and a mortgage liability of £1.65m (as he paid £350k in deposits). With income of £120,000 per year he could comfortably pay back £60,000 per year for the next 25 years or so to pay down his mortgage liabilities.

This would likely happen quicker as, over time, the rental income should increase and Martin can become more aggressive in paying down the mortgage. Martin could also choose to up the 50% to pay more in deposits and end up with less liability.

With the remaining 50% of the portfolio, a solid stocks portfolio would also make a lot of sense. Martin has time on his side, so the chances are he will gain on average 10% per year investing in the stock market. This will help Martin to beat inflation and continue to grow his already sizeable pot.

We also think it would be prudent for Martin to have around 10% of his portfolio allocated towards venture capital, crypto, and other such high-risk, high-reward investments. This is because with this kind of allocation, even if the investments completely failed, it would not derail Martin's goals. However, if they were to succeed, it would massively help Martin and accelerate his journey considerably. Therefore, our advice is given in Table 16.1.

Table 16.1 The conservative approach

Goal	Investment decision	Amount (£)	Potential investments	Time period (years)	Expected amount on exit (£)
Regular income	Low-risk, long-term	350,000	Property	10	2,000,000[1]
Portfolio growth	Medium-risk, long-term	250,000	Stock market	10	676,760[2]
Portfolio growth	High-risk, long-term	50,000	Venture capital	5–10	£200,000[3]

17 Case Study: Moderate

Madiha is a 35-year-old mother of two boys – one aged 5 and the other 6. She's got healthy savings of £30,000, she works as a dental hygienist and has goals of going for hajj in the short term and saving for her children's university fees in the long term, as well as building up a pension.

Her husband also works and they have recently bought their first home with the help of an Islamic mortgage. Madiha's husband takes care of day-to-day expenses as well as covering the monthly mortgage payments.

Madiha earns around £40,000 a year and ends up saving around £20,000 of that. That means, over the next 5 years she will need to deploy £100,000 in total, in addition to the £30,000 she already has.

Here, the goals are really clear. In the short term, she wants to go for hajj and in the long term she wants to build up around £150,000 to be able to pay for both her kids' university fees and she also wants to put any excess towards her retirement.

For the short-term hajj savings (let's assume it is £10,000), depending on when exactly she needs to pay the tour operator, she could lock this away in a savings account and make a small return. She should take care to make sure she locks into a savings account for only that amount of time that allows her to meet her hajj payments as they become due.

For the long term, she's actually got a considerable way to go. Although she has at least 10 years, she's starting from a base of around £20,000 and she needs 7.5× this if she wants to hit £150,000.

Here's how her initial deployment of £30,000 could look (Table 17.1). Then there's the matter of the additional £20,000 in savings that she has coming in annually too. A portion of this definitely needs to go into savings for her children's university fees as she's currently short on her target there. The remaining amount should then be allotted to her final goal – building a pension pot.

Table 17.1 The moderate approach

Goal	Investment decision	Amount (£)	Potential investments	Time period (years)	Expected amount on exit (£)
Saving for hajj	Low-risk, short-term	10,000	Savings account or sukuk fund	1	10,400
Kids' university fees	High-risk, long-term	20,000	Venture capital fund or property development projects	10	100,000
Pension pot	Blend of medium-risk, long-term and high-risk, long-term	0	N/A	N/A	N/A

The other thing to factor in here is that Madiha is in a stable household where her husband covers a lot of household expenses per traditional Islamic teaching. This means she can actually take a bit more risk than others who have dependents directly reliant on them financially.

Here's how the deployment could look after 5 years (note, we have removed the hajj saving goal, as she has now achieved that) (Table 17.2).

Assuming Madiha maintains a return of 7% per annum consistently over 20 years, and every year she adds in an extra £20,000, she'll end up with around £900,000 in her pension pot.

Table 17.2 The moderate approach after 5 years

Goal	Investment decision	Amount (£)	Potential investments	Time period (years)	Expected amount on exit (£)
Kids' university fees	High risk, long-term	40,000	Venture capital fund or property development projects	10	200,000
Pension pot	Blend of medium risk, long-term and high risk, long-term	80,000	Rental property, stocks, and property development	20	900,000

A £900,000 pot can very easily generate around £60,000 per annum as income – more than enough for Madiha to retire on.

As you can see, being consistent and disciplined with a relatively simple investment strategy over a few decades can return some pretty stellar returns and meet your key financial goals.

The key lesson to learn from Madiha's example is the virtue of starting early and matching investment goals with asset types that have the potential to meet those goals.

18 Case Study: Aggressive

Ali is a young man, just starting out in employment and because he is just starting out he can afford to take a fair amount of risk.

The first thing he should do is to focus on clearing any short-term debts and building his rainy day fund which he can keep either as cash or in an account where he can access the cash straightaway.

Ali has some clear short-term and medium-term goals. In no particular order they are:

- To get married (approximately £10,000–£20,000 for the wedding and associated costs).
- Buy a first house (expected required deposit of £30,000).
- Enjoy life while he is young with holidays and other nice things (expect to spend £5,000 per annum on these).
- Go for hajj with his future wife (expect to be £20,000 in total).

Ali's situation is that he is regularly saving money due to the fact that he is living with parents and therefore able to save £2,500 a month from his salary. Ali has around £10,000 in savings, and the short- and medium-term goals add up to around £75,000 combined. It would take him just under three years in his current situation to save that amount of money but of course once he gets married and buys a house, his savings will reduce drastically.

Ali is therefore on a quest to amass as much capital in as short a period of time as he can. This is always dangerous as it can lead to falling for scams, investing in the completely wrong things, and completely blowing up one's entire account.

We would therefore propose an approach here which is aggressive in nature, but limits the potential for a blow-up (Table 18.1).

Table 18.1 The aggressive approach

Goal	Investment decision	Amount (£)	Potential investments	Time period (years)	Expected amount on exit (£)
Marriage	Medium-risk, short-term	10,000	High-yielding sharia debt finance or property development project	2	13,225
Deposit	High-risk, long-term	20,000	Venture capital fund or property development projects	10	100,000
Holidays/ lifestyle	High-risk,[1] short-term	5,000	Stock trading	1	12,590[2]
Hajj	Medium-risk, long-term	10,000	Stock market	10	26,000[3]

Parting Thoughts

Over the years we've been privileged to talk to thousands of people about their wealth and their relationship to money and we have found that there are four types of people that crop up time and again when it comes to their relationship with money:

1. Those who have little interest in money other than as a necessary evil useful to achieve their goals.
2. Those who enjoy investing and entrepreneurship.
3. Those who are aggressive, risk-taking, and decisive.
4. Those who are indecisive and slow.

Character (1) will do perfectly fine as long as they make the necessary time to put their investment on autopilot.

Investor (2) will thrive, as they will naturally end up hunting down the better opportunities and unlocking higher returns.

Investor (3) can often have things work out for them and often the biggest profits and losses return to them. However, this group would do well not to get too optimistic and not to rush any investment.

Of this list, the worst of them is investor (4). Anything worth doing is worth doing fast, and with investment you end up actually losing money through indecisiveness.

So as our first bit of parting advice, please don't finish reading this book and then not invest for another few years. Use this moment as a turning point in your financial life and build up that momentum and urgency.

Our second bit of parting advice is not to measure yourself against anyone else. Investment success can come in many different shapes and sizes and the whole dance of investment is an art not a science. Everyone has their own relationship with money and their own life goals. Money and investments are a tool to be used to achieve yours, not a lodestone to hang around your neck.

Our third and final advice is to keep learning. The journey of investment has begun for you – you now have a strong base on which to build. But, like any expert in any profession knows, when you encounter a new problem or situation, you have to do your research afresh and deepen your knowledge. Take asset classes and investment strategies step by step and master each steadily, basing your actions on sound research you continue to do all the while. We have included a "Helpful Resources" chapter and a list of suggested readings in the "Continuing Education" chapter at the back of this book to give you some ideas of what else you might like to read.

It has been a privilege taking you through the essentials of halal investing and personal finance. We wish you all the best in your journeys and may Allah shower his blessings upon you and your investments!

Notes

Introduction

1. We'll be using "we" for much of this book but every so often we'll be speaking in the first person. Where we do this, we'll note who is speaking. In this instance, it is Ibrahim.
2. If we had known it would grow as big as it has done, we might have spent a bit more thought on the name. A mate of ours had a website called "transferguru" and it was about money transfer. So, in a leap of imagination, we thought to replace the word "transfer" with "Islamic finance", thus Islamic Finance Guru was born.
3. *Qur'an*. 92: 8–11. https://quran.com/92/8-11 (accessed 14 December 2022).
4. J. Davies, R. Lluberas, and A. Shorrocks, *Global Wealth Report* (13th edition) (Zurich: Credit Suisse Research Institute, 2022). https://www.credit-suisse.com/media/assets/corporate/docs/about-us/research/publications/global-wealth-report-2022-en.pdf (accessed 14 December 2022).
5. Naturally we assume you will be regularly revisiting this book, given the soft spot in your heart we will have won through notes like this one.
6. Halal Investment Checklist and Financial Journey. http://www.islamicfinanceguru.com/resources/investment-checklist.
7. We took our own lead and decided to Google Bulgarian tax incentives and we found a ton. Point proved!

Chapter 1

1. Never let it be said that we cannot flog a metaphor long enough.
2. Not to be confused with "getting even", a pursuit that is far more difficult and often comes with long criminal sentences.

Chapter 2

1. https://www.freeagent.com/.
2. We are keen to keep this book's size and weight below the level where you require a weightlifting belt to safely read it.
3. Should I Buy or Rent? Calculator: https://buy-rent.mortgage.islamicfinanceguru.com.

Chapter 3

1. Sahih Al Bukhari 2738, Book 55, Hadith 1. https://sunnah.com/bukhari:2738 (accessed 14 December 2022).
2. UK Government. How Inheritance Tax Works: Thresholds, Rules and Allowances. (2022). https://www.gov.uk/inheritance-tax (accessed 12 December 2022).
3. UK Government. Making a Will. (2022). https://www.gov.uk/make-will (accessed 12 December 2022).
4. C. Barratt. Are You Due a Share of £50bn in Lost Assets? *The Financial Times*, 21 July 2022. https://www.ft.com/content/e3e91313-fc53-495b-9281-0e80096c0a4b (accessed 29 October 2022).
5. The Best 3 Free UK Islamic Wills – and When They're Right for You: https://www.islamicfinanceguru.com/articles/personal-finance/the-best-3-free-uk-islamic-wills-and-when-theyre-right-for-you.
6. Islamic Will Guides and FAQs: https://www.islamicfinanceguru.com/guides-and-faqs/islamic-will-guides-and-faqs.

Chapter 4

1. We will discuss this later.
2. We will cover this concept later.
3. Pension legal opinion letter: https://f.hubspotusercontent-eu1.net/hubfs/24915384/IslamicFinanceGuru_September2021/PDF/Sharia-op-v2.pdf.

Chapter 5

1. Burial shrouds.
2. B. Feur, First-Time Investors Now Make Up 15% of Retail Market. *Institutional Investor*, 8 April 2021. https://www.institutionalinvestor.com/article/b1r9ycrxwlld7j/First-Time-Investors-Now-Make-Up-15-of-Retail-Market (accessed 13 December 2022).
3. Long-term users of Muslim matchmaking sites will know this feeling.
4. They spout a lot of bull sometimes too.
5. Try never to marry a bear. This is actually a serious point. All things considered, a generally optimistic attitude in the investment world is a better attitude to have. It means you are open to possibilities. We also have a vague suspicion that bears likely won't gift their spouses well. You have been warned.
6. Or, if you're like Ibrahim's brother, you just don't repair your car. Once Ibrahim borrowed his car to discover that you had to sit on the driver's seat at a particular angle in order for the car seat beeping to stay quiet. Move a fraction, and off it went. Four intense hours of driving later, Ibrahim handed the car back with strong exhortations to Mustafa to get it fixed. A year later, he borrowed the car again, and the problem persisted. Ibrahim got Mustafa into deep trouble with their father that night. A great victory.

Chapter 6

1. *Qur'an*. 2:278–279. https://quran.com/2?startingVerse=279 (accessed 14 December 2022).
2. Sahih Muslim 1015 (trans. I. Khan.) Book 12, Hadith 83. https://sunnah.com/muslim:1015 (accessed 14 December 2022).
3. I. Khan, Is My Job Haram? Islamicfinanceguru Ltd, 21 May 2021. https://www.islamicfinanceguru.com/articles/personal-finance/is-my-job-haram (accessed 12 December 2022).
4. Aviva. https://www.direct.aviva.co.uk/myfuture/FundChoice/FundHub/B1N94Q4 (accessed 30 October 2022).
5. Note that you shouldn't look to make non-compliant ETF investments subsequently and look to purify those. Only invest in sharia-compliant ETFs, now you know.

Part II

1. Ibrahim.

Chapter 7

1. As an aside, shorting is seen as impermissible from a sharia standpoint so don't go getting any ideas from this!
2. However, there is such a thing as too much research too. The reason so many people prevaricate too long over investing is that they don't actually know what they want out of it. If you don't know what you want out of something, how can you expect to know what to invest in? This is like staring eggs and flour in the face without knowing you want to ultimately make pancakes.
3. By the way, it might be the correct decision to have sold out of your position, but the way you decided that was not justifiable – it was just emotion. That is not a good basis to make decisions.
4. Mohsin.
5. Peter Lynch and John Rothchild, *One Up on Wall Street: How to Use What You Already Know to Make Money in the Market* (New York: Simon & Schuster, 2000).
6. Not least because if you start to make £2000 direct debits out to a certain "A J Bell" every month, your husband or wife may start enquiring who this is.
7. Ibrahim's wife is quick to remind him of his car crash investment in a company called KOOV, which promised to be the Indian ASOS, but delivered only heartache and losses.

Chapter 8

1. If you want to read more on this, we have written about it extensively on our website. You can find the various articles on this at: https://www.islamicfinanceguru.com/guides-and-faqs/islamic-mortgage-guides-and-faqs.
2. See Part I.
3. UK Government. Tax When You Get A Pension (2022). https://www.gov.uk/tax-on-pension/tax-free (accessed 12 December 2022).

4. The People's Pension, Minimum Pension Age Change (2022). https://thepeoplespension.co.uk/minimum-pension-age-change (accessed 12 December 2022).
5. If that is not reason alone to grimly hang on till the bitter end, we don't know what is.
6. Ibrahim's late grandfather, wheelchair-bound and very hard of hearing, famously got very angry with the local registrar at his citizenship ceremony and refused to accept British citizenship because he couldn't hear the oath he had to say. Eventually, after much difficulty, he was persuaded in a side room to continue, but not before he had made it clear he was only doing it for us.
7. Please see Chapter 13 in Part III dedicated to property, in particular, the section on getting access to REITs for examples of such options.
8. UK Government, Income Tax Rates and Personal Allowances (2022–2023). https://www.gov.uk/income-tax-rates (accessed November 2022).

Chapter 9

1. Mohsin.
2. There is a well-known crypto scam where deep-fake technology is used to impersonate someone like Elon Musk over a live YouTube stream. You are joined in this livestream by 25,000 bots, so you feel like this livestream must be legitimate. You are promised a large amount of bitcoin but first you have to send some bitcoin to a particular wallet to test out things. You never see that bitcoin again.

Chapter 10

1. This is illegal, so it would be pretty foolish of us to write a book encouraging this!

Chapter 11

1. "Leveraged" means a property that is financed through financing, therefore reducing the equity a buyer needs to put down initially.

Chapter 12

1. B. Sulivan, Average Stock Market Return. Forbes Media, LLC. 17 August 2022. https://www.forbes.com/advisor/investing/average-stock-market-return (accessed 12 December 2022).
2. A. Walker, Do Property Prices Double Every 10 Years? Monoperty. (2022). https://monoperty.com/do-property-prices-double-every-10-years (accessed 12 December 2022).
3. Peter Lynch and John Rothchild, *One Up on Wall Street: How to Use What You Already Know to Make Money in the Market* (New York: Simon & Schuster, 2000).
4. Mohsin.
5. Jim Slater, *The Zulu Principle* (Petersfield: Harriman House, 1992).
6. Benjamin Graham, *The Intelligent Investor* (New York: Harper and Brothers, 1949).
7. Mohsin.
8. Available at: https://www.berkshirehathaway.com/letters/letters.html.
9. Lynch and Rothchild, *One Up on Wall Street*, op. cit.
10. Mohsin.
11. Mohsin.
12. Slater, *The Zulu Principle*, op. cit.
13. Stan Weinstein, *Secrets for Profit in Bull and Bear Markets* (New York: McGraw-Hill, 1988).
14. William O'Neil, *How to Make Money in Stocks: A Winning System in Good Times or Bad* (4th edition) (New York: McGraw-Hill. 2009).
15. Exchange rate fees are the sneaky way "zero commission" apps make a healthy amount of money per transaction.
16. Quantofasia. 75% of S&P 500 Returns Come From Dividends: 1980–2019. GFM Asset Management, 25 July 2019. https://gfmasset.com/2019/07/75-of-sp-500-returns-come-from-dividends-1980-2019 (accessed 12 December 2022).
17. Unless with an Islamic bank.
18. This is on top of, or in lieu of the ways already listed for zero-fee brokers previously.
19. F. Mufti Adam,. Is Online CFD Trading Permissible? Darul Fiqh. https://darulfiqh.com/is-online-cfd-trading-permissible-2/ (accessed 12 December 2022).

20. The other thing to watch out for with less well-traded stocks is the spread can be enormous, i.e. the broker fees for executing the trade can sometimes be between 5–10% of the entire transaction.
21. Otherwise known as the Accounting and Auditing Organization for Islamic Financial Institutions.
22. We think that if you are a tiny investor in an enormous company, then due to your negligible impact you can forego this step.
23. Graham, *The Intelligent Investor*, op. cit.
24. Apps like Zoya, Islamicly, Musaffa, and others have made progress in this direction.
25. See National Zakat Foundation's analysis here: https://nzf.org.uk/knowledge/pensions.
26. IFG Zakat Calculator: https://www.islamicfinanceguru.com/zakat.

Chapter 13

1. Monoperty.
2. Ibrahim was once called up by a neighbour of a new buy-to-let his family had bought the day before, and the neighbour proceeded to fire swear word after swear word at him. It transpired that her nephew had been playing with Ibrahim's then-tenant's child and had tripped and hurt himself in the garden. There's a lot of nonsense like this that goes into being a landlord.
3. Houses in Multiple Occupation. This is the fancy name for a house where multiple individuals rent out rooms.
4. Ibrahim and his family have flipped four properties to date, each at a profit, but with plenty of frogs kissed along that particular journey. At times it seemed that every other builder in Leicester was of the amphibious persuasion.
5. Literally, this is a good idea. Property development with one's eyes shut is particularly challenging.
6. Mohsin.
7. National Zakat Foundation. Zakat on Property and Other Fixed Assets, 29 November 2021. https://nzf.org.uk/knowledge/zakat-on-property (accessed 12 December 2022).

8. An example of an exponential scale-up would be most technology companies. For each new search that takes place on Google, they don't have to attend a particular amount of staff to their team to service that. Effectively the marginal cost of a new item of produce becomes near zero.
9. Franklin Templeton. Franklin Global Sukuk Fund (accessed 30 November 2022). https://www.franklintempleton.co.uk/our-funds/price-and-performance/products/16214/Z/franklin-global-sukuk-fund/LU0792756115#performance (accessed 5 December 2022).

Chapter 14

1. Finoa. Crypto Adoption Among Retail and Institutional Investors in 2022, 29 September 2022. https://www.finoa.io/blog/crypto-adoption-growth (accessed 7 November 2022).
2. B. A. al-Marghinani, (530/1135). Al-Hidayah.
3. The other point to note here is that the distinction between positions 2 and 3 may not appear wholly crucial, and most of the time it isn't – especially where parties contract privately to designate X a currency for the purposes of their contract (even where others do not accept it as such yet). However, there are differences which are relevant, particularly in the ICO context. A currency exchange must not be deferred and must be hand-to-hand, whereas an asset exchange can involve either deferment of payment or delivery (but not both at the same time).
4. IFG. Wise up with Halal Crypto. https://www.islamicfinanceguru.com/crypto.
5. C. Wagner, Crypto Venture Funding Hits Year-Low in Q3 2022: Galaxy. Blockworks Advisors LLC., 28 October 2022. https://blockworks.co/news/crypto-venture-funding-hits-year-low-in-q3-2022-galaxy (accessed 13 December 2022).
6. M. Speiser, How Much Is Your Unicorn Investment Worth? AngelList, 24 March 2022. https://www.angellist.com/blog/median-multiple-unicorn-investment (accessed 13 December 2022).
7. C. Korver, Picking Winners Is a Myth, but the Powerlaw Is Not. *Medium*, 29 May 2018. https://medium.com/ulu-ventures/successful-vcs-need-at-least-one-outlier-to-have-a-well-performing-fund-c122c799dfb3 (accessed 15 November 2022).

8. *Forbes*. Profile: Larry Ellison. (2022). https://www.forbes.com/profile/larry-ellison/?sh=4dc1732924c2 (accessed November 2022).
9. G. Kay, Elon Musk's Private Signal Chats with Famed Investor Marc Andreessen Show How Short and Sweet Deal-Making Can Be If You're a Big Fish. *Business Insider*, 29 September 2022. https://www.businessinsider.com/elon-musk-signal-messages-marc-andreessen-deal-making-twitter-investment-2022-9?r=US&IR=T (accessed November 2022).
10. Accounting and Auditing Organization for Islamic Financial Institutions. Shari'ah Standards. Dar Al Maiman. No 12: Sharikah (Musharakah), and Modern Corporations. Provision 3/1/5/5, p. 333.
11. International Islamic Fiqh Academy. Resolutions and Recommendations (2000). Resolution No. 63/1/7: Concerning Financial Markets, p. 129.
12. M. Al-Suhaibani, and N. Naifar, Islamic Corporate Governance: Risk-Sharing and Islamic Preferred Shares. *Journal of Business Ethics* 124(2014): 623–632.
13. Calculated using BullionByPost gold pricing on 22 November 2022. https://www.bullionbypost.co.uk/gold-price//gold-price-history.
14. I. M. Majah, Hadith 2187, Chapter: 14, The Chapters on Business Transactions. https://ahadith.co.uk/chapter.php?cid=170&page=3&rows=25 (accessed 23 November 2022).
15. The Art Market 2022, an Art Basel and UBS Report by Dr Clare McAndrew, accessible at https://www.artbasel.com/about/initiatives/the-art-market.
16. For our views on the subject, you can visit: https://www.islamicfinanceguru.com/guides-and-faqs/islamic-mortgage-guides-and-faqs.
17. European Council for Fatwa and Research. Final Statements: The Fourth Ordinary Session of the European Council for Fatwa. (1999). https://www.e-cfr.org/blog/2017/11/04/fourth-ordinary-session-european-council-fatwa-research (accessed November 2022).

Chapter 15

1. Ibrahim's sister.
2. Real Estate Investment Trusts – effectively listed real estate funds that give you access to a basket of real estate assets through a stock.

Chapter 16

1. Assuming that the investment money is used for deposits and this is the worth of the properties.
2. Assuming 10 years at 10% growth each year with the growth re-invested.
3. Assuming a 4× cash-on-cash return which is about right for a well-performing VC fund, but not accounting for fees.

Chapter 18

1. There is an argument that this should be low risk since this money is earmarked already, however, we have put this down as a high-risk investment as, in reality, even the worst case scenario of capital blow-up, Ali has not really lost anything significant other than a nice holiday. But if he does well, he can finance his lifestyle for much cheaper and put away the rest towards his goals.
2. Assuming a monthly 8% gain, which is then added to the investment amount at the end of every month.
3. Assuming 10% annual return compounding annually.

Continuing Your Education

Like Zinedine Zidane at his industrious peak, we have covered vast swathes of ground in this book. But this book is still ultimately an introductory summary. For those of you who are happy to park your money with various providers and leave it at that, this book should suffice.

However, for those of you who want to go further and can feel the bug of investment slowly taking root within, we have compiled a reading list for you to continue your education with. We have organised the list into a general group and three distinct groups which can be found below.

Please also refer to the "Helpful Resources" chapter, which contains a number of online resources we have referenced throughout this book: we wanted to put these in one place for you to systematically refer to and work through.

General Economics and Investment Grounding

1. John Kay (2006) *The Truth about Markets*. London: Allen Lane.
2. Tim Hartford (2005) *The Undercover Economist*. New York: Little, Brown and Company.
3. Robert Kiyosaki and Sharon L. Lechter (2000) *Rich Dad, Poor Dad*. New York: Warner Brothers.

Islamic Investment

1. T. Diwany, T. Ahmad, H. Al-Haddad, A. Fazel, et al. (2010) *Islamic Banking and Finance: What It Is and What It Could Be*. 1st Ethical Charitable Trust.
2. W. Al-Zuhayli (2003) *Financial Transactions in Islamic Jurisprudence*. Vols 1 and 2 (trans. M. A. El-Gamal). Dar al-Fikr al-Mouaser.
3. Mufti Faraz Adam (2020) *Introduction to Islamic Fintech*. Amanah Advisors Press.
4. Harris Irfan (2015) *Heaven's Banker: Inside the Hidden World of Islamic Finance*. London: Constable.
5. Tarik El Diwany (1997) *The Problem with Interest*. Kreatoc Ltd.

Stocks-Specific Investing

1. Stan Weinstein (1988) *Secrets for Profit in Bull and Bear Markets*. New York: McGraw-Hill.
2. Peter Lynch and John Rothchild (2000) *One Up on Wall Street: How to Use What You Already Know to Make Money in the Market*. New York: Simon & Schuster.
3. Jim Slater (1992) *The Zulu Principle*. Petersfield: Harriman House.
4. Guy Thomas (2011) *Free Capital*. Petersfield: Harriman House.
5. Lee Freeman-Shor (2015) *The Art of Execution: How the World's Best Investors Get It Wrong and Still Make Millions in the Markets*. Petersfield: Harriman House.
6. William O'Neil (1988) *How to Make Money in Stocks: A Winning System in Good Times or Bad*. New York: McGraw-Hill.

Startup Investing

1. Ben Horowitz (2014) *The Hard Thing About Hard Things: Building a Business When There Are No Easy Answers*. New York: HarperCollins.
2. Blake Masters and Peter Thiel (2014) *Zero to One: Notes on Start Ups, Or How to Build the Future*. London: Crown.
3. Reif Hoffman and Chris Yeh (2018) *Blitzscaling: The Lightning-Fast Path to Building Billion Dollar Companies*. New York: HarperCollins.
4. Brad Feld and Jason Mendelson (2011) *Venture Deals: Be Smarter Than Your Lawyer and Venture Capitalist*. Hoboken, NJ: Wiley.

Helpful Resources

Halal Investment Checklist and Financial Journey: http://www.islamicfinanceguru.com/resources/investment-checklist

IFG. Wise Up with Halal Crypto: https://www.islamicfinanceguru.com/crypto

IFG. Zakat Calculator: https://www.islamicfinanceguru.com/zakat

Islamic Mortgage Guides and FAQs: https://www.islamicfinanceguru.com/guides-and-faqs/islamic-mortgage-guides-and-faqs

Islamic Will Guides and FAQs: https://www.islamicfinanceguru.com/guides-and-faqs/islamic-will-guides-and-faqs

Khan, I. Is My Job Haram? Islamicfinanceguru Ltd. (21 May 2021). https://www.islamicfinanceguru.com/articles/personal-finance/is-my-job-haram

National Zakat Foundation. Does Zakat Need to Be Paid on Pension Assets? https://nzf.org.uk/knowledge/pensions

National Zakat Foundation. Zakat on Property and Other Fixed Assets https://nzf.org.uk/knowledge/zakat-on-property (accessed 29 November 2021).

Pension Legal Opinion Letter: https://f.hubspotusercontent-eu1.net/hubfs/24915384/IslamicFinanceGuru_September2021/PDF/Sharia-op-v2.pdf

Should I Buy or Rent Calculator: https://buy-rent.mortgage.islamicfinanceguru.com

The Art Market 2022, an Art Basel and UBS Report by Dr Clare McAndrew: https://www.artbasel.com/about/initiatives/the-art-market

The Best 3 Free UK Islamic Wills – and When They're Right for You: https://www.islamicfinanceguru.com/articles/personal-finance/the-best-3-free-uk-islamic-wills-and-when-theyre-right-for-you

UK Government. (2022a). How Inheritance Tax Works: Thresholds, Rules and Allowances: https://www.gov.uk/inheritance-tax

UK Government. (2022b). Making a Will: https://www.gov.uk/make-will

UK Government. (2022c). Tax When You Get A Pension: https://www.gov.uk/tax-on-pension/tax-free

Warren Buffet's Shareholder Letters: https://www.berkshirehathaway.com/letters/letters.html

Index

A

AAOIFI, 113, 149, 182, 190
Aberdeen Standard Physical Gold Shares ETF (SGOL), 199
advanced subscription agreements (ASA), 177
Aghaz Investments, 118
AIM (Alternative Investment Market), 90, 107
  index, 78
AirBnB, 171
AJ Bell, 93, 117, 160
Al Rayan, 206
Al-'Aqar Healthcare REIT, 135
Algebra, 118
Almalia Sanlam Active Shariah Global Equity UCITS ETF, 118
Al-Salam REIT (Bahrain), 135
Al-Suhaibani, M. 183
alternative cryptocurrencies ("alts"), 162
Alton Towers, 155
Amazon, 114
AMD, 165
Andreesen, Marc, 175
Andreesen Horowitz, 175-6
Angel syndicate, 185-6
Angellist, 187
annual reports, 96
annuity, 61, 62-5
  enhanced rates, 63
Antofagasta, 200
Anything World, 166
Arabesque, 208
Arcapita, 191
Artwork, 203-4
ASAs, 177-8
ASOS, 78
asset risk, 83
AstraZeneca PLC, 31
Automated Market Maker (AMM), 160
Aviva, 69
  pension fund, 32
Axis Real Estate Investment Trust (Malaysia), 135

B

Bank of England, 142
Barroso, 173
bear market, 23, 43, 95
Beyond Meat, 171

BIMB Investment Management, Malaysia, 208
Binance, 158, 160, 161
bitcoin, 72, 153, 157, 159, 160, 162
Bitcoin ETF, 164
Bitcoin Fund, 164
Bitwise Crypto Industry Innovators ETF, 164
black swan event, 60
blockchain technology, 154-5, 165
bonds, 30, 32. 145
  vs sukuk, 146
Boohoo, 78
BP PLC, 31, 200
breaking even, 4, 5-11
British American Tobacco PLC, 30, 31
BT, 90
Buffett, Warren, 98-9, 115
build-to-rent model of property investing, 129
bull market, 23, 42-3
Bullion by Post, 198
BullionVault, 193, 198
buy-to-let properties, 131
  REITs for, 135
buy vs. rent, 51, 52-5

C

capital gain
  investing for, 95-7
  purification on, 114-15
capital gains tax, 78
capital growth vs. dividends, 91-4
case studies
  aggressive approach, 229-30
  conservative approach, 221-3
  moderate approach, 225-8
casino chip 155
Centamin, 200
CFD costs, 110
Chaarat Gold Holdings, 201
Charles Schwaab, 117
chart patterns, 101-2
child education trust (CET), 79
Coca-Cola, 170
Coinbase, 158, 161
collectibles, 22
commercial properties, 123-4
commodity *Murabaha* structure, 140, 145, 206
convertible loan notes (CLN), 177-8
corporate sukuk defaults, 148
corporate tax, 78
COVID-19 pandemic, 13, 21, 94
  vaccination passports. 165
credit, lines of, 24-5
credit cards, 24, 29
Crowdcube, 176, 185
crowdfunding, 174
crypto adoption156
crypto broker, 162
crypto ETFs, 164
crypto investing, 153-69
  access, 161-9
    non-fungible tokens (NFTs), 167
    metaverse, 167-9
    through startups, 166
    through stock market, 163-6
      crypto ETFs, 164
      crypto mining stocks, 163
      early adopters, 165-6
      funds/trusts, 163
      picks and shovel plays, 165
  definition, 153-5
  getting money back, 158
  returns on offer, 155-7
  safety, 157-8
  Sharia considerations, 158-61
    crypto staking sharia analysis, 160-1
    Zakat, 161
  styles of, 155-7

crypto lending, 157, 161
crypto market, performance of, 154
crypto miners, 157
crypto mining stocks, 163
crypto staking, 156-7, 158, 160-1
crypto trading, 155
crypto value investors, 156
cryptocurrencies, 22, 72, 82, 84, 153-5
  linked to education, 155
  value of, 155
cryptocurrency mining, 157
Cur8 app 14
Cur8 Capital, 78, 138, 140, 149, 151, 166, 184, 187, 191, 209
currency conversion fees, 110
currency risk, 148

D

debit card, 29
debt ratio, 115
debts, repaying, 8-9
decision-making, family, 48-9
declaration/announcement date, 92
deferred tax assets, 116
DeGiro, 107
Delaware Statutory Trust (DST), 78
deposit fees, 109, 111
Diageo PLC, 30, 31
dividend cover, 94
dividend history, 94
dividend payout ratio, 94
dividend tax, 79
dividend yield, 93-4
dividends
  ETFs, 105-6
  investing during a crash, 95
  vs. capital growth, 91-4
"diworsification" 104
DIY investing, 117
DJIM, 113
DocuSign, 165
Dogecoin, 22
Dow Jones Sukuk Index, 150
drawdown, pension, 61, 65-6, 67
due diligence, 35, 96
  into investment company, 71-5
Dyson, 90

E

emerging markets ETFs, 102
Emirates REIT (UAE), 135
Emma, 7
enhanced rates on annuity, 63
enterprise investment schemes (SEIS/EIS), 78
equities-only fund, 18
Erad, 140
ETCs (Exchange Trade Commodities), 200
ETFs *see* exchange-traded funds (ETFs)
ethereum, 162
Ethis, 140, 185
European Council for Fatwa and Research, 205
Exchange Trade Commodities (ETCs), 200
exchange-traded funds (ETFs), 102-5, 115-16, 134
  "Acc." 106
  benefits, 103
  crypto, 164
  "Dist." 106
  dividends, 105-6
  drawback, 103-4
  gold, 102, 199-201
  "Inc" 106
  fees, 105
  net asset value (NAV), 105
  with other traded investments, 106
ex-dividend date, 92-3
expenses, cutting, 7-8

F

Facebook, 8, 165, 171, 172
Fajr Capital, 191
family decision-making, 48-9
Fasset, 161
Federal Reserve, 141
Fidelity, 117
financial advisors, 46
financing, 29
Finviz, 97
fixed income funds, 26
fixed income products, 65
flipping, property, 124-5
Flyp.co, 125
Forbes, 153
foreign currency exchange fees, 105, 109
forestry, 201-2
  taxation, 78
Forge Global, 176
forward dividend yield, 93
Franklin Templeton Sukuk fund, 150
FreeAgent, 7
Freecycle, 8
FreeTrade, 107
Fresnillo, 200
FSCS (Financial Services Compensation Scheme) protection, 108
FTSE (Financial Times Stock Exchange), 90, 113
  FTSE100, 107
  FTSE, 250 Gold Stocks. 200
Funding Souq, 140

G

GameStop 37, 38
Gatehouse, 206
gharar (uncertainty), 28
Glencore PLC, 31
global financial crisis (2008), 21
  real estate and, 52
Global X Blockchain ETF, 164
gold, 83, 106
  access, 197-8
  benefits, 191-2
  CFDs, spread betting or other derivative Products, 201
  definition, 191-4
  disadvantages, 192
  ETFs, 102, 199-201
  getting money back, 195
  gold bullion, 197-8
  gold coins, 197-8
  investment timing, 192-3
  jewellery, 198
  returns on offer, 194
  safety, 195
  Sharia considerations, 195-7
  storage costs, 192
  strategy, 193-4
  Zakat on, 197
Gold Bullion Securities, 199
Google, 171
Graham, Benjamin, 98
  Intelligent Investor, The, 98, 115
GraniteShares Gold Trust (BAR), 199
Grayscale Bitcoin Trust. 164
Greatland Gold, 201
GSK PLC, 31
Gulf Finance House, 191
Gumtree, 8

H

Hakim bin Hizam, 196
halal, going, and purifying historic investments. 4, 27-33
hands-on, types of, 45-8
  hands-off, 46-7, 117-18

hands-on, 46, 47
hands-on plus, 46, 47-8
HANetf The Royal Mint Physical Gold ETC Securities (RMAP), 199
Hargreaves Lansdown, 109, 117, 160
Hedera Hashgraph (HBAR), 81-2
Heylo Housing, 206
higher-risk portfolio, 84
Highland Gold Mining, 200
high-risk investments, 84
HMOs (house in multiple occupation), 127
Hochschild Mining, 200
HODLing163
home financing. 9-11
home transformation, 126
house buying vs renting, 9-11
housing ladder, 9-11
Halal, degree of, 204-6
property, 205-6
sharia wrappers, 206
stocks, 204-5
HSBC, 7, 30, 208
HSBC Holdings PLC, 31
hurdle, 179

I

IBM, 165
idea generation, 96
Ideagen, 96, 97
IFG zakat calculator, 117
IG, 117
Ignatova, Dr, 72
ijarah (lease;rental) sukuk, 146, 150
impact investing, 207
impermissible income, 114-15
income, 29
increasing, 6
inflation rate, 141-2
inheritance tax, 14
inheritance tax-free, 78
Inovest REIT (Bahrain), 135
Instant Access Savings Accounts, 26
Interactive Brokers, 117
interest-bearing debt, 115
interest rates, 141
Invesco Alerian Galaxy Crypto Economy ETF, 164
Invesco DB Gold Fund (DGL), 199
Invesco DB Precious Metals Fund (DBP), 199
Invesco Physical Gold A (SGLP), 199
investment company, 74
investment mindset, 35, 37-49
hands-on, degree of, 42-5
planning for exit and the unexpected, 39-42
investments, 29-32
taxation on, 77-9
investment stages, 23
Investors Chronicle, 97
IRA, 77
ISA, 77
allowance, 62
fees, 109
iShares, 208
iShares Gold Trust (IAU), 199
iShares MSCI EM Islamic UCITS ETF, 118
iShares MSCI USA Islamic UCITS ETF, 118
iShares MSCI World Islamic UCITS ETF, 118
iShares Physical Gold ETC (SGLN), 199
Islamic banks, 141, 143, 144, 190, 206
Islamic bonds *see* Sukuk
Islamic Wills, 4, 13-15
Islamicly, 113

J

JCB, 90
JISA, 216
job posts, 96-7
Junior ISA, 216
Jupiter, 208

K

KFH Capital REIT (Kuwait), 135
KLCC, 135
KLCC REIT (Malaysia), 135
Koyfin, 97
Kraken, 158, 161
Kwarteng, Kwasi, 5

L

land
  development, 128-9
   planning permission on, 130
Larry Ellison, 175
leases, 123
Lendo, 140
life's Big Events
  planning for, 55-8
  preparation for, 51
lifestyling, 61
line of credit, 26
liquidity, 25, 59
liquidity mining, 161
loans, long-term, 29
  student, 29
London Stock Exchange, 111
long-term investments, 39, 46
lower-risk portfolio, 84
low-risk investments, 82-3
LSE (London Stock Exchange), 90
Lynch, Peter, 104
  One Up On Wall Street, 42, 96, 99

M

M1 Finance, 107
MACD, 101
Māl, 158, 159
margin lending. 109
marketplace, 8
MarketSmith, 97
Mastercard, 165
medium-risk investments, 83
memecoin, 82
Meta *see* Facebook
Microsoft, 73, 170
Minted, 193, 198
Money Dashboard, 7
Monzo, 7
mortgage
  Islamic, 142, 145
  refinancing, 7
MSCI, 113
mudarabah structure, 143, 145
mudarabah sukuk, 146, 149
Mufti Faraz Adam, 159
Mufti Taqi Usmani, 149
murabaha-based mortgage, 132
murabaha sukuk, 146
Musaffa, 113
musharakah-based mortgage, 132
musharakah sukuk, 146, 149
Musk, Elon, 175, 176
Muslimxchange, 113

N

Naifar, 183
Nando's, 90
NASDAQ (National Association of Securities Dealers Automated Quotations), 90
nickel, 106

NVIDIA, 165
NYSE (New York Stock Exchange), 90

O

offshore entities, 78
offshore real estate, 79
Omegas, 202
OneCoin, 72, 74
O'Neill, William: *How to Make Money in Stocks, 100*
Oracle, 175
outgoings, decreasing, 6-9
overdrafts, 29

P

Pan African Resources, 201
Pancake, 160
Patek Philippes, 202
patent boxes, 79
payment date, 93
payment for order flow (PFOF), 109, 110
pension pot, 60
- leaving money in, 61
- tax free allowance, 61, 62
- workplace, 68-9

pensions, 4, 17-19, 59-67
- business owners, 68-70
- countries that charge tax, 17-19
- countries that do not charge tax, 19
- defined benefit, 66-7
- drawdown, 61, 65-6, 67
- family, 70
- self-employed, 68-70
- self-invested personal pension, 18
- sharia-compliant option, 19
- taxation, 17-19, 77
- workplace, 18

personal finance, taxation, 79-80
Perth Mint Physical Gold ETF (AAAU), 199
Petronas Twin Towers, Kuala Lumpur, 135
Petropavlovsk, 200
picks and shovels startups, 165, 166
planning permission, 128-9
- on land, 130

Polymetal International, 200
Ponzi scheme, 73, 155
portfolio theory, 213-19
- goals, 213-18
  - saving for additional income, 217-18
  - saving for children's university fees, 216
  - saving for house, 216-17
  - saving for luxury, 217
  - saving for rainy day fund, 215
  - saving for retirement, 215-16
- role time horizons play in battle plans, 218-19

portfolios, 57
power law distribution, 173
preference shares (PS), 177, 178-9
- Islamic issues with, 179-80
- Sharia-compliant solutions, 183-4
  - best solution, 184
  - negligence solution, 184
  - next-best solution, 184
  - *wa'd* solution, 183-4
- venture capitalists and, 181-2

preferred return (PR), 177, 179
- Islamic issues with, 179-80
- Sharia-compliant solutions, 182-3
- venture capitalists and, 182

primary finance, 206
private equity, 188-91

private equity (*continued*)
access, 191
betting money back, 189
definition, 188
returns on offer, 188-9
safety, 189
Sharia considerations, 189-91
private sukuk funds, 149
profits, definition, 114
Proof of Stake ("PoS") crypto project, 160
property, 73, 122-37
access, 133-7
DIY, 133
private funds, 136-7
REITs, 134-5
stocks, 136
commercial, 123-4
definition, 121-2
getting money back, 131
legal process, 130
leverage, 83
residential, 123-4
returns on offer, 122-9
buy-to-let, 123-4
land development, 128-9
property development/ flipping, 124-8
safety, 129-31
Sharia considerations, 131-3
Zakat, 132-3
property financing (bridge and development finance), 144-5
access, 145
definition, 144
getting money back, 145
returns on offer, 144
safety, 144
Sharia considerations, 145
Zakat, 145
property financing (savings accounts), 140-3
access, 143
definition, 140-1
getting money back, 142-3
returns on offer, 141-2
safety, 142
Sharia considerations, 143
Zakat, 143
property prices
UK (1985–2025), 52
United Arab Emirates (2005–2021), 53
ProShares Bitcoin Strategy, 164
publicly listed sukuk funds, 149, 150
purification on capital gain, 114-15
Purpose Bitcoin ETF, 164

Q

Qardus, 140
Qatar Investment Authority, 175
quantitative easing191

R

r/wallstreetbets, 37
Rain, 161
rainy day fund, 4, 21-6
necessity of, 26
saving into, 24-5
investing, 25-6
real estate, 64
private funds, 65
see also property
Real Estate Investment Trusts *see* REITS
real-world indicators, 96-7
Record date, 93
Reddit, 35-7
Redditors, 38
rehypothecation, 109

REITs, 68, 131
for buy-to-let, 135
publicly listed, 64-5
zero-debt, 135
renting vs. buying, 51, 52-5
renting out, 127
Republic, 185
research & development tax credits, 79
residential properties, 123-4
retirement (and pre-retirement) 51, 59-67
investments, 60
planning for, 59
social side of, 59
strategy, 60
Return on Capital Employed (ROCE), 96, 97
returns on offer, 90-102
reward vs. risk, 35, 81-5
continuum, 147
riba (interest), 28, 195
rights of way, 130
Rio Tinto PLC, 31
risk, 59
risk curve, 82
risk vs reward, 35, 81-5
continuum, 147
Robinhood, 107, 109, 117
roboadvisor, 118
ROCE, 96, 97
Rolexes, 202
RSI, 101
rule of, 72 90

S

S&P 113
S&P 500, 105, 111, 112
Sabana REIT (Singapore), 135
SAFENotes, 177-8
SAFES, 177-8
salaries, 56, 58
savings accounts, 142
buying a government sukuk bond, 83
rates, 141
savings lifecycle, 22
Schwab, Charles, 23
Scottish Widows, 69
seasoned finance professionals, 46
Securities and Exchange Commission (SEC), 110
Seedrs, 176, 185
Seekingalpha, 97
SEIS/EIS schemes, 78
self-employment pensions, 17
self-invested personal pensions *see* SIPPs
Sequoia Capital, 175
Sh. Qaradawi, 205
Shanta Gold, 201
Sharepad, 97
shares *see* stocks
Sharia-compliant annuity replacement options, 64-5
Sharia-compliant debt, 190
Sharia-compliant financing on a property, 130
Sharia-compliant investing
overarching impact considerations 206-8
investing in esg, 208-10
Sharia wrapper, 189, 190
Shell PLC, 31, 90, 200
short-term fixed-income products, 61
short-term investing, 39
shorting, 37 8
Shuaa Capital, 191
simple agreements for future equity (SAFE), 177-8

SIPPs, 42, 68, 69
fees, 109
UK, 108
Slater, Jim: *Zulu Principle, The,* 97, 99
Small Cap Gold Stocks, 200
small cap investing, 84
smaller companies ETFs, 102
small self-administered pension scheme, 70
SME financing, 138-40
access, 140
definition, 138-9
getting money back, 139
returns on offer, 139
safety, 139
Sharia considerations, 140
Zakat, 140
social investing, 37
SolGold, 201
Sovereign sukuk defaults, 148
SP Funds Dow Jones Global Sukuk ETF, 118
SP Funds S&P 500 Sharia Industry Exclusions ETF, 118
SP Funds S&P Global REIT Sharia ETF, 118
Spacex, 176
SPDR Gold MiniShares Trust (GLDM), 199
SPDR Gold Trust (GLD), 199
spreads, 110
SSAS, 70
stamp duty on share purchases, 107
Starling, 7
startups, 73, 169-87
access, 184-6
defensibility, 172
definition, 169-72
getting money back, 176
investing, 84
Returns on Offer, 172-3
safety, 173-6
Sharia considerations, 176-84
VC Fund, 186-7
stock brokers, 108
administration fee, 108-9
charges, 108-11
ease of use, 111
getting money back, 112-13
product range, 111
reputation, 108
safety, 111
Sharia considerations, 113-17
business, 113-14
debt ratio, 115
ETFs, 115-16
impermissible income, 114-15
Zakat, 116-17
stock market, 22, 89-90
funds, 83
starting investing in, 106-7
stock stages, 101
stocks, 73, 89-119
access to, 117-18
capital gain, investing for, 95-7
capital growth vs. dividends, 91-4
dividend investing during a crash, 95
DIY investing, 117
fundamental analysis, 95-7
popular fundamental styles, 97-100
safety of investment, 107-1
technical analysis, 100-6
chart patterns, 101-2
trends, 101
vs. funds, 102-7
stocks and shares ISA, 108
Strideup 206
Stripe, 176
student loans, 29

Sukuk, 65, 106, 145-7, 173
access, 150-1
bond vs, 146
definition, 145-7
funds, 26
getting money back, 149
ijarah structure, 150
Returns on Offer, 147-8
safety, 148-9
Sharia considerations, 149-50
types, 146
Zakat, 150
Super-Hands Off, 118

T
tax avoidance, 78
tax evasion, 78
tax rebates, 6
tax recoverables, 116
tax-saving strategies, 35, 77-80
taxation, 6
basic rate taxation, 66
capital gains, 78
corporate, 78
dividend, 79
higher rate taxation, 66
inheritance, 14, 78
TD Ameritrade, 117
technical analysis, 100-6
Tesco Clubcard, 7
Tesco Cola, 170
Theil, Peter, 172
tokens, theme park, 155
Total Expense Ratio (TER), 105
trade and other receivables, 116
trade cryptocurrencies, 162
TradingView, 97
Trading212, 107, 110, 117
trailing dividend yield, 93
Trans-Siberian Gold, 201
Twitter, 42, 175

U
Uber, 171
UK Gold ETFs, 199
Unilever PLC, 31
Uniswap 160
uranium, 106
US Gold ETFs, 199

V
Valkyrie Bitcoin Strategy, 164
Van Eck Bitcoin Strategy, 164
Van Eck Merk Gold Trust (OUNZ), 199
venture capital (VC) funds, 166
venture capitalists (VCs), 177
Visa, 165
Vodafone, 90
volatility, 25-6

W
Wafra Capital, 191
Wahed Invest, 118, 208, 209
wakalah structure, 143, 145
watches, 202-3
Wayhome, 206
Wealthsimple Shariah World Equity Index ETF, 118
Weinstein, Stan, 101
Secrets for Profit in Bull and Bear Markets, 100
WhatsApp 73
Wills, Islamic, 4, 13-15
Windows Office, 365 170
WisdomTree Physical Gold (PHGP), 199
WisdomTree Physical Swiss Gold (OGZU), 199
WisdomTree Physical Swiss Gold (SGBX), 199
Withdrawal fees, 109
Wood, Cathie, 106
www.muslimxchange.com, 113

X

Xetra-Gold (OGLD), 199
Xtrackers IE Physical Gold ETC Securities (XGDU), 199
Xtrackers Physical Gold ETC (EUR) (OXA5), 199
Xtrackers Physical Gold ETC (XGLD), 199

Y

Yahoo stock screener, 97
yield farming, 161

Z

Zakat, 33, 184
  on cryptoinvesting, 161
  on gold, 197
  on private equity, 190–1
  on property, 132–3
  on property financing (bridge and development finance), 145
  on property financing (savings accounts), 143
  on SME financing, 140
  on stock brokers, 116–17
  on stocks, 116–17
  on *Sukuk*, 150
zero-debt REITs, 135
zero-fee brokers, 109
Zoya, 113
Zuckerberg, Mark, 172